Harold W. Picton

The story of chemistry

Harold W. Picton

The story of chemistry

ISBN/EAN: 9783742830142

Manufactured in Europe, USA, Canada, Australia, Japa

Cover: Foto ©ninafisch / pixelio.de

Manufactured and distributed by brebook publishing software (www.brebook.com)

Harold W. Picton

The story of chemistry

JOHN DALTON.

From an Engraving by C. H. Jeens.

(By permission of Messrs. Macmillan & Co.)

ISBISTERS' HOME LIBRARY

THE STORY OF CHEMISTRY

By HAROLD W. PICTON B.Sc.

With a Preface by SIR HENRY ROSCOE
M.P., D.C.L., LL.D., F.R.S.

LONDON
ISBISTER AND COMPANY Limited
15 & 16 TAVISTOCK STREET COVENT GARDEN

PREFACE.

AM pleased to be asked to introduce this little book to the notice of the English public. The author has, in my opinion, told his story brightly and truly, and in a way to interest those who have some knowledge of our science, as well as those who wish to gain that knowledge.

A short and attractive history of Chemistry

has long been wanted, and my friend the author seems to have written just such a book as was needed.

H. E. ROSCOE.

10, Bramham Gardens,
    Wetherby Road, S.W.
        October, 1889.

CONTENTS.

CHAP.		PAGE
	PREFACE. BY SIR HENRY ROSCOE	5
	INTRODUCTION	13
I.	CHEMISTRY BEFORE THE ALCHEMISTS—EMPIRICISM	23

FIRST PERIOD: ALCHEMICAL MYSTICISM.

II.	ALCHEMICAL MYSTICISM	37

SECOND PERIOD: MEDICAL MYSTICISM.

III.	BASIL VALENTINE	55
IV.	PARACELSUS—VAN HELMONT	79

THIRD PERIOD: THE DECLINE OF MYSTICISM.

V.	GLAUBER	97

FOURTH PERIOD: THE BEGINNINGS OF SCIENCE.

VI.	THE BEGINNINGS OF SCIENCE	113
VII.	THE ACKNOWLEDGMENT OF NESCIENCE	119
VIII.	HOOKE—MAYOW—HALES	137

FIFTH PERIOD: THE CHILDHOOD OF TRUTH.

CHAP.   PAGE
IX. CULLEN—BLACK   .   157

SIXTH PERIOD: THE CONFLICT WITH ERROR.

X. THE BIRTH OF ERROR   175
XI. THE FIRST OF AUGUST, 1774   .   .   . 185
XII. TRUTH IN DISGUISE 211

SEVENTH PERIOD: THE TRIUMPH OF TRUTH.

XIII. LAVOISIER .   .   . 231

EIGHTH PERIOD: THE ATOMIC THEORY.

XIV. DALTON'S IDEA 257
XV. THE DEVELOPMENT OF DALTON'S IDEA   . 277
XVI. THE ATOMIC THEORY OF TO-DAY .   . 293
XVII. DAVY AND FARADAY 317

NINTH PERIOD: THE MODERN SCIENCE.

XVIII. MODERN INORGANIC CHEMISTRY   .   . 343
XIX. ORGANIC CHEMISTRY TO-DAY .   .   . 360
    CONCLUSION 382

INTRODUCTION.

THE ALCHEMIST.

THE early history of chemistry sounds more like fiction than fact. A romance clings about the stories of the old alchemists which lends them irresistible charm. We may perhaps best get a notion of their character by paying an imaginary visit to an alchemistic laboratory of, say, the fourteenth century.

It is a winter's evening and the wind moans melancholy without. We are in a long gloomy room. Above us age-grimed oak rafters stretch away into the dim shadows of the roof. Smoke and furnace-fumes hang dusky in the air. Glowing eyes seem to gleam at us through chinks in furnace doors. Strange distorted alchemistic vessels stand silently working out their secret wonders, or lie carelessly neglected on their shelves. Phials filled with deep-coloured liquids stand here and there picturesquely tinged by fitful gleams of fire-light. Open folios lie scattered here and there, the pages covered with mystic writing and cabalistic signs. And there, bending over a heated crucible and watching its contents with grave concern, stands the alchemist himself.

Beside him an assistant is urging the bellows, and the fire throws a ruddy glow on the face of each. The alchemist is venerable and careworn. His dark eyes look out from under shaggy eyebrows, and just now the forehead is knit in anxious thought. Will his labour succeed? For years he has sought the true method of preparing the substance at whose touch all metals shall become gold. Now at last the time of successful trial seems at hand. In that small crucible his whole labour is to find its issue, and here and now the great secret is to be won or lost. Two metals are here molten together, and upon them the miracle is to be worked. From their baseness is to come forth pure, lustrous gold.

The alchemist knits his brows a little closer as the time seems ripe for projection; he motions his assistant to stop the blast, and taking from his breast a small piece of yellow wax enclosing a few red grains drops it upon the molten mass. A quick bubbling is heard and light puffs of smoke are blown out from the crucible. Presently the bubbling ceases, but the smoke is pouring out faster than ever. It mounts in the air and floats in light wreaths round alchemist and servant. It grows denser and obscures the light of the furnace, rolls upwards among the rafters and down into the dark corners, making all darker and mistier and more unreal. Crucibles, folios, alembics, and alchemist are fast vanishing in it, and at length, puff! the whole room, with its workers and their mysteries, has vanished into the dreamland of fancy from which it sprang. We are back in the nineteenth century again; but, for all that, we have caught a glimpse of the alchemist at his task.

Now let us ask who were the alchemists, and what was their work? The alchemists were a body of men who flourished from the early centuries of the Christian era to the close of the seventeenth century,* and whose main guiding star in their search for knowledge was their belief in the transmutation of the baser metals into gold. They sought to prepare the "philosopher's stone," and it was at the touch of this that transmutation was to occur. Some, it is true, sought in the stone a universal medicine rather than inexhaustible lucre. It was to cure all diseases and ills of flesh. Among such seekers was Geber, perhaps the first alchemist of whom we have record. But Geber seems to have been far more truly scientific than, with very few exceptions, any of his successors for the next six hundred years.

* Even at the close of the eighteenth century a few scattered alchemists like Peter Woulfe were known. Woulfe died in 1805.

It cannot be said then that these men were in the main moved by any very noble ambition. On the whole their object was to find a way to make gold—a desire indeed not yet extinct. Still, the alchemist usually had some other interests as well as this which distinguished him from his modern counterpart. Where in his search he chanced to discover other interesting bodies he would not seldom describe them with some care, and in this way made real contributions to science. The alchemists, we may with much probability say, never achieved the main hope of their quest, but in their search for it they achieved much that was far better. Their dreams were not healthy enough to be realised, but the cold realities with which they were disappointed were to fall as cherishing snow-flakes above the hidden seeds of truth, which else had withered with the frost. Put in its most matter of fact way they looked for gold, and instead of it they found nitric and sulphuric acids, many other chemicals, and much useful apparatus.

This may seem somewhat paltry by comparison, but is really not so. It reminds us of an old tale of long ago in which a dying countryman informs his sons that in the farm he is leaving them there lies a hidden treasure. The man has much neglected his farm, and it is thickly grown with weeds; but among them the treasure must be sought. The sons naturally set about digging over the land here and there in their search. But dig where they will the mine of gold and gems they pictured is not found. At

THE ALCHEMIST.

last every inch is dug over, and they think their father must have been wandering in his mind. But now, things being as they are, they determine to make the best of a bad business, and as the ground is open they proceed to sow and plant. This is done, and in due season, when the crops are growing and the fruit is rounding on the branch, they bethink them once more of the promised treasure. As the money comes in for the immensely increased produce of the farm it strikes them that the treasure their father meant was the unused fruitfulness of the soil; and now, in seeking for the apparently delusive promise, they have found what was much better, the reward of honest industry.

Having thus briefly seen who were the alchemists and how their work was connected with the chemistry of to-day, we shall in the next chapter sketch in outline the chemical knowledge already acquired before their time, the material ready to hand for their use. In the sequel we shall pass briefly in review some of the more renowned and interesting alchemists in chronological order, and endeavour to see more clearly what they actually did for chemistry.

But before closing this chapter it may be suitable to give one of the many stories of transmutation, which we find related by writers of repute with apparently the sincerest belief in their truth. The story is told by Mangetus, the editor of "Bibliotheca Chemica curiosa . . . ." (1702) on the authority of M. Gros, a clergyman of Geneva, said to be of the most unexceptionable character, a skilful physician and an expert chemist. About the year 1650 an unknown Italian came to Geneva and took lodgings at the sign of the Green Cross. Wishing to see what was to be seen at Geneva he requested his landlord, De Luc, to procure him a guide to the town. De Luc was acquainted with M. Gros, at that time about twenty, and a student of Geneva, and knowing his proficiency in Italian requested him to accompany the stranger about the town. M. Gros at once acceded to this request, and for the space of a fortnight acted the part of guide to the Italian. When this time had elapsed the stranger began to complain of want of money. M. Gros became somewhat alarmed, fearing that he might be asked for a loan, and not being in a position to lose much money without inconvenience. But the Italian only asked to be conducted to a goldsmith who would lend him his blowpipe and utensils for a short space.

Such a goldsmith was found in the person of M. Bureau, to whom M. Gros conducted his acquaintance. M. Bureau courteously placed his workshop at the Italian's disposal, and there left him with M. Gros and a workman. The Italian then at once proceeded, before the astonished gaze of the clergyman, to melt tin in one crucible and heat some quicksilver in another. When the crucibles were hot he poured the mercury upon the molten tin and projected upon it "a red powder enclosed in wax." A rapid reaction seemed to occur, the mass became agitated, fumes were exhaled, and the metals were forthwith converted into pure gold, yielding six heavy ingots. The identity of the product with gold was not allowed to rest upon its appearance alone, for it was submitted to all the tests then known and certified by the goldsmith to be pure. Furthermore the ingots were taken to the mint, so says the account, and there exchanged for a large sum in Spanish coin. As some token of his indebtedness, the stranger presented M. Gros with twenty pieces, while fifteen more were given jointly to M. Gros and M. Bureau for their own entertainment.

And now comes the dramatic climax to the scene. The mysterious Italian proceeded to order for that evening a sumptuous supper for the three with which to celebrate the occasion. He then went out, and as the day passed and the evening came they waited in vain for his return. He never came back, and the secret of the transmutation had gone with him.

This is a very circumstantial account; but as no detailed directions have ever been given for successfully performing such transmutation, and as the subject is one where imposture or inaccuracy must be peculiarly liable to creep in, we can only conclude, with a very high degree of probability, that the above is not a case of the actual transmutation of metals into gold. There is no doubt that the alchemists' ideas gave rise to a vast amount of deliberate deception of others, and still more muddleheaded deception of self. A race of jugglers, severely satirised in Ben Jonson's *Alchemist*, arose who traded upon the gullibility of their dupes most successfully and most mercilessly. To these latter they could give easy evidence of their power by stirring the mixture in their crucibles with hollow rods containing oxide of gold or silver within and having the lower end closed with wax. In this way by the reduction of the oxide they could obtain particles of metallic gold.

Another form of imposture, it is said, was to use crucibles having a false fusible bottom, below which oxide of gold or silver was contained. Or nails were dipped into an appropriate liquid and drawn out half converted into gold. The nails consisted of gold soldered to iron, and covered so as to conceal their colour. It was possible also for the alchemist himself to be deceived by such an operation as that of cupelling argentiferous lead* in a crucible of ashes or pulverised bones. The lead then disappears, being oxidised and sinking into the porous crucible, leaving the silver behind. To one having imperfect knowledge of what took place, it might well seem that the lead was converted into silver. And so, indeed, the main fabric of alchemy was a fairy palace resting upon the basis of a false dream. Its ruin was sure, but from its shattered fragments the workers of to-day are building a fabric which to-morrow will be fairer than the fairest dream.

* That is lead containing silver.

CHAPTER I.

CHEMISTRY BEFORE THE ALCHEMISTS.—EMPIRICISM.

LIKE so many other accomplishments of civilisation chemistry may probably be traced back to an Egyptian origin. In the mysteries of the Egyptian temples is found the beginning of the sacred art. In the third and fourth centuries the learning of Egypt was the fashion. As the power of Egypt declined the art passed thence, and from Greece, about the beginning of the ninth century, into the hands of the Arabians, who produced some of the earliest true men of science.

The Arabians were certainly real enthusiasts, and in their treaties with the Greeks of Constantinople there occurred repeated stipulations for the surrender of particular manuscripts. To show how strangely in some respects knowledge remained for a long period quiescent we may mention, as a small, though striking instance, that in Part V. of his *Opus Majus* Roger Bacon quotes from the Arabian philosopher Alhazen a description of the anatomy of the eye which, in all essential particulars, is identical with that set forth in modern anatomical text-books. Having got so far, the progress of knowledge for several centuries well-nigh ceased. Indeed, as for chemistry itself, it has only since the opening of the present century thrown off its swaddling clothes.

Alexander of Aphrodisia invented the term *chymike* to describe the operations of the laboratory. Hence the word *chemics*, a word unknown in the fourth century, and only popular some centuries later. Later, when men reflected that the old name of Egypt was Cham or Chemia, it flattered the chemists to call their art the art of the ancient Chemi. Such is the power of words that this false derivation gave fresh impulse to the science.

We must now give some account of the chemical knowledge acquired, and the chemical notions entertained, by the ancients previous to the time of Geber (eighth century), and may in passing point out some of its connections with the knowledge of a later day. Their ideas were of course very vague, and their knowledge had been arrived at by chance and empirically* rather than by intelligent research. Aristotle, the

---

* Empiric, empirical, empiricism, are words that need careful definition. They are derived from a Greek word signifying experience. But all knowledge is derived from experience, and, therefore, at

CHEMISTRY BEFORE THE ALCHEMISTS.

great Greek philosopher, looked upon the universe as built up from the four "elements," earth, fire, air, and water, and with such theories science could not progress far. We shall see later on how at the present time we have come to regard an "element" as any substance which we cannot by any known process split up into two or more different things.

Seven metals were known to the ancients*—gold, silver, mercury, copper, tin, lead, and iron. None is more commonplace to us now than the last, but in these early days it was thought very precious indeed, owing to the difficulty of working it. Copper was then more extensively used than any other metal, and generally alloyed with tin to form *bronze*. This alloy, bronze, was much used for coinage and for statuary. Here is an analysis of three different bronzes for comparison. Each gives the amount of copper and other metals in one hundred parts of the bronze.

	I.	II.	III.
Copper	84·53	99·3	88·77
Tin	6·82	0·7	9·25
Lead	8·65	..	0·70
Zinc	..	..	1·28

first sight, it would appear that empiricism must be the right method of acquiring knowledge. The meaning of words, however, depends not only on derivation, but on accidental use, and "empiricism" happens to have been used chiefly of chance experiences occurring irregularly and without any ordered plan of research An instance of empiricism is found in the discovery of glass, described in Chapter II. The researches of Black on lime and magnesia, described in a later chapter, afford an example of ordered research or induction of a high order.

* Many of the facts in this chapter are obtained from Thomson's *History of Chemistry*.

I. A Roman bronze coin of Justinian.
II. Bronze statues of horses in the portal of St. Mark's, Venice (about A.D. 430).
III. Thorwaldsen's " Shepherd " (cast in Berlin, 1825).

In working and casting metals the ancients were very advanced. The bronze statue of Apollo placed in the capitol in the time of Pliny* was forty-five feet in height and cost five hundred talents, equal to about £50,000. The statue of the sun at Rhodes (the "Colossus of Rhodes") was the work of Chares, a disciple of Lysippus. According to one account it was a hundred and five feet† in height, was twelve years in making, and cost three hundred talents (£30,000). It bestrode the entrance to the harbour, and ships could pass full sail between its legs. A winding staircase ran to the top, and the shoulders afforded an excellent point of view. For about fifty-six years this tower of bronze stood unhurt and was then overthrown and partly ruined by an earthquake. Money was subscribed to the Rhodians to restore it to its place. This they divided among each other and excused themselves by an oracle from Delphi which forbade them to raise the statue. For nine hundred years it lay on the ground and was at last sold to a merchant who loaded nine hundred camels with its fragments. Iron and steel were used in the time of Pliny, but of the method of working them there is little record.

Various mineral colouring matters were used, as for instance, minium (red lead), which is an oxide of

* First century A.D.
† Thomson gives ninety feet.

lead; cinnaberis (cinnabar) or sulphide of mercury, &c. Some dyes were also prepared, the most important being the celebrated Tyrrhian purple discovered about 1500 B.C. This colouring matter was extracted from two kinds of shell-fish found in the Mediterranean. The ordinary process of calico-printing is to stamp the material at certain parts with "mordants" which fix the colour in its meshes. It is then steeped in the dye, after which the colouring matter may be washed out from the unmordanted portion, leaving the pattern stamped in colour on the material. This process seems to have been known in ancient times in India and the East, and probably to the Egyptians.

Among the most important chemical products known to the ancients was the invaluable substance, glass. Glass beads are found on Egyptian mummies which date back to some thousands of years B.C. Glass consists mainly of a compound of silica with soda and lime. Silica is a white substance occurring in nearly all rocks and existing almost pure in white sand. The glass is made by fusing soda-ash with sand, the lime being added in various forms such as calc-spar, chalk or limestone, according to circumstances. Its original discovery as described by Pliny has thus by no means any great improbability. According to his account some Phœnician merchants, in a ship loaded with carbonate of soda from Egypt, stopped and went ashore on the banks of the river Belus. Having nothing to support their kettles they used lumps of carbonate of soda; the fires melted this and fused it into the sand of the river, thus forming glass. In Pliny's time too, coloured glasses were decolourised by the addition of manganese in the making, just as now.

Starch was known to the Greeks and its manufacture is described by Pliny. It was prepared by washing wheaten flour by processes similar to those of the present day. It may not be out of place to shortly describe these here. Wheat, maize, rice, and potatoes consist very largely of starch. From these sources it is obtained by rasping or grinding the vegetable structure to pulp and washing the mass upon a sieve, by which the torn cellular tissue of the plant is retained. The starch passes through and settles down from the liquid in the form of a fine white powder. Examined by the microscope it is seen to consist of little rounded, concentrically striated particles, the appearance of which differs characteristically in different plants. The chemical constitution of starch is a subject which has given rise to much labour and discussion. We may gain some insight into the amount of labour involved in the thorough study of one apparently commonplace body by noticing that in a recent famous paper upon starch by two chemists, Brown and Heron, the authors in their introduction remark that more than four hundred papers have already appeared on the same subject.

Porcelain and stoneware are made by heating various clays with a "frit," "flux," or fusible material. Porcelain is obtained when the whole mass is thoroughly permeated by the frit, and is thus semi-transparent or translucent. Earthenware is made from a coloured plastic clay which forms a porous mass when baked. It is then glazed. The history of porcelain is of no little interest. The first discovery is lost far back in the unrecorded ages of the great Chinese empire. Like much other knowledge which Europeans had painfully to rediscover for themselves it lay there totally hidden. To the Romans the art was wholly unknown,* and remained so to the rest of Europe for many centuries, till in 1709 the method of making it was discovered by Bötticher and a manufactory was established at Meissen, in Saxony. This manufacture was kept strictly secret, and the King of Prussia instructed the celebrated chemist Pott to find the secret out. Pott could obtain no details as to the materials actually used. His only plan was to choose those which seemed suitable, to mix them together in varying proportions and see what happened. It is said that Pott's experiments in this way reached the enormous total of thirty thousand. After all he did not discover what he sought, but to his work we owe much valuable information. He was followed in the search by Réaumur and other French chemists, and finally the lost art was rediscovered, and in 1769 the great Sèvres manufactory was founded. It is only

* The art of *pottery*, *i.e.* the opaque ware, of course never became extinct.

during the present century that porcelain has become an article of every-day use and is known to us more familiarly as china. The knowledge of earthenware or faience dates back to equally early times, but this did not in the same way suffer extinction. In more recent times it was the renowned Bernard Palissy whose disinterested labours spread abroad a thorough knowledge of this important product.

We shall next discuss the knowledge which the ancients had attained of a very important article—important at least to us moderns. "The quantity of soap," says Liebig, "consumed by a nation would be no inaccurate measure whereby to estimate its wealth and civilisation. Political economists, indeed, will not give it this rank; but whether we regard it as joke or earnest, it is not the less true, that, of two countries with an equal amount of population, we may declare with positive certainty that the wealthiest and most highly civilised is that which consumes the greatest weight of soap. This consumption does not subserve sensual gratification, nor depend upon fashion, but upon the feeling of the beauty, comfort and welfare attendant upon cleanliness; and a regard to this feeling is coincident with wealth and civilisation. The rich in the Middle Ages who concealed a want of cleanliness in their clothes and persons under a profusion of costly scents and essences, were more luxurious than we are in eating and drinking, in apparel and horses. But how great is the difference between their days and our own, when a want of

CHINESE PORCELAIN.

cleanliness is equivalent to insupportable misery and misfortune!"

Before the time of Pliny soap seems to have been unknown. The word is used in the Old Testament, in one case for the Hebrew word *nether*, which probably signifies trona or native carbonate of soda, and in the other for *borith*, meaning the lye or solution obtained from the ash of a plant, and which contains the same ingredient. In the older Greek period garments were washed with water only, and oil was used to soften the skin after bathing.

Pliny is the first to mention soap. He describes it as made from wood-ashes and tallow, and says it was used as a pomade, and more among men than women. In a work published in the second century soap is stated to be used both as a medicine and for cleansing purposes. In early times, however, other cleansing agents seem to have been more frequently used. These included native carbonate of soda, the ashes of sea-plants, and putrid urine. Among the many secrets which the buried remains of Pompeii have disclosed is the fact of the use of soap among the Romans, at least in later times, for a complete soap-boiling establishment has there been discovered. At present soap is made from caustic alkalies (soda and potash) and fats.

The ancients were acquainted with only one acid—vinegar, which is merely dilute acetic acid. It is formed when alcoholic drinks turn sour, and is obtained from alcohol by further fermentation. Its solvent properties are said to have been known to Cleopatra when she boasted to Anthony that she would consume an incredible value of food to her own share at one meal. Towards the close of the appointed meal she produced a goblet containing some weak vinegar and dropped into this the two finest pearls then known in the world. They at once dissolved in the acid and in this way her one draught cost ten million sestertii. This story is, however, of very doubtful authenticity, pearls, indeed, being insoluble in *weak* vinegar.

Of gases we find in these times really no knowledge at all. Pliny's whole account of the air is that it condenses itself in clouds and rages in storms. So too of that most common body, water, little was known. Its properties were too simple to be explained without much greater progress, and our knowledge of water may be said to commence with Cavendish in 1785.

Another substance which has acquired a rather questionable importance among us, and which was known to the ancients, is the old English beverage, beer. The story of beer is a very old story indeed, and, as Prof. Huxley says, "among the earliest records of all kinds of men you find a time recorded when they got drunk." The process of fermentation has apparently been made use of from the earliest periods of which we have any records handed down. The question may be asked—what is fermentation? Well, in spite of the long ages it has been in use it is impossible to say certainly what it is. But the way

c

CHEMISTRY BEFORE THE ALCHEMISTS.

in which it is brought about is simple enough, and much the same now as in ancient times. Grain—barley, for instance—is steeped in cold water and spread out, when it begins to sprout. In this process part of its starch is changed into sugar. The grain is now killed by heating it, and in this state is called *malt*. The crushed malt is run into a large vessel, the "mash tun," where it is mixed with warm water. Here the rest of the starch becomes changed into sugar, and it is this *solution of sugar* which is fermented by adding common yeast. Yeast is made up of a number of little round bodies which are really small plants. These grow in the liquid, and by their growth they somehow manage to attack the sugar and form alcohol from it. If beer is being made the wort or infusion of malt is first boiled with hops before fermenting. This gives its characteristic bitter taste to the beer.

YEAST CELLS.

The Egyptians appear to have prepared beer from malted grain, while wine, prepared by allowing grape-juice to ferment, is mentioned in Homer and the Old Testament. But as the ordinary methods of distillation were in those times unknown, ardent spirits and spirits of wine could not be obtained. Thus, although alcohol had been for ages produced as a drink, it was never obtained in anything like purity till probably the time of the alchemist, Raymond Lully, at the close of the thirteenth century.

FIRST PERIOD.

CHAPTER II.

FIRST PERIOD—ALCHEMICAL MYSTICISM.

E shall now pass in review some of the work of the alchemistic teachers, and see how air-built were their castles, and how they failed to put foundations under them. We shall find out how involved and mysterious were their writings, but also how distinct was their service to knowledge, and how patiently they followed their lode-star even though it proved a will-o'-the-wisp. In this way we may seek not in vain among their broken alembics for some grains of a wisdom whose price is more precious than gold or rubies.

According to Suidas (who flourished in the eleventh century), the art of alchemy was known as early as the Argonautic expedition, the golden fleece being actually a treatise written on skins concerning the making of gold. Such is the subtlety of exegetics.

Alchemy was also said to have originated with a mysterious Hermes Trismegistus, an Egyptian. In a reputed writing of Albertus Magnus it is said that Alexander the Great discovered the tomb of Hermes, in which were many golden treasures, and, most precious of all, an emerald table on which was inscribed a description of the preparation of the philosopher's stone capable of curing all diseases. The description is of course unintelligible, and after an immense amount of controversy as to the claims which these directions have to authenticity, it is now almost certain that both they and the tract, attributed to Albertus Magnus, in which they were inserted, are altogether forgeries. The Tractatus Aureus is attributed to Hermes and is of the same type. To prepare this mystic philosopher's stone we are directed to "catch the flying bird," by which is meant quicksilver (mercury), "and drown it so that it may fly no more." This is what was afterwards termed the *fixation* of mercury by uniting it to gold. And so on; the total result in the end probably being to increase the weight of the gold by addition of impurity. So much for the reputed founder of alchemy!

The first alchemist of whom we have probably any authentic record is Geber, an Arabian of the eighth century, also known as Djafar, or in full as Abu Musa Dschabir Ben Haijan Ben Abdallah el-Sufi el-Tarsusi Kufi. If his writings are indeed authentic, they present us with one of those extraordinary instances of a man born hundreds of years before his time, for which it is difficult on any hypothesis to account. Geber's reputed works are precise and clear to a degree surpassing the best writers in the later alchymical period. Older writings there are none. Subsequent treatises as clear do not appear till far more knowledge had been acquired. His work stands out alone. There seems indeed to linger in it the after-glow of some previous sunset of knowledge, soon to be plunged in almost starless night.*

Geber describes a number of metallic compounds, such as green vitriol (a sulphate of iron), saltpetre, corrosive sublimate (a chloride of mercury). Possibly the accounts given of various acids and salts may have been added to at a later date. But his claims to be considered the first propounder of a chemical theory are probably valid. According to Geber's views

* Geber is mentioned in the Kitab-al-Fihrist (tenth century), by Ibn Khallickan (thirteenth century) and others. If these references are correct he flourished in the eighth century. His birth-place was probably Tarsus and he resided at Damascus and Kufa, but some have gone the length of altogether questioning his existence. The titles of no less than five hundred of Dschabir's works on chemistry are given in the Fihrist, and have been catalogued by Hammer-Purgstall; nothing more is known about the majority of them. Arabic manuscripts on alchemy bearing the name of Dschabir Ben Haijan exist in Leyden, Paris, and London. Geber describes many chemical operations, such as filtration, crystallisation, and sublimation, and was able, it seems, to prepare nitric acid, or *aquafortis*, and from it the mixture *aqua regia*, a liquid almost fulfilling, at least in its solvent properties, Van Helmont's dreams of the *alcahest* or universal solvent, and the only acid dissolving gold. It consists of mixed nitric and hydrochloric acids.

all the metals are composed of the same "elements," so that the less perfect may be developed into the more perfect, or as he somewhat fantastically puts it, "Bring me the six lepers, so that I may heal them," that is transmute the six imperfect metals into gold. The elements which he considered to be combined in various proportions to produce the different metals are sulphur and mercury. The mercury was supposed to give the body its metallic characteristics. The more mercury the substance contained the more truly metallic it became, and the less readily altered by heat or chemical agents. If much sulphur were present the metal would, said Geber, be less perfectly metallic and would lose its metallic properties in the fire. But this was not all; the mercury and sulphur could exist in different degrees of purity and of division, and these conditions also affected the character of the metal so composed. Thus either by changing the proportion of mercury and sulphur, or by altering their condition, or by combining both changes, we might reasonably hope to convert one metal into another, and to convert all metals into gold. Gold and silver were supposed to contain a very pure mercury, combined in the first case with a red, and in the second with a white sulphur. These ideas are, as we shall see, adopted by Roger Bacon in his *Mirrour of Alchemy*.

Now what are we to say of such ideas as these? Are we to treat them scornfully as unscientific and as unworthy of recapitulation? The suppositions have been disproved, it is true, but then so have innumerable hypotheses which were useful in their time. The Copernican system which represented the planets as moving round the sun in circular paths was given up in favour of the view which regarded those paths as an ellipse, but it was only by constructing the first hypothesis and *finding that to be insufficient*, that the second could ever have been arrived at.

Again, the theory according to which matter is built up of multitudinous minute particles called atoms which cannot be divided, when philosophically considered, involves us in absurd inconsistencies. Nevertheless it has been an especially useful hypothesis in helping us to a proper classification of chemical facts for purposes of research. It is quite true that it will not suffice in science to set about weaving fancies without reference to fact; but in trying to explain things we are bound to make guesses at truth, and some of our first guesses are sure to be wrong. The proper way to treat the guesses which we call hypotheses is to think out what logically follows when we assume that they are true. If our deductions are found to coincide with fact the hypothesis is probably valid, if not it is invalid. Thus if we were to assume that the moon is made of green cheese, it would follow from this that the weight of the moon would be for its bulk very small, but this is known not to be the case; and moreover as many other absurd and impossible or improbable results would follow, such a hypothesis is obviously invalid. Newton assumed that the force of gravity varied inversely as the square of the distance, and the validity of this hypothesis was proved by showing that Kepler's laws of planetary motion, which were known to be true, followed naturally from this assumption.

When we have got a hypothesis which in many cases is workable but in some cases also fails, it may still be of immense service, but we should not hastily describe it as a fact. Of such a hypothesis, for instance, as the atomic theory* we can say that there is between this idea and the actual constitution of matter sufficient analogy to make the former a great help towards the appreciative study of many scientific facts. But we have no right whatever to say that this theory in any form rightly represents what *is* the constitution of matter. Shortly then the use of any hypothesis is to lead to a more appreciative study of facts. One of the first fruits of this study may be the proof that the hypothesis itself was invalid, but that does not destroy its value as a means to progress. In this light Geber's idea was a first guess. It was wrong, but it at least led people to think of the metals together, and as a class; and was the first step in a series of conjectures as to what were the "elements" or simple substances out of which complex bodies were composed. It was a decided advance on the old Aristotelian notion of the four elements, earth, fire, air, and water; and it was something to have escaped so early from the thraldom

* For the atomic theory see p. 257

in which the ideas of Aristotle were destined to hold the world for centuries to come.

After Geber we seem almost to go back. The writings of his successors, for a long period, are in most cases a farrago of mysterious nonsense broken by rare deviations into sense. Their descriptions of their experiments are among the most wonderful specimens of a falsely metaphorical style on record. These treatises are interesting, however, for the occasional gleams of light they shed on the development of what was to become a science. Some of the alchemists, too, certainly did good work. After all they had few means then of attaining their knowledge, and we cannot justly scoff at those who, while seeking their unsubstantial dreams, were unconsciously preparing the ground for the seed which later generations sowed, seed now, though the sowers have long slept, springing forth into a full harvest of ripe grain.

Albert Groot, better known as Albertus Magnus (1193—1282), was a German; a universal genius he would probably be termed now, who after being made Bishop of Ratisbon, gave up his bishopric to follow science. He was theologian, physician, astrologer, and alchemist. In his chemical ideas, he followed Geber, considering all metals to be composed of sulphur and mercury. He describes various apparatus, such as alembics and aludels, but it is difficult, of course, to say how many of his ideas were original. He is chiefly renowned as the commentator of Aristotle. Alembics were used for distilling liquids. The aludel was used chiefly for distilling solids which vaporise without melting, *i.e.* for *sublimation.*

We next come to a name which, like Geber's, stands out alone, though the bearer of it was greater as a philosopher than as a chemist. Roger Bacon was a contemporary of Albertus Magnus, though the dates of his birth and death are somewhat uncertain (perhaps 1214—1284). In the course of his life he passed through many vicissitudes. After studying at Oxford, he enrolled himself as a Franciscan friar, probably in order to pursue his meditations in peace. He engaged in experimental research, thereby acquiring an unenviable notoriety. One who cared to study God's work, must, it was thought in those days, be in league with the devil. Accordingly Bacon was ordered to Paris, and there confined to his cell, without writing materials, it is said, for ten years. Imagine the torment this insane act of barbarity must have caused to a man whose brain was seething with thoughts struggling to be uttered, and theories waiting to be tested by fact. For ten mortal years to be compelled to silence, when some of the greatest purposes of life could only be fulfilled in speech; for ten years to be forced into idleness, when a millennium would be all too short to accomplish the work waiting to be done!

But at length there intervened one whose soul seems, at least, to have been above the superstitious prejudices of his subordinates. Pope Clement IV. was appealed to, and ordered Bacon forthwith to send him any writings he might prepare. The restrictions as to writing materials were then removed, and Bacon was at work once more. The long pent-up flood of his thoughts seems to have burst forth then in an overwhelming torrent. In the next eighteen months three large treatises were dispatched to the Pope—the *Opus Majus, Minus,* and *Tertium*—the first itself filling a large folio volume of print. In 1268 Bacon returned to Oxford, and characteristically undaunted by the penalties he had suffered, forthwith produced a strongly-worded attack upon the Church, for which he was once more promptly thrown into prison. There it appears he remained for fourteen years, being released in 1282, after which he published his *Compendium Studii Theologiæ* and died probably in 1284.

Condemnation of this treatment could not be expected for a long time after his death. The greater a man is, indeed, the longer period must elapse after his death before he is thought of as even not below the level of the ordinary man. The ordinary man is apt to honour people with reverence in proportion as they conform more nearly to his own type, so that a few flashes of diplomatic tact superimposed upon invulnerable mediocrity afford an immediate passport to popularity, though not to lasting fame. Roger Bacon could not be mediocre, nor did he stoop to be diplomatic. He was centuries in advance of his contemporaries, and such presumption was reckoned, as it ever is, unpardonable. It is only of late years, indeed, that his position has come to be appreciated, though some indignation had been aroused at a much earlier date. Here is an extract, for instance, from a writer of the seventeenth century.

"But such was the stupid ingratitude of Bacon's age that it almost repented this learned man of his knowledge. For his own order would scarce admit his books into their libraries. And great was this poor man's unhappiness: for being accused of magick and heresy, and appealing to Pope Nicholas the Fourth, the Pope liked not his learning, and by his authority kept him close prisoner a great many years." *

The stories told about Bacon were, of course, of the wildest and most extraordinary kind. The best known of them is embodied in a play of Robert Greene's (1594), entitled *The Honourable History of Friar Bacon and Friar Bungay*. The story is here told of the famous brazen head, by the enchantments of which the whole of England was to have been walled with brass. Bacon sent his servant Miles to watch it while he slept, with exhortations to waken him if the head should speak. The head merely uttered the words "Time is," for which Miles thought it not worth while to waken his master. The second speech, "Time was," did not suffice to rouse

---

* *Bacon, Roger: His Discoveries of the Miracles of Art, &c.* Translated by T. M. (London, 1659).

him, and finally came the fatal words, "Time is past." Then, as they have it in the play, "a lightning flashes forth, and a hand appears that breaks down the head with a hammer." Miles now roused his master at once, but it was, of course, too late. In *The Famous Historie of Fryer Bacon*, a chap-book of the year 1527, will be found this and many other amusing stories. There seems no doubt that Roger Bacon was one of the several people incorporated in the old Faust legend. This will be seen by reference to a curious old book, *The Surprizing and damnable life of Dr. Faustus*.*

Of Bacon's works, we must make reference to the *Opus Majus*, though this is not strictly chemical, but rather a treatise on the general principles of science.† But as these principles have a bearing upon chemistry as well as upon other sciences, and as, moreover, Bacon insists strenuously upon the value of experiment—a doctrine the acceptance of which is peculiarly necessary to the advance of chemical science—his work should have interest for every chemist.

In Part IV. of the *Opus* Bacon upholds the value of mathematics. Force, according to him, is invariably subject to mathematical laws. If we recollect, and it is certainly difficult to realise it, that such ideas were promulgated in the thirteenth

* London (1608).
† Roger Bacon: *Opus Majus* (London, 1733, folio). See also an interesting paper by Prof. R. Adamson (1876), on *The Philosophy of Science in the Middle Ages*.

century, while the great Kepler thought the revolutions of the planets might be accounted for by guiding spirits, we may be able to appreciate Bacon's pre-eminence. In Part VI., Bacon treats of experiment, and in a way more truly philosophical than that of his successor Francis Bacon, who is generally referred to as the founder of the inductive philosophy. Francis Bacon's system rests wholly upon induction; Roger Bacon grants the validity, indeed, the necessity, of theorising, but the hypothesis must be *verified* by appeal to observation and experiment. As he says in Part VI., "Argument shuts up the question, and makes us shut it up too; but it gives no proof, nor does it remove doubt, and cause the mind to rest in the conscious possession of truth, *unless the truth is discovered by way of experience.*"

The strange resemblance in many points between Roger Bacon's ideas and those of his illustrious namesake has been noticed by Hallam in his *History of the Middle Ages.* "Whether Lord Bacon," he says, "ever read the *Opus Majus*, I know not, but it is singular that his favourite quaint expression, *prærogativæ scientiarum*, should be found in that work; and whoever reads the sixth part of the *Opus Majus* upon experimental science, must be struck by it as the prototype in spirit of the *Novum Organum.*" But we must not further discuss the *Opus Majus* here. So far as it has bearing upon the general principles of scientific research, it deserves a prominent place in the history of every science. The practice of spinning wordy cobwebs without appeal to fact was the fashion for centuries after Bacon's death, and we all owe reverence to the man who so early saw that a theory or hypothesis cannot stand "unless the truth is discovered by way of experience." But having thus far glanced at the importance of Bacon's logical work, we must now turn to more strictly chemical matter.

Bacon has been usually alluded to as the discoverer of gunpowder, at least as far as Europe is concerned. That he was acquainted with it is certain from the following passage in the sixth chapter of his *De secretis operibus artis et naturæ.** "Mix together saltpetre, luru vopo vir conutiret (*sic*), and sulphur, and you will make thunder and lightning, if you know the method of mixing them." By the extraordinary term "luru vopo vir conutiret," he presumably refers to charcoal. But it is not certain that he invented this mixture. On the authority of an Arabic writer in the Escurial collection, referred to by Hallam, it seems that gunpowder was introduced by the Saracens into Europe before the middle of the fifteenth century. Whether Bacon had gathered his information at an earlier date from some Eastern source is uncertain and may be doubted. And, whoever first prepared this substance, it is difficult to say whether it has done much credit to its inventor.

Bacon's *Mirrour of Alchimy* is written in a style

* Hamburg (1618). Also a translation by T. M.: London (1659).

similar to that of other alchemistic writing of his and a later period. In it he adopted Geber's ideas as to the constitution of the metals :—" All metals and minerals .... are begotten of Argentvive and sulphur." The book, as a whole, does not seem worthy of its author.

Raymond Lully's name may perhaps be mentioned in connection with Roger Bacon (1235—1315). He wrote a great deal, but for the most part it was jargon. He had a romantic life, beginning as a lover of the Lady Eleanor of Castello. She cured him of his passion by showing him an ulcer eating away her breast. At her request he consecrated himself to God and missionised the Mussulmans. He died in sight of Minorca after being stoned at Tunis. He was acquainted, it seems, with nitric acid, which he obtained by distilling saltpetre with the lower sulphate of iron, and he knew that on adding potashes to a liquid containing alcohol the alcohol rose to the surface or was salted out. His opinion of alcohol seems to have been high, for he terms it *consolatio ultima corporis humani*. His missionising propensities notwithstanding, Lully seems to have been somewhat of an impostor, and his chemical opinions are not of much moment.

Bernard of Trevisa spent his whole life in searching for the secret. In one striking chemical passage he asserts that the alchemists are mistaken in supposing that with acids they obtain solutions of the metals *as such*, or, as he puts it, as with mercury, for by the action of these acids the metals are *severed* or "decomposed" (*separabuntur*). The truth, of course, is that the acid is decomposed, the metal forming a soluble *salt*. When we dissolve copper in nitric acid a chemical change occurs and the metal disappears. We obtain a blue solution, but this is not a solution of copper, it contains a *salt* of copper, viz. copper nitrate. The writings of this time are romances, and indeed so far did the writers carry their hyperbole and mysticism that we find treatises on alchemy almost unrecognisably disguised in what on the surface seems merely a romantic tale.

But the darkest age of alchemy was now drawing to a close, and although for a long time the alchemists held the field, yet more and more of them were chemists as well. The time of the mere gold-searcher, the mere alchemist, whose desires consumed themselves like his furnace fires to white profitless ashes which could be rekindled no more, was almost past.

SECOND PERIOD.

CHAPTER III.

SECOND PERIOD: MEDICAL MYSTICISM.
BASIL VALENTINE.

BRANDE rather rashly utters a sweeping condemnation of the history of the alchemists up to the date at which the last chapter closes: " It presents nothing that the mind rests upon with satisfaction; nothing that it reverts to with interest or profit." This is certainly going too far; for Geber and Roger Bacon both afford us interest and profit. But it was a dark age for chemistry to this time. In the present chapter we shall meet with people who directed many experiments to the elucidation of other mysteries than that of the preparation of gold. It is true their writings are still written in a very inflated and often unintelligible style, but we find a greater tendency to attempt accurate description.

Basil Valentine is the first of these new chemists whom we shall notice. Valentine was a native of Erfurth, and wrote towards the close of the fifteenth century. He strangely combines the incoherent jargon of the older alchemist with really rational descriptions of experiments. The period which opens with Valentine is a new one in more than one characteristic. The era of medical chemistry, iatro-chemistry as it is called, was ushered in by Valentine's *Triumphant Chariot of Antimony*, in which the medicinal properties of antimony were insisted upon with strenuous vehemence. The search for transmutation was to some extent exchanged for the pursuit of the *elixir vitæ*, which was to cure all the ills of flesh, and by means of which, even so far back as 1130, Artephius was said to have lived to the advanced age of 1,025. The term philosopher's stone has also been applied to this elixir, and probably some thought that the same body was to transmute the metals and prolong life. However, Valentine's purpose was in the main medical, and his work in this direction led him to important results. Before considering what services he rendered to science we may quote a passage from him where the alchemistic taint is pronounced.

The following is from *The twelve Keys of Brother Basil Valentine, of the Benedictine Order. By which the doors to the ancient stone of our forefathers is opened, and the unfathomable well-spring of all health*

THE KING AND HIS BRIDE.

From a Woodcut in *Die Zwölf Schlüssel*
(illustrating the quoted passage).

is discovered.* "The crown of the king must be of pure gold, and a chaste bride must be given to him in marriage. Therefore if you wish to work through our bodies then take the greedy, grey wolf, so-called because he is subject to the warlike Mars, but who is by birth a child of old Saturn, found in the valleys and hills of the world and possessed by great hunger, and throw to him the body of the king that he may make it his food, and when he has devoured the king make a great fire and throw the wolf into it, that he may be wholly burned, and by this means will the king be again released. When this has happened three times the lion will have conquered the wolf, and will find nothing more of him to consume, and in this way our body is made perfect for the beginning of our work."

This is a fair example of the falsely metaphorical style, and it is a similar passage which is chosen for satire by Glauber at a later date. If this is indeed one of the keys to the stone it is itself shut within what at first seems a keyless lock. If we merely read the prescription as it stands it is indeed senseless jargon, but it becomes more intelligible when we make some attempt to interpret these alchemical terms. The *king* signifies sulphur, the *wolf* is antimony, *Mars* is iron. By thus substituting rational equivalents for this fanciful nomenclature something may be made of it, but, as a rule, *le jeu ne vaut pas la chandelle.*†

* Basilius Valentinus: *Chymische Schriften*, Hamburg (1677).
† Not content with these fanciful names they represented the metals by the curious symbols still not entirely obsolete. These symbols are given below; each of them is enclosed in a square as they occur in

Valentine's important chemical work is concerned with the metal antimony, and with nitric, hydrochloric, and sulphuric acids. Of antimony and its medicinal uses he writes at length in his best-known work, *The Triumphant Chariot of Antimony.* His other principal writing is the *Haliographia*, which appeared in 1644 at Bologna. It embodies a mass of information on the mineral, vegetable, and animal salts. It is scattered through this and the former work that his references to nitric, hydrochloric, and sulphuric acids will be found.

Nitric acid is a very old chemical product. The acid was in common use among the early alchemists, but we find in Valentine the first mention of a simple preparation, according to which a mixture of three parts of powdered earthenware with one of nitre is distilled. The method remained in use for a long period. Other methods are given by Valentine and sufficiently clearly

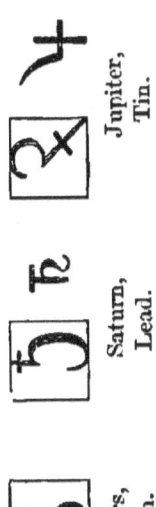

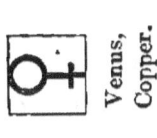

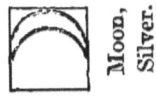

Glauber's *Treatise of the Signature of Salts, Metals, and Plants.* The extent to which the symbol touches the enclosing squares is intended, says Glauber, to indicate the relative perfection of the metal. "Now if into one of these I put the character of the sun or gold, viz., a round circle, it touches four parts of the square and filleth it up, signifying that among celestial and terrestrial creatures, the sun and gold do excel all other things in their perfection."

described. The method at present in use was not discovered apparently till the time of Glauber. It consists in distilling mixed nitre (saltpetre or nitrate of potash) and sulphuric acid (oil of vitriol), and will be further mentioned when Glauber's work is considered. Valentine termed it *water* or *acid spirit* of nitre. It was afterwards called *aquafortis*.

Hydrochloric or muriatic acid was known to the Arabian alchemists, as was its mixture with nitric acid or *aqua regia*. But it is in Basil Valentine's work that we first find mention of the pure acid under the name *spiritus salis*, prepared from *guter vitriol* and *sal commune*, that is from the green sulphate of iron and common salt.

Sulphuric acid was apparently known to Geber, but its preparation from green vitriol is first fully described by Valentine. He refers to the product as *oil of vitriol* in the *Haliographia*, while the directions for preparing the green vitriol, or lower sulphate of iron, by dissolving iron filings in dilute oil of vitriol, are also there given. "The solution," he says, "when put aside in a cool place, soon forms beautiful crystals;" while elsewhere he states that "this salt is an excellent tonic; that it comforts weak stomachs; and that externally applied it is an admirable styptic."

In references like these we see a distinct desire to examine chemical products for their own sake, and not merely because they might lead to the discovery of the philosopher's stone. Further we see in the medical tendency which the science was now assum-

From *Die Zwölf Schlüssel*.

ing the awakening of a conviction that some everyday good might be hoped for from its earnest study. It does not do to love your science any more than to love a person with an entirely abstract and fanciful passion. One must love as well

> "to the level of every day's
> Most quiet need by sun and candlelight;"

and the alchemists were only just realising that their science must be an every-day science as well as a beautiful dream.

As the main facts concerning the preparation of this most important substance, sulphuric acid, were by this time discovered, we may here find an appropriate place for a general sketch of its history. Valentine, as just stated, prepared it from ferrous sulphate by heat. The liquid so obtained fumes in the air, and is thus distinguished from the acid as ordinarily prepared by the name of *fuming sulphuric acid*. It is also now known as *Nordhausen sulphuric acid*, from the fact that it was prepared at Nordhausen, in the Hartz. It consists really of a solution of sulphur trioxide in sulphuric acid. It is now prepared in Bohemia in the works of J. D. Starck. It is a colourless, thick, oily liquid when pure, but is generally coloured slightly brown from the presence of organic matter. The oxide of iron left behind in the retort when the distillation is complete was termed *colcothar* or *caput mortuum* of vitriol. This last term arose from the fanciful practice by which the old chemists symbolised the dregs and last products of substance by the figure of a death's head and crossbones. Sulphur trioxide (SO^3) is also prepared in large quantities, near London, by Dr. Messel.

Another and more important method of preparing sulphuric acid is for the first time described by Basil Valentine, and it is a modification of this which is now in general use. It consists in burning a mixture of sulphur and nitre (nitrate of potash), whereby the sulphur is oxidised or burnt up by the oxygen of the nitre, and sulphuric acid is formed. The following are his words: "Take of antimony,* sulphur, salt nitre, of each equal parts, fulminate them under a bell, as oil of sulphur *per campanam* is made, which way of preparing hath long since been known to the ancients; but you will have a better way if instead of a bell you take an alembic and apply to it a recipient, so you will obtain more oil, which will indeed be of the same colour as that made of common sulphur, but in powers and virtues not a little more excellent."†

The present method of manufacturing sulphuric acid was, according to some accounts, introduced into England from the Continent by Cornelius Drebbel; but the first authentic information is that a certain Dr. Ward obtained a patent for its manufacture. He employed glass globes of about forty or fifty gallons capacity. A little water was poured into the globe,

---
* The antimony forms a sulphide with the sulphur present and is not essential to the reaction.
† *Triumphant Chariot of Antimony.*

a stoneware pot introduced and on this was placed a red-hot iron ladle. A mixture of sulphur and saltpetre was then thrown into this ladle, and the vessel closed to prevent the escape of the copious fumes evolved. The vapours were absorbed by the water

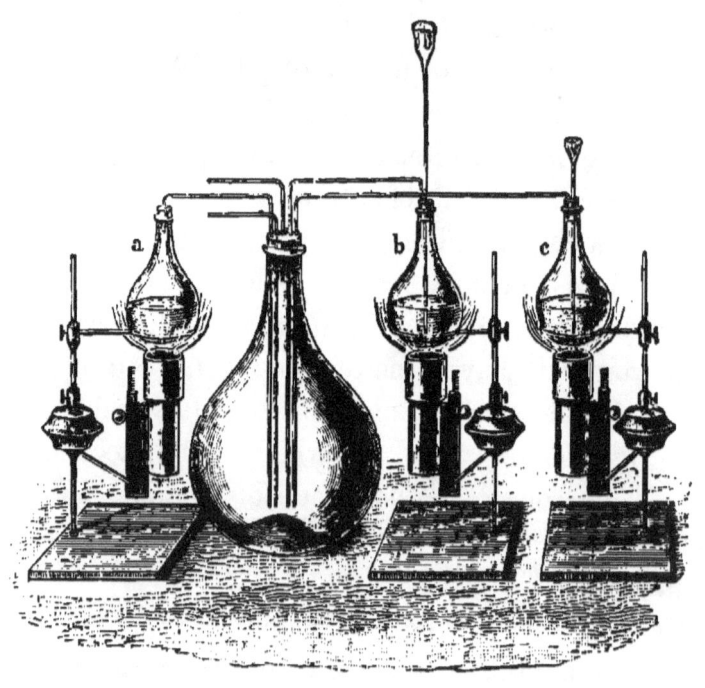

APPARATUS TO ILLUSTRATE THE MANUFACTURE OF SULPHURIC ACID.

a, flask for boiling water.
b, flask containing copper and sulphuric acid to evolve sulphuric dioxide.
c, flask containing copper and nitric acid to evolve nitrous fumes. The other tubes in the large flask are to admit air.

and sulphuric acid thus formed. To distinguish it from the acid obtained from the iron sulphate it was termed oil of vitriol made by the bell. It was priced at from 1s. 6d. to 2s. 6d. per pound. The next advance was effected by Dr. Roebuck, a physician of Birmingham, who replaced the glass globes by leaden chambers. These chambers were first erected in Birmingham in 1746, and in 1749 at Preston Pans in Scotland. As before, the charge of sulphur and nitre was placed within the chamber, ignited, and the door closed. After the lapse of time sufficient for the absorption of the product by the water in the chamber the doors were opened and the charging repeated.

The size of the leaden chambers was at first limited to six feet square, and for many years did not exceed ten feet square. By 1783 Messrs. Kingscote and Walker had erected chambers forty-five feet long and ten feet wide. Berthollet's application of chlorine to the bleaching of cotton goods (1788) gave at once an enormous impulse to the manufacture, and in the following way : Hydrochloric acid is largely used in the preparation of chlorine, and sulphuric acid in the preparation of hydrochloric. The reaction of the manufacture of each upon that of the other is thus readily seen. The final improvement, chiefly proposed by Chaptal, resulted in making the process continuous. To this end the sulphur* is burnt separately to form sulphur dioxide, and this is sent into the leaden chambers mixed with steam. Nitre is heated in separate vessels and the *nitrous fumes* resulting from its decomposition also passed into the chambers.

* Iron pyrites, a sulphide of iron, is actually used in practice.

To show the extent to which the sulphuric acid industry has developed we must recall that in Dr. Ward's time the commercial acid was priced at from 1s. 6d. to 2s. 6d. per lb. It may now be obtained at the price of 1d. per lb., while the annual product in Great Britain cannot fall far short of 1,000,000

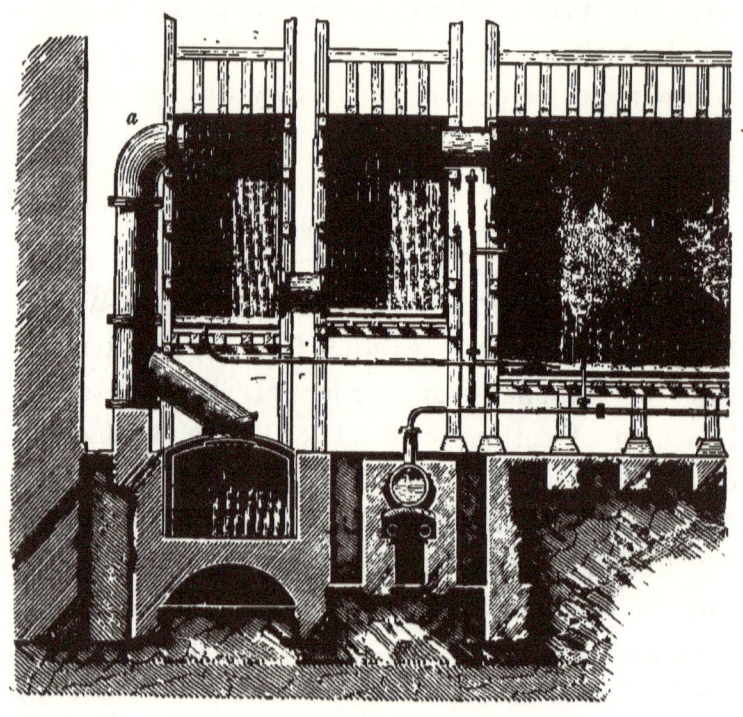

MANUFACTURE OF SULPHURIC ACID.

Steam passes in from the boiler (i); sulphur dioxide and nitrous fumes through the large pipes (a).

tons. In the South Lancashire district alone the quantity manufactured some years ago amounted to 3,000 tons *per week*. Dyeing, bleaching, and the alkali industry consume enormous quantities of sulphuric acid, and there are innumerable manufactures in which it is more or less employed. Such is the development presented to us by a single chemical industry. The figures are impressive enough, and we are apt to become elated by mere contemplation of a long succession of noughts when anything commercial is concerned. Perhaps it may be well, therefore, to remind ourselves that the mere production of sulphuric acid, even to the amount of inland seas, is in itself no special boon. Chemistry has so far been applied to manufacture. Good, but how far has the manufacture increased the happiness of life?

Having now shown the wider development and application of some ideas known in all their essential details so far back as the time of Basil Valentine, and brought to their present enormous range of application by only very slight additions and changes, we must return to our alchemist. We have discussed to some extent his position as a chemist, and we need now only treat of the work upon which he himself most strenuously insisted—the elucidation of the properties and virtues of antimony.

This metal occurs native as stibnite or antimony sulphide, a mineral known in very early times, and employed by women in the East for painting the eyebrows. In St. Jerome's translation of the Hebrew of Ezekiel xxiii., 40, we read "circumlinisti stibio oculos tuos,"—"thou hast painted thine eyes around with stibnite."

The word *alkohol* was originally used to distinguish

this mineral. The Arabic name was "Kohl," and this word passed as *alcool* or *alkohol* into other languages, as, for instance Spanish, where the above biblical passage is rendered "alcoholaste tus ojos." At a later date the term alcohol was applied to any fine powder and, finally, spirits of wine. How this last transition was effected it is difficult to say. We know that strong alcohol was formerly termed *vinum alcalisatum* (wine strengthened with alcohol), and it has been suggested that by some misunderstanding this came to be written *vinum alcoholisatum*, and then *alcohol vini*. At best this is a somewhat doubtful conjecture. Pliny termed the mineral *stibium*, while in the Latin translation of Geber the word *antimonium* is used. The German name *spiessglas* is first found in the writings of Basil Valentine.*

How the word antimony was derived it seems impossible to say. A fanciful story is related to the effect that Valentine, intent upon discovering the medicinal properties of this substance, used his brother monks as "subjects" for his experiments, and administered it in some form to several, some of whom succumbed to its powers. Upon this it is said that Valentine invented for this body the term *antimoine*, *i.e.*, "hostile to monks." (!) To dispose of this story it is only necessary, apart from its inherent absurdity, to cite Kopp's remark to the effect that this word would have been invented by a Frenchman, while Valentine wrote in German.

* This account is taken from Roscoe and Schorlemmer's *Treatise*.

Valentine's monograph indicates a really epoch-making advance on previous chemical writings. It is a thoroughly earnest attempt to study in detail the properties of one substance and its derivatives. We find here the first description of the mode of obtaining the metal, though this is not mentioned as a new discovery. Numerous antimonial preparations are described, and special stress is laid upon their medicinal properties.

The metal antimony, as already stated, is found in nature chiefly as the sulphide. It forms with other metals some important alloys which may here be mentioned. Valentine alludes to the existence of alloys of antimony. *English type-metal* is an alloy of lead, antimony, and tin. The antimony gives the alloy the property of expanding as it solidifies. From this it results that when used to make a cast of a letter it presses itself into all the interstices, and a very accurate reproduction is obtained. The tin gives the metal toughness and coherence. Three analyses of English type-metal are here given :—

	I.	II.	III.
Lead	50	55·0	61·3
Antimony	25	22·7	18·8
Tin	25	22·1	20·2

German type-metal contains about 15 per cent. of antimony.

Britannia Metal and Pewter.—This is a silver-white alloy largely used for spoons, tea-pots, and other "silver" articles. It is mainly composed of tin and antimony.

	Britannia Metal.	Plate Pewter.	Ashbury Metal.
Tin	85·7	81·9	89·3	77·8
Antimony	10.4	16·2	7·1	19·4
Copper	1·0	—	1·8	—
Zinc	2·9	1·9	—	2 8
Bismuth	—	—	1·8	—

White or anti-friction metal is used for lining the brasses of various parts of locomotive engines. It is composed of tin, antimony, and copper. The variety of this alloy known as Babbit's metal, also contains a considerable percentage of lead.

Two processes may be used to extract metallic antimony from the native sulphide. In either case the sulphide is subjected to the *liquation* process. In this process the mineral is melted in vertical cylinders, through a hole in the bottom of which it flows out leaving the *gangue* behind. The sulphide, thus purified, is known as *crude antimony*. By one process the metal is obtained from it by heating to redness with scrap iron. The iron takes away the sulphur from the antimony sulphide, leaving the metal behind.* The metal is fused with sodium carbonate (*pearl-ash*)

---

* Where Fe stands for iron, Sb for antimony, and S for sulphur we have:—

$$Sb^2 S^3 + 3 Fe = 3 Fe S + Sb^2.$$

to purify it from foreign metals, and poured into moulds where it is allowed to cool slowly. During this slow cooling the metal assumes a crystalline

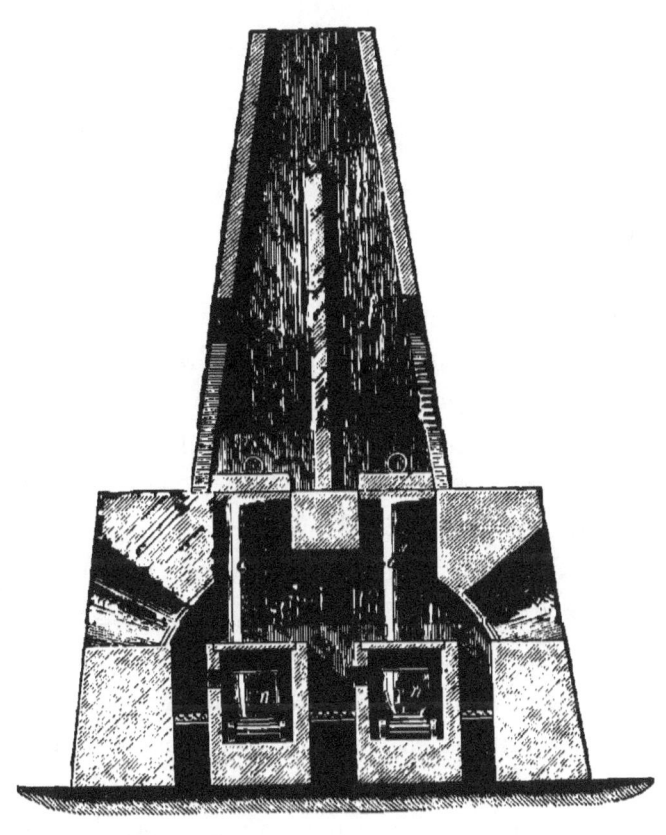

structure and exhibits on its surface very beautiful fern-leaf markings. It has a white colour and is very brittle. In the second process the purified sulphide is roasted in order to convert it into oxide, and the oxide is "reduced" to metal by melting in a large earthen crucible with charcoal or crude tartar. The construction of a common form of liquation furnace is shown in the illustration on the previous page. The ore is placed in the cylinders c, c' and the molten sulphide collects in the pots n, n'.

Both of the above methods were known to Basil Valentine: "Antimonium is a master in medicine, and from it by means of cream of tartar and salt a king (regulus) is made, steel-iron being added to the spiessglas during fusion. Thus by an artifice a wonderful star is obtained which the learned before my time have termed the philosophical signet star." Again: "Take good Hungarian spiessglas with the same quantity of crude tartar, and half as much saltpetre; rub these small and let them fuse well in a wind furnace; afterwards pour out into a mould and allow to cool, when a regulus is found." The preparation of the stellated antimony was asserted by different alchemists to be due to the action of various occult influences. Valentine thought the appearance only resulted when iron was employed in the preparation; many on the other hand asserted that the stars were in some way answerable for the result, and that it was only during some propitious conjunction that the stellated metal could be obtained. We see here once more an indication of the parting of the ways between alchemy and chemistry. The path of the former, leagued with astrology and other mystic arts, was to tend ever downwards towards deeper degradation, until it was represented only by a race of ignorant impostors and a few perplexed fanatics. That of the latter was to ascend by ways that were often steep and barren, but became ever more prosperously fruitful, to the lonely Pisgah heights beyond which the land of promise stretched no longer as an unfulfilled dream but as the realisation of unbaffled hope.

Of Valentine's description of his antimonial preparations we may here give some samples. After a very lengthy introduction, the greater part of which is devoted to violent abuse of the doctors of his day, and during the perusal of which we wait with growing impatience for matter which is really to the point, Basil Valentine at last rewards us by describing the preparation of "antimony-glass" which consists of the oxide usually coloured by sulphide. "Take Hungarian antimony, or any other (the best), grind it upon a marble into most subtile powder, lay this powder thin and sparingly in a plain earthen vessel, round or square, which let be made with rims about the height of two fingers' breadth; place this vessel on a calcining furnace, administer at first a gentle fire of coals and when the stibium begins to fume, stir it with a little iron rod to and againe, without ceasing, until it ceaseth to emit any vapour; but if in the calcination the antimony chanceth to melt and run into balls, take off the vessel from the fire and let the stibium cool, and grind it again, and doe as afore, which must be so often done, until it neither fumes nor runs together any more, but remains in the form of white ashes; for then is your calcination perfect.

"Take now this stibium thus calcined, put it into a goldsmith's crucible, place it at a violent fire, that the antimony may flow like pure clear water, and that you may know when the glasse of stibium has attained a perfect and pellucid colour, put into the crucible a long cold iron, and the glasse will stick thereunto, which strike with an hammer, and so separate it, and hold it up against the light, which if it be transparent 'tis good and perfect glasse."*

The above quotation is given to show that the alchemist's style is here passing into the clear and accurate language of the chemist. It contrasts strangely indeed with the language used by the same writer in *Die Zwölf Schlüssel*.

We must lastly refer to the marked medical tendencies of Basil Valentine's work. We have already said that with him the era of medical chemistry opened. His naïve enthusiasm for the union of chemistry and medicine is often irresistibly amusing, but is at the same time of grave significance. Medicine had indeed up to this date been a very unscientific affair, and, when we recollect that up to this day we are almost wholly ignorant of the true functions of such a well-known organ as the spleen, this will not

* *Triumphant Chariot of Antimony*, London (1661).

surprise us. With regard to the chemical changes which go on in the body we are far more ignorant. The question of the clotting of blood and its precise causes is still *sub judice*, and the common ideas of yesterday on this matter have been strongly combated of late. We know that phosphorus and arsenic are both very poisonous bodies, but *why* they are so it seems impossible to say. We can conjecture that phosphorus affects the oxidation processes of the body, but when we have said so much we have not got far and can go no farther.

The case of arsenic is made doubly mysterious by the fact that people can accustom themselves to take poisonous doses of the substance without harm. Roscoe has contributed to the Literary and Philosophical Society of Manchester an interesting paper "On the alleged practice of arsenic-eating in Styria," from which it appears that in one case a wood-cutter was seen by a medical man to eat a piece of arsenious acid (arsenic trioxide) weighing 4·5 grains, and the next day he crushed and swallowed another piece weighing 5·5 grains, and the following morning was in his usual state of health. A dose of one grain is, with those who are not of the cult, very dangerous, while one of two to four grains is *almost always fatal*. How individuals can thus by practice withstand fatal doses it is at present simply impossible to say. When then on such simple matters we are at the close of the nineteenth century so ignorant, it is startling to find any writer at the close of the fifteenth century who could discern any relation between chemistry and medicine, or could conceive that the latter was to be dealt with scientifically at all.

Antimony was the substance above all others whose medicinal properties Valentine was sworn to defend. In *The Triumphant Chariot* he approaches his subject with almost awed devotion: "He that will write of Antimony needs a great consideration and most ample minde .... in a word one man's life is too short to be perfectly acquainted with all its mysteries. It is to be administered for inward and outward diseases, which to many moles will seem incredible." Valentine is not given to compliment those who oppose him. "Whoever, therefore, will be a true antimonial anatomist, let him first consider the division or operation of his body." For the unchemical medicine-man Basil Valentine entertains the loftiest scorn, and upon such men he pours out the vials of his wrath. They do not even know how to prepare their own medicines; "they know not whether they be hot or dry, black or white, they only know them as written in their books, and seek after nothing but money. Labour is tedious to them, and they commit all to chance; they have no conscience, and coals are outlandish wares with them; they write long scrolls of prescriptions, and the apothecary thumps their medicine in his mortar, and health out of the patient." Probably Valentine's denunciations might apply to some medicine men even now, for it is said that they have been known to mix in a prescription substances which by interaction would lose their characteristic medicinal properties; "they only know them as written in their books."

Valentine finds it difficult to repress his wrath against these "moles," and especially such as refuse to recognise the surpassing value to the human organism of antimony. Thus we find him breaking forth in this strain:—"So I know that many trifling wanderers, lazy doctors, empericks, and many other intruders into physick, will clamour out against antimony, crying a crucifige, but yet it will endure, when those ignorant medicasters shall be broken in pieces." Farther on he gives two ways of extracting a poison, first by its contrary, second by its like: "which proudly arrogant medicasters or physicians, by reason of their sluggish and droanish laziness, are unacquainted with." A plain-spoken man is this Basil Valentine.

Again: "Ah, wretched men, unlearned doctors, unexperienced physicians, who write tedious receipts on a long paper. O ye apothecaries that set over the fire great cauldrons sufficient to boil the meat of noblemen's houses, and to hold enough for a hundred persons, how long will ye be blind . . . ? . . . O deplorable, putrid and stinking bag of worms . . . "

These vigorous onslaughts are amusing enough now, but they must have called for some courage when they were made, and at least their tendency was in the right direction. And this must close our account of Valentine. He rendered some sterling services to knowledge by his discoveries, by his advocacy of really scientific aims, by the dauntless courage of his attacks upon an effete empiricism, and by his early inauguration of the union between medicine and chemistry.

CHAPTER IV.

SECOND PERIOD: MEDICAL MYSTICISM.
PARACELSUS: VAN HELMONT.

THE scientific sky was now for a moment illuminated by the flash of an erratic meteor, which after some moments of dazzling brilliancy plunged back into cimmerian gloom, and left behind it only the feebly glimmering track of light surviving until now. The name of Paracelsus carries with it a mysterious suggestion of power. But it was power for the most part expended in fitful and unproductive bursts. According to Van Helmont's account Paracelsus came to Constantinople during 1521 and received there the philosopher's stone. The adept from whom he received the stone was said to be a certain Solomon Trismosinus, a countryman of Paracelsus. This man appears also to have been in possession of the Universal Panacea and is said to have been seen still alive by a French traveller at the end of the *seventeenth century!* * The details left us of his career are all too few, but as we read even these scattered fragments we continually expect some consummation of achievement from so mysteriously isolated a man. But we await in vain; "we have a careless and insolent indication of things that might be—not the splendid promise of a grand impatience, but the scrabbled remnant of a scornfully abandoned aim."

Phillipus Aureolus Theophrastus Bombastus Paracelsus von Hohenheim was by birth Philip Hochener, but he changed his name on commencing his professional career. He was the son of a physician and born in 1493 at Einsiedeln, a small town in the canton of Schwitz, distant some leagues from Zürich. At an early age he quitted his native country and wandered over Europe, visiting the most important towns. This restless spirit characterizes the whole of his future career, and was one great reason why so much of his influence was dissipated and lost.

In 1526 he returned to his native land and was recommended by Œcolampadius to the chair of physic at Basle. Here Paracelsus commenced his career by burning publicly in the hall the works of Avicenna and Galen. These two physicians were not together

---

* F. Hartmann: *Life of Paracelsus and the Substance of his Teachings;* a curious work in which the author professes belief in all the mysteries of alchemy.

possessed of so much knowledge, he assured his audience, as were his own shoe-ties; all the universities and all the writers united were less instructed than the hairs of his beard, and he was to be regarded as the sole monarch of physic.

After such proceedings Basle soon ceased to be able to contain him. According to some accounts he was obliged to leave the town owing to his dissolute habits and the wild extravagance of his life. On the whole one may fairly incline to doubt some of these worst stories that were told of him. The force of impact with which this strange being met the stormy opposition of his age is sufficient proof of some nobler aims; and the blindness of his enemies to these leads one to suspect that their condemnation was not unmingled with spite. Besides, Paracelsus was essentially of an aggressive nature, he wanted to do things in a way of his own, and moreover he wanted people to see that that way of his own was a good one. The mildest-mannered man would be sure to incur some hatred as soon as he suggested that things might be done better than they are, and Paracelsus does not seem by any means to have been mild or bland.* Indeed we may fully expect that such a character would have to take an unusually large share of envenomed hatred and scorn.

Let us make allowance for the hatred he inspired

---

* See his works *Opera omnia medico-chemico-chirurgica*, Geneva (1658). Some of his chemical writing was translated by R. Turner: London (1657).

and consent to take him at his best. Another account is given of the reasons which obliged him to leave Basle and it seems the more probable story. A rich canon, it is said, fell sick and offered a hundred florins to any one who could cure him. Paracelsus, with characteristic daring, at once offered to cope with the disease. He administered three pills and the canon got well. We all know the old rhyme:—

> " The devil was ill,
> The devil a monk would be;
> The devil got well,
> *The devil a monk was he.*"

And the Canon of Basle seems to have acted in this case after the pattern of one who should not have been his patron saint. Being so soon restored he felt too confident to part readily with his money, and he refused to pay the promised sum.* The matter was brought before the judicial powers, who decreed that the physician should only receive his customary fee. Probably, such a decision was capable of being called legal; it was certainly not just. Incensed at his treatment by the canon, and at the absurd partiality of the judicial decision, Paracelsus retired in high dudgeon, declaring he would leave the inhabitants of Basle to the eternal destruction which they deserved. In 1527, therefore, he quitted Basle for Strasburg, then travelled into Hungary, and after wandering all

---

* Testimonials to his cures of cases of elephantiasis placed under his care by the City Council of Nuremberg may be found in the archives of that city. (*Hartmann*.)

over Europe in restless discontent, returned to Salzburg to die in poverty in 1541, at forty-eight years of age.

It is difficult to speak very definitely of the discoveries made by Paracelsus. It was, as already hinted, by the impact of his masterful personality that he made the impression that he has left behind. To him was due the growing closeness of union between chemistry and medicine. An alchemist, he yet despised the *mere* search for gold; a physician, he despised the ordinary rote and rule of his profession; a learned professor, he yet determined, in spite of all precedent, to lecture in the common people's tongue. He aimed at making knowledge at once more useful and more widely known. The hide-bound pedants of his age were all against him, and this the more because, even making all allowance for exaggeration, we must admit he was most extravagantly aggressive. But, in spite of the pedants, his work produced a resistlessly expansive impression.

Of the discoveries of Paracelsus as a chemist we may mention that he was the first to prepare hydrogen gas. That alone is sufficient to lend deep interest to his name. He obtained an inflammable gas by the action of dilute acids on metals; this gas was certainly hydrogen, though its true nature and its importance lay undiscovered till the time of Cavendish in 1766. Paracelsus adopted the views taken by Basil Valentine as to the universal constituents of matter, supposing them to be three in number, sulphur, mercury, and salt. It appears, however, that these constituents were not regarded as identical with the common substances recognised by these names, but that, for instance, salt was taken in the sense of *the principle of saltness*, and so on; it was the something which gave rise to the saltness of salt itself. But it is difficult to enter into the subtlety of these views and if we appreciate their general bearing we may be content.

Paracelsus was the first who included animal and vegetable bodies in the same classification, and, according to his theories, health was supposed to result from the presence in the organism of the above constituents in their normal proportions, while a disturbance of these relations led to disease.

In his desire for the union of chemistry and medicine Paracelsus introduced a variety of mercurial preparations in certain diseases. The use of mercury for these purposes is strongly maintained at this day. Opium also came into general use as a medicine owing to the influence of Paracelsus. In such ways he took the initiative in establishing the class of chemical-physicians which now arose.

These men were of course treated as possessed of very questionable powers. It was not "the thing" to administer chemical preparations for medicine; it was not done; and what more condemnation could be needed of those who should try to do it? That mercury and antimony should be used as medicines was certainly too heterodox to be allowed. Their fathers had lived and died without antimony or calomel, and why should these new-fangled faddists think they knew better? And the superior people among them said it was all very well in theory no doubt; but in practice—! and they shook their heads silently and with infinite wisdom.

This made the introduction of chemical preparations by no means easy, and so, when the physicians wanted to administer chemical substances, they disguised them under pretty and fanciful names and their patients were quite satisfied and happy. If these subterfuges were not resorted to, woe betide the physician. Towards the end of the fifteenth century the use of antimony was prohibited at Paris, and Besnier was expelled from the faculty for having persisted in administering it. Chemical medicines came into use in England in the reign of Charles I., and shortly after 1644 the London College of Surgeons made its appearance. We must be ready to recognise the good done by the line of medical chemists. As Brande says, "The foundations of chemical science are to be found in the medical and pharmaceutical writers of the sixteenth century, who rescued it from the hands of the alchemical pretenders, and gave it a place and character of its own." As time went on and the medical sect grew, the alchemists were becoming more and more pretenders indeed, and more and more justly typified by the Subtle of Ben Jonson. The finest talent was enlisted in the ranks of the medical chemists to whose work Paracelsus had given such impetus. It is true that Paracelsus had often raved rather than reasoned, but his ravings, like those of Cassandra, were at least prophetic, and, unlike hers, were never doomed to be impotent.*

Van Helmont, a Dutchman, was one of the followers of Paracelsus, and flourished in the early part of the seventeenth century. He was, it seems, a conscientious enthusiast, but of his additions to knowledge nothing very definite can be said. That the character of the man was of interest is sufficiently shown by the following extract from an autobiographical fragment which he left :—†

"In 1594, being then seventeen years of age, I finished my courses of philosophy, but upon seeing none admitted to examinations at Louvain who were not in a gown and hood, as though the garment made the man, I was struck with the mockery of taking degrees in arts. I therefore thought it more profitable, seriously and conscientiously, to examine myself; and then I perceived that I really knew nothing, or, at least, nothing that was worth knowing. I had, in fact, merely to talk and to wrangle, and therefore refused the title of Master of Arts, finding that nothing was sound, nothing true, and unwilling to be declared master of the seven arts, when my conscience told me I knew not one. The Jesuits, who then taught philosophy at Louvain, expounded to me the

* Those who wish for an *idealised* and poetical sketch of the career of Paracelsus should of course read Browning's poem, published under that name.

† Quoted in Brande's *Chemistry* (2nd ed., 1821).

disquisitions and secrets of magic but these were empty and unprofitable conceits; and instead of grain I reaped stubble. In moral philosophy, when I expected to grasp the quintessence of truth, the empty and swollen bubble snapped in my hands. I then turned my thoughts to medicine, and having seriously read Galen and Hippocrates, noted all that seemed certain and incontrovertible; but was dismayed upon revising my notes, when I found that the pains I had bestowed, and the years I had spent, were altogether fruitless; but I learned at least the emptiness of books and formal discourses and promises of the schools. I went abroad and there I found the same sluggishness in study, the same blind obedience to the doctrines of their forefathers, the same deep-rooted ignorance."

Van Helmont (1577—1644) adopted neither the Aristotelian nor the Paracelsian doctrine as to the constituents of matter. He admitted that air and water were elements. Yet he was the first to recognise the existence of different kinds of "air," and was apparently the inventor of the word "gas." He gave his attention to the "air" which is given off during the process of fermentation, and gave to it the name of *gas silvestre*, or "the gas that is wild and lives in out-of-the-way places." Later this gas was called *fixed air*, and is of course carbonic acid gas, carbon dioxide, or the gas which is obtained on burning charcoal in air. Van Helmont identified this gas with that given off during combustion, with that found in the "Grotto del Cane," near Naples, and also with that obtained by the action of acids on calcareous substances, such as marble. He mentions a *gas pingue* which is evolved from dung, and is inflammable. This is probably impure ammonia. Van Helmont also showed that when a metal is dissolved in an acid it is not destroyed, but may be recovered from solution in the metallic state by suitable means.

Van Helmont was a representative of a different sect of the alchemists from any we have yet discussed. As his ideal and goal he set before himself the discovery, not of transmutation nor of the medicinal "philosopher's stone" as usually understood, but of the universal solvent, or *alkahest* as it was termed, which at the same time was to serve as the cure of all diseases.

Apart then from his interest as a man of penetrating judgment, sufficiently discernible in the short autobiographical extract quoted above, Van Helmont's chief merits lie in his discovery of the existence of different kinds of gases, which had hitherto been all generally confused under the one name of "air." This discovery was indeed one of the very first importance, and required at that time great keenness of observation and alertness of attention. If we recall how in all their superficially observable properties atmospheric air and carbon dioxide are exactly similar, we shall be more in a position to appreciate the talents which, in that condition of knowledge, could discern the differences. In the first place one cannot see air, and in the ordinary sense cannot feel it, cannot take it up and inspect it as one does a mineral; and these peculiar attributes are characteristic of most gases. This of course makes the discovery of their properties a work of quite peculiar delicacy.

Then too such bodies are always tending to escape from us. If one takes a handful of carbonic acid gas out of a jar it at once streams away into the surrounding air. They will not remain, or at least not remain

PREPARATION OF CARBONIC ACID.

long, in a vessel which is open at top, as water will do. We cannot pour hydrogen into a basin and then examine it at leisure, as could be done with a liquid. Carbonic acid, however, being a very heavy gas, and thus tending to sink rapidly in the air, will in this respect to some extent behave like water. If marble, which is calcium carbonate (carbonate of lime), is treated with hydrochloric acid, carbon dioxide is given off and we may conduct the gas so evolved out of the evolution flask into a collecting cylinder as shown. The gas being so much heavier than air it will lie in the cylinder, and only be disturbed quickly by a considerable draught. And having got this gas in the cylinder we may indeed pour it out into another, much as we should do with water, though some will certainly be lost in the process. It will stream downwards into the lower cylinder, and by simple tests, such as pouring in a little lime water which will at once be turned milky, we can readily show that it is there.

Such being the properties of carbonic acid gas it is readily seen that it presents us with fewer difficulties than do other gases; we can more easily get hold of it and deal with it. And carbonic acid, indeed, was the first gas distinguished from ordinary atmospheric air, and this work was accomplished by Van Helmont. In the fermenting vats of breweries this gas is evolved in large quantities. Being heavy and not exposed to rapid air-currents it collects there, and it was there that Van Helmont discovered it. He found that it extinguishes flame and, when inhaled for some minutes, is fatal to animal life.[*] These properties were at once sufficient to distinguish it from atmospheric air, and this and others were sufficient to identify it with the gas obtained by other processes, such as the action of acid upon marble, and found by Van Helmont in the Grotto del Cane, the

[*] It should be noted, however, that this gas taken into the stomach as in aerated drinks is quite harmless and even beneficial.

mineral waters at Spa, and at other places. Carbon dioxide is formed during combustion, the carbon of the burning body, such as a candle, combining with the oxygen of the air to form the oxide.* It is also given off in large quantity in the breath of animals, being formed by the burning up of the waste products in the tissues. It occurs in *chalybeate* and *acidulous* waters, and in volcanic districts escapes in large volumes from the fumeroles and rents in the ground. The Poison Valley in Java is remarkable for the evolution of this gas in very large quantities. In the Grotto del Cane the gas issues from fissures some two or three feet below the mouth of the cave. Up to this depth the gas, by reason of its great density, collects. The cave is thus fatal to small animals thrown into it, while men breathing the pure air above this level are unaffected.

It is interesting to remind ourselves that carbon dioxide has now became a commercial article in every-day use. Aerated waters in almost every case hold carbonic acid gas in solution.† The gas is forced in under pressure, and in these circumstances the water will take up more than its usual amount. On opening a bottle, therefore, of one of these aerated waters, and thus releasing the pressure, the gas begins to escape, thereby causing effervescence and the peculiar *sparkling* appearance seen in the liquid. The consumption

---

* $C + O_2 = CO_2$; or carbon $+$ oxygen $=$ carbon dioxide.

† The *eau oxygené* now somewhat in vogue contains oxygen in place of carbonic acid.

of these drinks is now enormous. Forty years ago two hundred thousand bottles of aerated waters were consumed annually in France. Ten years ago two hundred *million* bottles were scarcely sufficient to satisfy the demand. Some natural waters are aerated, for example, Apollinaris, Carlsbad, and Friedrichshall waters.

To make the water strongly effervescent the gases which escape from the Apollinaris Brunnen, and which contain more than 99 per cent. of carbonic acid, are condensed into the water by machinery specially erected at the spring. The Apollinaris spring furnishes a regular supply of water amounting to 6,000 quart bottles per hour, or more than forty million (40,000,000) bottles per annum.*

In manufacturing the artificial water the gas evolved by treating marble with a mineral acid is first passed through water in the purifier, then stored in a gas-holder, and next passed into a machine for mixing it thoroughly with water. The bottling of the water is also effected by machinery, and in bottles now generally used, small glass balls are inserted as a substitute for corks.

Such then is the importance of carbonic acid gas, which to Van Helmont was known as the wild or out-of-the-way gas, "*gas silvestre.*" It would have seemed to him strange and even incredible that so subtle and intangible an essence should be bottled every day for the use of thousands of quite ordinary mortals at quite

* Spon's *Encyclopædia.*

ordinary dinner-tables. The wandering, mysterious *gas silvestre* sparkling before us on our table of an evening in the light shed by the burning of a still more wonderful "gas" than any known to Van Helmont, that is a strange picture to contrast with the knowledge of his day.

Van Helmont was bitten with the Paracelsian spiritualistic madness and was by this led to form some very curious ideas. The archeus or sentient soul he conceived as having its seat in the stomach, where it directs the first digestion; other digestions being carried on with the aid of the *vital spirits* in different parts of the body. There are in all six digestions described by him; *the number seven has been chosen by nature for the state of repose.* The mystical tendency of Van Helmont is sufficiently indicated by the last clause. It permeated his whole being. He had striven in vain to find any satisfactory knowledge till he secured the works of Thomas à Kempis and John Tauler. He then thought he perceived that wisdom is to be obtained only by humility and prayer. Though a gentleman of means and lord of Merode, of Royenbock, of Oorschot, and of Pellines, he gave up all his property to his sister and renounced all the privileges of his birth. After this a genius appeared to him in all important circumstances of life, and in 1633 his own soul appeared to him in the form of a resplendent crystal. Having followed the ordinary courses of medicine and discarding their doctrines with disgust, he turned his attention to Paracelsus, of whom he became in most respects a warm follower. After the year 1599 he travelled for some time, and on his return married a rich Brabantine lady and passed the rest of his life on his estate at Vilvorde.

Van Helmont achieved for himself immortal fame by his discovery of the *gas silvestre*, but for a long period his work sank into obscurity and was forgotten. Such strange halts are there in the progress of science that it was left to Dr. Black, in the middle of the eighteenth century, to rediscover in *fixed air* the forgotten gas of Van Helmont.

THIRD PERIOD.

CHAPTER V.

THIRD PERIOD: THE DECLINE OF MYSTICISM.

GLAUBER.

AN HELMONT as a disciple of Paracelsus was mentioned immediately after him, but the name of Agricola, who was a contemporary (1490—1555) of Paracelsus, must not pass unnoticed. He was the author of a remarkable work, *De Re Metallica*, containing a complete treatise on metallurgy and mining, and most clearly written. Many of the processes described by him are now actually in use.

The next name of importance is that of Glauber (1603—1668), who still shares a somewhat hazy popular fame as the discoverer of "Glauber's salt," or sodium sulphate. This was the piece of work which seems to have been Glauber's favourite, and his admiration for this substance certainly led him to much magnify its value. The hydrated* sodium sulphate, known as Glauber's salt, is first mentioned in his *De Natura Salium* published in 1658. His collected works were translated into English and published in a folio volume " for public good, by the labour, care, and charge of Christopher Packe, *Philo-Chemico-Medicus*, in 1689. In Glauber's works we find the first clear description of the preparation of ammonium sulphate (sulphate of ammonia), formerly known as *sal ammoniacum secretum Glauberi*. This salt is now used for the manufacture of other ammonia salts, and is also largely employed as a fertiliser in artificial manures. Its conversion into sal ammoniac,† or ammonium chloride, by distillation with common salt (sodium chloride), was also first described by Glauber. Ammonium nitrate, too, was first prepared by him and known as *nitrum flammans*. The production of copper sulphate or blue vitriol by boiling copper with sulphuric acid (oil of vitriol) was first proved by Glauber in 1648. The sulphate is now obtained on the manufacturing scale by roasting the copper ores and digesting with sulphuric acid. It is largely used in calico-printing, and in preparing copper pigments, such as Scheele's green and emerald green. It is also used in electro-metallurgy.

The production of vinegar by the distillation of wood is described by Glauber, but not as a new dis-

* *I.e.*, combined with water.
† Sal ammoniac, the reader may be reminded, was known to Geber.

covery. He mentions that the *acetum lignorum* so obtained may, by redistillation, be made as virtuous as the common *acetum vini*. At a later date his wood vinegar came to be known as *pyroligneous acid*, a name which is indeed preserved still. The method of preparing this acid and its derivatives is described by Glauber in great detail and, apparently, with original improvements. He tells us of the power possessed by wood-tar, or the oily product of the distillation, which is less volatile than the acid, of preserving wood. "Any wood exposed to the Rain, or standing in the water, easily rotting, being anointed with this Oil will be preserved so that it will not so easily rot." In closing this portion of his discourse Glauber says: "Nevertheless I easily persuade myself, that this discourse of mine will not be credited by many, which I cannot help. It contenteth me that I have written the Truth and lighted a candle to my neighbour."

But Glauber's chief claim to immortality rests in his being the first to describe the preparation of hydrochloric (muriatic) acid, by distilling common salt with sulphuric acid, and the first to obtain by this same operation the sodium sulphate so long to be known to posterity as "Glauber's salt." The preparation of the hydrochloric acid, or *spirit of salt*, is described in the first section of the second part of the *Miraculum Mundi*. Here also is given the method for obtaining the Sal Mirabile, which is, of course, obtained in the same process and the discovery

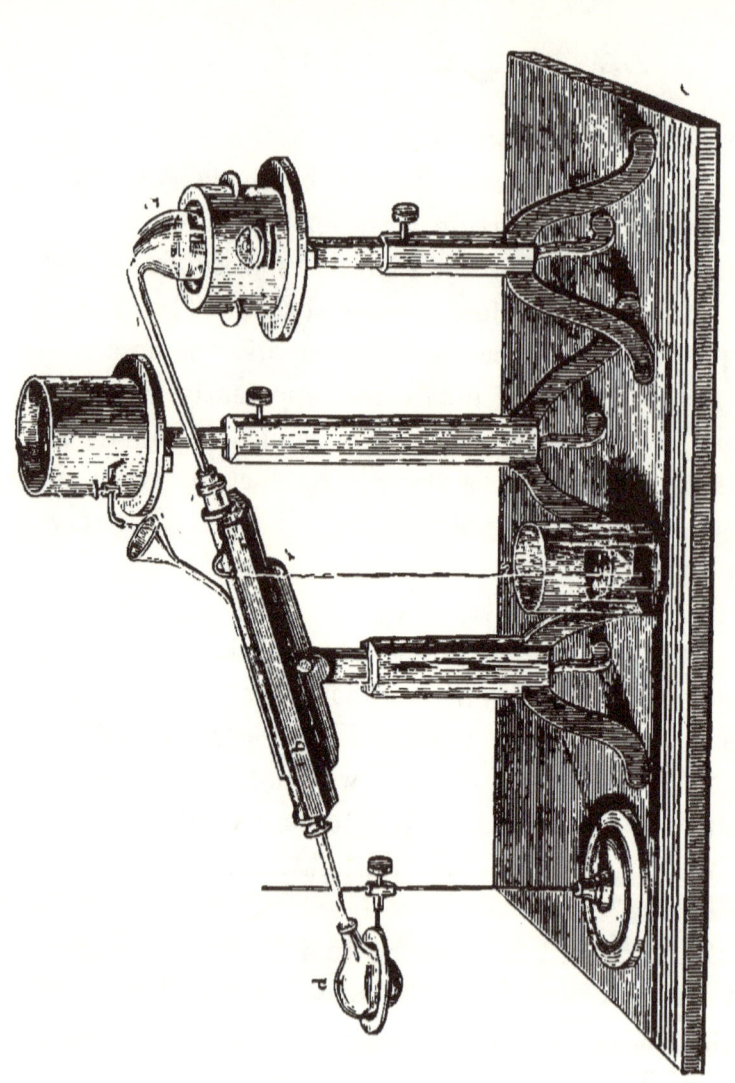

PREPARATION OF NITRIC ACID ON THE SMALL SCALE.
a, retort; b, condenser; d, receiver.

of which first appeared in Glauber's *De Natura Salium* in 1658. To the discussion of the spirit of salt Glauber acutely adds: " Plainly after the very same manner as we have taught spirit of salt to be prepared, so may also be made *Aquafortis** . . . . Instead of salt take nitre, and you will have *Aquafortis*."

The present method of preparing nitric acid from nitre and oil of vitriol (sulphuric acid), would thus appear to have been first used by Glauber, and, indeed, for a long time afterwards the acid thus obtained was known as *Spiritus nitri fumans Glauberi*. Glauber entertained somewhat grandiose ideas as to the uses and virtues of his salt. " Husbandmen, physicians, apothecaries, and chirurgeons are to receive in it a priceless boon." Again, " I believe every Artificer and Trading Man when he can perform his work with less labour and charge, and acquire his wares for less trouble and cost, will sell his commodities to his neighbours at a cheaper rate than he could before he found the benefit of this salt." He then goes on to enumerate fifty-nine of its uses in Medicine, the Arts, and in Alchemy.

As a stage in the manufacture of carbonate of soda in the alkali works, the sulphate is now produced on an immense scale. In the year 1876, no less than

---

* Nitric Acid. This acid is now prepared on the manufacturing scale from sodium nitrate and oil of vitriol. It is largely employed in the manufacture of coal-tar colours, nitro-glycerine, gun-cotton, sulphuric acid, and nitrate of silver (now much used for photography).

700,000 tons were in this way prepared in the United Kingdom. The pure sulphate is used in the production of various kinds of glass—chiefly bottles; in certain medicinal preparations, and to some small extent in dyeing and printing. Here again, as in the case of Helmont's *gas silvestre*, a wonder of the world has become a commonplace. It is, however, none the less wonderful for that.

Salt was regarded by Glauber as one of the principles of matter, and he assigns more power to it than to the others. "This known salt I here call (and not injuriously) the universal treasure, and general riches." Again, "It is the beginning and end of all things, and it increases their powers and their virtues."

Glauber invented and improved chemical apparatus to a large extent, and in his *Furni Novi Philosophic* many useful and interesting furnaces may be found described.

We cannot forbear, before closing our comments upon Glauber, to quote the following amusing imitation by him of the style adopted by Basil Valentine in a paragraph already quoted. This passage occurs in the discussion on *concentrating and amending metals by nitre*. "First a man is to be made of iron, having two noses on his head, and on his crown a mouth which may be opened and again close shut. This if it be to be used for the concentration of metals is to be so inserted into another man made of iron or stone, that the inward head only may come forth of the outward man, but the rest of his body or belly

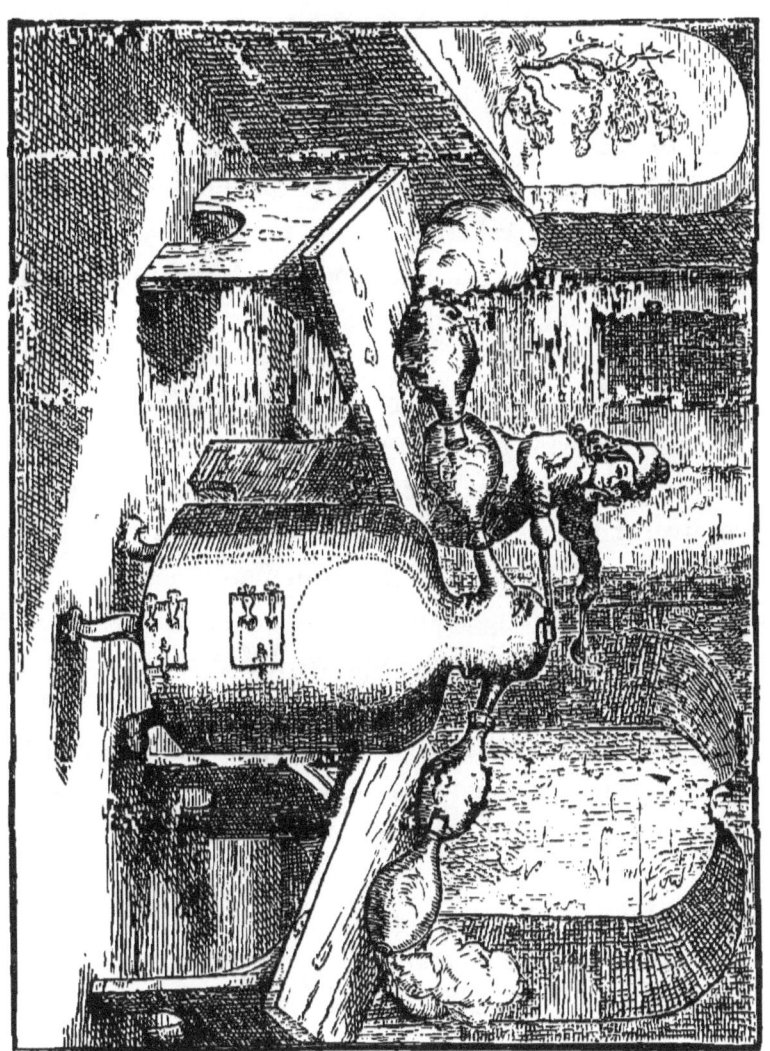

THE IRON MAN WITH TWO NOSES.

may remain hidden in the belly of the exterior man. And to each nose of the head glass receivers are to be applied, to receive the vapours ascending from the hot stomach. When you use this man you must render him bloody with fire to make him hungry and greedy of food. When he grows extremely hungry he is to be fed with a white swan. When that food shall be given to this iron man, an admirable water will ascend from his fiery stomach into his head, and thence by his two noses flow into the appointed receivers; a water, I say, which will be a true and efficacious aqua-vitæ; for the iron man consumeth the whole swan by digesting it, and changeth it into a most excellent and profitable food for the king and queen, by which they are corroborated, augmented, and grow. But before the swan yieldeth up her spirit she singeth her swan-like song, which being ended, her breath expireth with a strong wind, and leaveth her roasted body for meat for the king, but her anima or spirit she consecrateth to the gods that thence may be made a salamander, a wholesome medicament for men and women." This is a very good imitation of the style of the older alchemists. It has the advantage, too, of being more humorously absurd. The iron man with two noses to which receivers are attached is seen in the illustration which is taken from a woodcut in Packe's edition of Glauber's collected works.

We may get a further glimpse into the character of our author from the following quotation taken from a paragraph on gunpowder :—

"Of this mischievous composition and diabolical abuse of gunpowder much might be written; but because the present world taketh only delight in shedding innocent blood, and cannot endure that unrighteous things should be reproved, and good things praised, therefore it is best to be silent, and to let every one answer for himself when the time cometh that we shall give an account of our stewardship, which, perhaps, is not far off; and then there will be a separation of good and bad by him that trieth the heart, even as gold is refined in the fire from dross. And then it will be seen what Christians we have been. We do all bear the name, but do not approve ourselves to be such by our works. Ever one thinketh himself better than others, and for a word's sake which one understandeth otherwise, or takes in another sense than the other (and though it be no point whereon salvation doth depend), one curseth and condemneth another, and persecuteth another unto death, which Christ never taught us to do, but rather did earnestly command us that we should love one another, reward evil with good and not good with evil as now-a-days everywhere they use to do. Every one standeth upon his own reputation; but the honour of God and his commands are in no repute, but are trampled under foot, and Lucifer's pride, vain ambition, and pharisaical hypocrisy or show of holiness hath so far got the upper hand with the learned, that none will leave his contumacy or stubbornness or recede a little from his opinion, although the whole world should be turned upside down thereby. Are not these fine Christians? By their fruit you shall know them, and not by their words. Wolves are clothed with sheep's skins, so that none of them almost are to be found, and yet the deeds and works of wolves are everywhere extant."

This is not chemistry, it is true; but we are concerned here also with character, and of that the previous passage gives much indication. What a man visibly *does* may not be so important as what he *is*. As Emerson puts it, " we do not want actions, but men." So in studying the lives of the workers in any technical branch of human labour, the study is generally pleasant in proportion to the space in their hearts which we find unoccupied by technicality. The quaint moralizing of Glauber in the foregoing passage and in other places shows us a man who had a good deal of earnestness in his heart, and it is all the pleasanter on that account to read of his chemical work.

Glauber was a truly scientific worker and had a fertile mind. We see in his work a distinct advance in method upon that of Basil Valentine. It is certainly more sane, though not so striking, as that of Paracelsus. We are indeed approaching, though slowly, to a more quietly scientific age. Mysticism had received some mortal wounds to which, in spite of its intense vitality, it must gradually succumb. Theory was gradually to become more closely inseparable from observation and experiment.

An interesting alchemical work may next be referred to—*The Brief of the Golden Calf: discover-*

ing the Rarest Miracle in Nature, how by the smallest portion of the Philosopher's Stone a great Piece of common Lead was totally transmuted into the purest transplendent Gold, at the Hague in 1666. This work is by Johann F. Helvetius, and contains one of the most celebrated records of transmutation, which, as it is of considerable interest, may be here quoted at some length :—*

"The 27th day of December, 1666, in the afternoon, came a stranger to my house at the Hague, in a plebeick habit, of honest gravity and serious authority, of a mean stature and a little long face, black hair and not at all curled, a beardless chin, and about forty-four years (as I guess) of age, and born in North Holland. After salutation he besceched me with great reverence to pardon his rude accesses, for he was a lover of the Pyrotechnian art, and having read my treatise against the sympathetic powder of Sir Kenelm Digby, and observed my doubt about the philosophic mystery, induced him to ask me if I really was a disbeliever as to the existence of a universal medicine which would cure all diseases, unless the principal parts were perished or the predestinated time of death come. I replied I never met with an adept, or saw such a medicine, though I had frequently prayed for it.

"Then I said, 'Surely you are a learned physician.' 'No,' said he, 'I am a brass-founder and a lover of

---

* The original version is, like most of these documents, exceedingly prolix and abounds in unnecessary details. That here given is from an abridgment in Brande's *Chemistry*.

chemistry.' He then took from his bosom-pouch a neat ivory box, and out of it three ponderous lumps of stone, each about the bigness of a walnut. I greedily saw and handled for a quarter of an hour this most noble substance, the value of which might be somewhere about twenty tons of gold; and having drawn from the owner many rare secrets of its admirable effects, I returned him this treasure of treasures with a most sorrowful mind, humbly beseeching him to bestow a fragment of it upon me in perpetual memory of him, though but the size of a coriander seed. 'No, no,' said he, 'that is not lawful, though thou wouldst give me as many golden ducats as would fill this room; for it would have particular consequences, and, if fire could be burned of fire, I would at this instant rather cast it all into the fiercest flames.' He then asked if I had a private chamber whose prospect was from the public street; so I presently conducted him to my best furnished room backwards, which he entered without wiping his shoes, which were full of snow and dirt.

"I now expected he would bestow some great secret upon me, but in vain. He asked for a piece of gold, and opening his doublet showed me five pieces of that precious metal which he wore upon a green riband, and which very much excelled mine in flexibility and colour, each being the size of a small trencher. I now earnestly craved a crumb of the stone, and at last, out of his philosophical commiseration, he gave me a morsel as large as a rapeseed; 'But,' I said, 'this scant portion will scarcely transmute four grains of lead.' 'Then,' said he, 'deliver it me back;' which I did in hopes of a greater parcel; but he, cutting off half with his nail, said, 'Even this is sufficient for thee.' 'Sir,' said I, with a dejected countenance, 'what means this?' And he said, 'Even that will transmute half an ounce of lead.' So I gave him great thanks and said I would try, and reveal it to no one. He then took his leave and said he would call again next morning at nine.

"I then confessed that while the mass of his medicine was in my hand, I had secretly scraped off a bit with my nail which I projected on lead, but it caused no transmutation, but the whole flew away in fumes. 'Friend,' said he, 'thou art more dexterous in committing a theft than in applying medicine; hadst thou wrapped up thy stolen prey in yellow wax, it would have penetrated and transmuted the lead into gold.' I then asked if the philosophic work cost much or required long time, for philosophers say that nine or ten months are required for it. He answered, 'Their writings are only to be understood by adepts, without whom no student can prepare his magistery. Fling not away, therefore, thy money and goods in hunting out this art, for thou shalt never find it.' To which I replied, 'As thy master showed it thee, so mayest thou perchance discover something thereof to me, who know the rudiments, and therefore it may be easier to add to a foundation than begin anew.' 'In this art,' said he, 'it is quite otherwise; for unless thou knowest the thing from head to heel, thou canst not break open the glassy seal of Hermes. But enough; to-morrow at the ninth hour, I will show thee the manner of projection.'

"But Elias never came again; so my wife, who was curious in the art whereof the worthy man had discoursed, teased me to make the experiment with the little spark of bounty the artist had left me. So I melted half an ounce of lead, upon which my wife put in the said medicine; it hissed and bubbled, and in a quarter of an hour the mass of lead was transmuted into fine gold, at which we were exceedingly amazed. I took it to the goldsmith, who judged it most excellent, and willingly offered fifty florins for each ounce."

Comment upon this story is needless. If the events narrated were not very much out-of-the-way we should believe Helvetius at once, but, of such a very extraordinary occurrence we should probably feel uncertain on all evidence short of ocular demonstration.

FOURTH PERIOD.

CHAPTER VI.

FOURTH PERIOD: THE BEGINNINGS OF SCIENCE.

AN event of importance belonging to the period with which we have been dealing may here be referred to. The Royal Society was founded by Charles II., and incorporated by him in 1662, under a Royal Charter, for the improvement of natural knowledge. The first volume of the *Philosophical Transactions* of that Society bears date 1665. With occasional intermissions the *Transactions* were published by the successive secretaries of the Society till the year 1750. At that date the publication was put into the hands of a Committee of Papers, and since 1762 a volume has annually appeared.

In 1666 the Royal Academy of Sciences was instituted in Paris under the protection of Louis XIV.

In its early annals we find the names of Homberg, Geoffrey, and the two Lemerys. Homberg discovered boracic acid, which he prepared by decomposing borax by means of a mineral acid, and termed *sal sedativum*. Geoffrey made contributions to pharmaceutical chemistry, and was probably the first compiler of the "Paris Pharmacopœia." Of the Lemerys more will be said in the sequel.

Ever since its foundation the Royal Society of London has been a nucleus round which has clustered the scientific genius of Great Britain. In the earlier years of its infancy it helped to fan the few glowing sparks of the desire for truth into a broadening blaze. It brought together those who were in sympathy through their devotion to knowledge, and who in their union found double strength. By the interchange of their ideas thought was quickened and the advance of science aided. By the publication of original papers new discoveries were placed on record, and thus preserved from being lost, as had too often happened before. The discussion of these papers helped more thoroughly to sift the evidence on which their conclusions were based, and promoted much increased accuracy and simplicity of thought and expression.

Research, too, was stimulated by the increased definiteness of boundary between the known and the unknown. Before such societies had existed the magic-mongers, who then so frequently took the place of men of science, were accustomed to produce their questionable results in mystical folios, or still stranger manuscripts, the few copies of which became dispersed and too often lost. It was, therefore, almost impossible to tell what subjects were really uninvestigated, and hence arose much repetition of already accomplished work, and delay in the real advancement of learning. Research was also more directly encouraged by the Royal Society, by awarding grants of money to defray the expenses of those investigations which seemed worthy of such aid.

Having now left Glauber behind us, we are entering upon a new epoch once more, the period with which the names of Boyle, Hooke, and Mayow are indissolubly connected.

But, before passing on to consider Boyle and his assistant, Hooke, mention must be made of a chemist whose work, though not of so great importance, is yet of considerable interest. Nicholas Lémery (1645—1715) was the well-known author of the *Cours de Chymie* (1675). This book embodied his ideas and teachings, and, being translated into Latin and most modern languages, enjoyed a wide popularity and produced great effects upon the progress of the science. He still retained the belief in salt, mercury (or spirit), sulphur (or oil), as elements, but to these were added water (or phlegm), and earth. The former set were the active, the latter the passive elements. As already stated these terms when thus used did not necessarily signify only the bodies more specially known by those names. "Sulphur," although used for brimstone, was also more generally applied to oils (perhaps from their usually having a yellow colour), and hence we also find the plural "sulphurs" in use. The substances included under one of these names were also supposed to share the same essential nature exhibited under different forms. It is difficult to state clearly what these ideas were; the fact being that the ideas themselves were not clear. But if we bear this in mind we shall be able to appreciate the advances made as the theoretical notions of the chemists become more intelligible.

Lémery, in his work, defines the aim of chemistry to be a knowledge of the various substances "qui se rencontrent dans un mixte" (which meet in a compound), understanding by this term natural products in general. He classifies the products as mineral, vegetable, and animal, placing among the first, metals, minerals, earths, and stones; among the second, plants, resins, gums, fungi, fruits, acids, juices, flowers, mosses, manna, and honey; and among the third, the various parts of the animal organism. Lémery thus established the distinction, now become so broadly defined, between inorganic and organic chemistry. The difference between the two realms of the science was for long a subject of dispute. It became gradually evident that the chemistry of minerals or unorganized structures obeys certain well-defined and never abrogated laws. A true inorganic chemical compound, say, for instance, mercuric oxide, is found on analysis to have always the same composition; in this case, 100 parts of mercuric oxide always contain 92·6 parts of mercury to 7·4 parts of oxygen. Now, owing to the difficulty of purifying substances found in the vegetable and animal kingdoms, it was for a long time considered that these bodies did not obey those and other laws of combination.

As discovery advanced, however, substances, unmistakably organic, were found which distinctly obeyed these laws; and when finally it was found possible artificially to prepare compounds previously known only as existing in the organized structure of plant or animal, the gulf, hitherto separating the organic and inorganic realms of the science, was at last bridged, and the universal reign of consistency and law became apparent.

But the gulf although bridged did not cease to exist, although it has been subsequently narrowed. Broadly, the distinction is now between compounds of carbon, and compounds of not-carbon. The element carbon is sharply distinguished from the other elements by the immense number and complexity of its compounds, while among these compounds nearly all the substances playing an active part in the life and decay of an organized structure are to be found. Becher, in 1669, argued that the same elements occur in the three natural kingdoms, but more simply combined in the mineral than in the vegetable or animal. Stahl, in 1702, asserted that in vegetable as well as animal substances a larger proportion of watery and combustible principles is to be found; a view in which he was perfectly at one with the more exact science of a later day, for hydrogen and carbon are as a rule the main and characteristic constituents of organic bodies. Van Helmont had held before Stahl that organic substances can be resolved by heat into their constituent elements, aqueous and combustible principles, or water and fire. This idea was, as we shall see, controverted by Robert Boyle in his "Sceptical Chemist" (1661). He pointed out that heat leads to different results under different conditions. As an example of how near the light truth may rest hidden for long periods before being discovered, it is interesting to note that, in spite of these suggestive discussions regarding the composition of organic bodies, it was not till **1784** that the existence of carbon and hydrogen in alcohol was a proven fact.

CHAPTER VII.

FOURTH PERIOD.—THE BEGINNINGS OF SCIENCE. THE ACKNOWLEDGMENT OF NESCIENCE.*

WE have already observed that the progress of chemistry was once more carrying it into a new era far more nearly allied to the present. Like the dawn of much new knowledge which the world slowly wins from darkness, the first brightening touch on the horizon was to creep upwards in a tremulous twilight of doubt. It is ever difficult to unsay what is said, or to combat an error that has become a habit of thought. Old instincts and old superstitions when they have ceased to be openly loud in their insistence, fall back upon whispering persuasion, to which, because we are often unconscious of its seductive suggestion, we easily fall a prey, and before

* The term nescience is a convenient one to signify the negation or absence of knowledge.

we can dare to openly defy a principle which has lived long in our hearts, we pass through a time of half-timid wonderment, and doubt if, after all, it be infallibly true. Then, after a long period of lingering doubt, our mind is made up, and we combat the false thought until we think that we have slain it. But a false confidence in our victory often deludes us, and the day comes when we discover in some fresh bias our old enemy in a new disguise.

A parallel to this frequent course of progress in the individual human mind is found in the changes passed through by the science we are considering. Alchemy and mysticism had ruled the older chemists, the latter partially crystallizing in the form of fantastical notions concerning the fundamental principles of matter. Slowly but surely uncertainty and doubt was creeping into the minds of the workers as to the so-called truths of transmutation. For some time yet the doubt was not to become open denial, and the idea was to spring up again and again even until the present century, at the commencement of which Peter Woulfe lived. The curious mysticism embodied in the notions entertained about the elements was to prove a phantom even less easily exorcised, and more powerful to do harm. The period of doubt was beginning, as will be seen in the discussion of Robert Boyle, and true ideas concerning the nature of an "element," and hence of combustion and other important natural phenomena, seemed about to spring up. But soon after this the apparently-slain demon was to be resuscitated as a giant of invulnerable strength. The *phlogistic* theory was started, and, as we shall see, for half a century it held chemistry in thrall, and caused men of remarkable brilliancy and power to grope blindly in the darkness for truths which, except for the baleful shadow that enshrouded them, would have been as clear as day. Chemistry had to wait for the steady lustre of Lavoisier's talents to dispel the gloom.

In entering upon this period of doubt, we shall discuss the three chemists, Boyle, Hooke, and Mayow; and first of all let us take the man who is most fitly representative of this era—Robert Boyle.

Robert Boyle (1627—1691) was the seventh son and fourteenth child of Richard, Earl of Cork. He was born at Lismore, in Munster. At eight years of age he was sent to Eton, where, says he, a perusal of "Quintus Curtius" "conjured up in me that unsatisfied appetite for knowledge that is yet as greedy as when it was first raised." It is related that while recovering from a fever at Eton he was induced to read "Amadis de Gaul" and other romantic books. The effect of the romance of that period upon him was to produce an intolerable restlessness and unsettlement in his mind, which he determined to end. To counteract these tendencies, he, therefore, set himself, being then ten years old, to extracting square and cube roots and other laborious and uninteresting calculations, in order to calm his brain.

Such strength of mind in one so young was perhaps to be condemned as dangerously prophetic of too great austerity. As a matter of fact, however, he seems through life to have kept his heart readily open to human sympathies and to have been quite free from the cynical reserve which has characterized a few intellectual workers. While at Eton his life was greatly endangered by the fall of the room in which he was sleeping, and had he not, with striking presence of mind, wrapped the sheet of the bed round his face he would probably have been suffocated with the dust.

After about four years at Eton, Boyle went to his father's seat in Dorset, and afterwards travelled abroad with his brother Francis and tutor. He took a view of those wild mountains where Bruno, the first founder of the Carthusian monks, lived in solitude, and where the first and chief of the Carthusian abbeys was built. Boyle relates that "the devil, taking advantage of that deep, raving melancholy, so sad a place, his own humour, which was naturally grave and serious, and the strange stories and pictures he found there of Bruno, suggested such strange and distracting doubts of some of the fundamentals of Christianity that, though his looks did little betray his thoughts, nothing but the forbiddenness of self-despatch hindered his acting it."*
He shortly after became fully converted to Christianity, though "the fleeting clouds of doubt and

* *Biographia Britannica.*

disbelief did never after cease to now and then darken the serenity of his quiet." Boyle was in Marseilles in 1641 at the outbreak of the Irish Rebellion. His father transmitted his brother £250, but it never reached them, and they were left almost penniless. They made their way to Marcombes, and then to Geneva, where they lived for two years on credit, and at length, by the sale of some jewels, got together enough money to bring them home. They reached England in the summer of 1644. Their father was dead, and so confused was the state of the country that for nearly four months Boyle could not make his way to the manor of Stalbridge, which he had inherited.

But through all this turmoil the scientific men were steadily, though secretly, at work. Through all the din of conflicting faction and disputed power they held calmly on towards the goal which to them was highest and best. There is something perhaps rather coldly grand about their impenetrable patience, but grand it certainly is. The "Philosophical Society," or, as Boyle preferred to call it, the "Invisible Society," met secretly in London in 1645, and from these meetings he derived fresh impulse. "Vulcan has so transported and bewitched me," he wrote from Stalbridge to his sister, Lady Ranelagh (1649), "as to make me fancy my laboratory a kind of Elysium." In 1652—3 he visited his Irish estates, and on his return in 1654 settled at Oxford in the society of some of his early philosophical associates. Meetings were held amongst them and experiments performed and discussed.

In 1659 Boyle perfected his air-pump, and in 1660, amongst other results, he published "Boyle's Law," confirmed by Mariotte in 1676. This well-known law asserts that the volume* of a gas varies

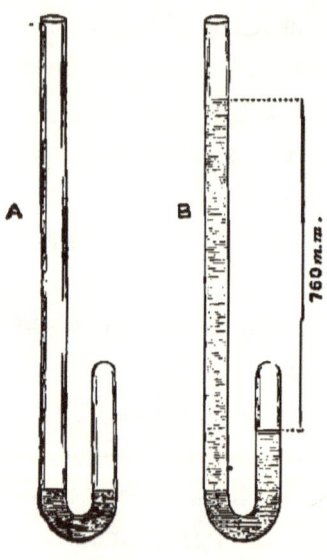

inversely as the pressure. For instance, if a certain volume of air be contained in the closed end of the U-shaped tube shown in the illustration, let us call this volume 1, and the pressure to which it is at first subjected 1. If we double the pressure we shall halve the volume. The volume 1 under pressure 1 becomes the volume ½ under pressure 2, the

* "Volume" means the amount of cubic space occupied by any substance.

volume $\tfrac{1}{4}$ under pressure 4, and so on. Similarly the volume 1 under pressure 1 becomes the volume 2 under a pressure $\tfrac{1}{2}$, the volume 4 under pressure $\tfrac{1}{4}$, &c. Of the two cases shown in the illustration the first shows the gas at the ordinary pressure of the atmosphere, the mercury standing at the same height in each limb of the tube. Now the ordinary pressure

SIMPLEST FORM OF THE BAROMETER.

of the atmosphere, as recorded by the barometer, is sufficient to support a column of mercury 760 millimetres high. If therefore we pour mercury into the long limb of the bent tube till the height of the column in it is 760 millimetres higher than the height of the column in the short limb, the gas enclosed behind the mercury which was formerly at the ordinary atmospheric pressure will now have to sustain *twice* that pressure, and its volume is accordingly halved, as is seen in the second illustration. This law, though not exactly true for all degrees of pressure, has yet been of very great service.

It may be objected that this is a question of physics rather than of chemistry. But it is a law, which is in every-day use by the chemist in calculating the amount of a gas the volume of which is not observed under the normal pressure of 760 mm. A further complication arises from the fact that these gases are observed at various temperatures and not often at the *normal* temperature, which is taken as the melting point of ice, or 0° centigrade. Now gases expand on heating, and it was Gay-Lussac who at a much later date discovered the laws of their expansion. Each gas expands for one degree centigrade $\frac{1}{273}$ of its volume at 0° C. Thus 273 volumes of gas at 0° C. become at 1° equal to 274 volumes, and so on. From these laws we can readily reduce the volume of a gas observed at any given temperature and pressure to the volume the same weight of gas would occupy at 0° C. and 760 mm. pressure. Once this is known the weight of the gas may be very simply deduced. In this way, if in analysing a nitrogenous organic body a certain volume of nitrogen is obtained, the *weight* of nitrogen contained in the body is readily calculated.

In 1668 Boyle came to London and was a prominent member of the then newly constituted Royal

Society. He was elected president in 1680, but refused to act, owing to a scruple he entertained as to taking oaths. In 1689 his health began to fail and he issued an advertisement restricting the visits of his acquaintances. He also had a board put up outside his house announcing when he received visits. Boyle's health had never been good; from the age of twenty-one he suffered from stone, and much feared that if it forced him to take to his bed the pain of it would become insupportable. He died, however, without pain, and almost without serious illness.

Boyle developed talent early, and at twenty-one he had already written on ethics and published several moral and religious essays. In 1665 he published his "Occasional Reflection upon Several Subjects," which procured him the satire of Swift in "A pious Meditation upon a Broomstick, in the style of the Honourable Mr. Boyle."

Personally Robert Boyle is described as pale, emaciated, and very delicate, so "that he had divers sorts of cloaks to put on when he went abroad, according to the temperature of the air, and in this he governed himself by his thermometer .... For almost forty years he laboured under such a feebleness of body and lowness of strength and spirits that it was astonishing how he could read, meditate, try experiments and write as he did." To these disabilities was added that of a memory by his own account so treacherous that he was often tempted to abandon study in despair.

He "wore the white flower of a blameless life." Naturally choleric he controlled himself to mildness; he was unostentatiously liberal, unselfish, and unambitious. He refused to take orders, excusing himself on the ground of not having an inner call, though this involved refusing the provostship of Eton. He also repeatedly declined a peerage. There is something very attractively quiet and simple about such a nature. It is an example of a man who worked quietly and peacefully at the problems toward which his nature felt drawn, undisturbed by feverish unrealities of ambition and unsullied by the desire of worldly fame. His work never led him into the bitter controversies in which others have sometimes too readily engaged, it did not lead him to forget the claims of human sympathy and sorrow, or to doubt the existence of knowledge beyond his own. The work itself has proved of lasting and notable service, and perhaps even more serviceable when we read of it, was the calm, unsullied purity of his soul.

Boyle's principal chemical work was published in 1661, under the title of *The Sceptical Chymist; or Chemico-physical Doubts and Paradoxes, touching the Experiments whereby vulgar Spagyrists are wont to endeavour to evince their Salt, Sulphur, and Mercury to be the true Principles of Things.* We see here the beginning of the time of doubt. It is in this work that the first rational notion of an element, and of the difference between an element and a compound, is contained. The book is written in the form of a discussion between a party of learned gentlemen, of whom one, Carneades, plays the part of the *Sceptical Chymist*. The earlier portions of the book are devoted to a demolition of the Aristotelian doctrine of the elements, which is amusingly and interestingly defended by one speaker in the following passage :—

"I speak thus, Eleutherius (adds Themistius), only to do right to reason, and not out of diffidence of the experimental proof I am to allege. For though I shall name but one, yet it is such a one as will make all other appear as needless, as itself will be found satisfactory. For if you but consider a piece of green wood burning in a chimney, you will readily discern in the disbanded parts of it the four elements of which we teach it and other mixed bodies to be composed. The fire discovers itself in the flame of its own light; the smoke by ascending to the top of the chimney and there readily vanishing into air like a river losing itself in the sea, sufficiently manifests to what element it belongs and gladly returns. The water in its own form boiling and rising at the ends of the burning wood betrays itself to more than one of our senses ; and the ashes by their weight, their firiness, and their dryness put it past doubt that they belong to the element of earth. If I spoke (continues Themistius) to less knowing persons I would perhaps make some excuse for building upon such an obvious and easy analysis, but 'twould be I fear injurious not to think such an apology needless to you, who are too judicious either to think it necessary that experiments to prove obvious truths should be far-fetched, or to wonder that among so many mixed bodies that are compounded of the four elements some should, upon a slight analysis, manifestly exhibit the ingredients they consist of." There is a delicious naiveté about the concluding portion of this speech, a blind simplicity that is almost charming. The absurdity of the suppositions implied in the experiment are so quietly put aside, that we become aware of the figure of Boyle behind Themistius with a satirical smile upon his face.

Carneades, after some preamble, replies thus : " To begin then with his experiment of the burning wood, it seems to me to be obnoxious to not a few considerable exceptions. And first, if I would now deal rightly with my adversary, I might here make a great question of the very way of probation which he and others employ without the least scruple to evince that the bodies commonly called mixed are made up of earth, air, water, and fire, which they are pleased also to call elements ; namely, that upon the supposed analysis made by fire of the former sort of concretes, there are wont to emerge bodies resembling those which they take for the elements. For . . . . if I were disposed to wrangle I might allege that by Themistius, his experiments, it would appear rather that those he calls elements are made up of those he calls mixed bodies, than mixed bodies of the elements ; . . . . it appears . . . . that which he takes for elementary fire and water are made out of the concrete, but it appears not that the concrete was made up of fire and water. Nor has .... he .... yet proved that nothing can be obtained from a body by the fire that was not pre-existent in it."

There is some very shrewd reasoning here. How, indeed, are we to know that heat thus applied splits a body up into its constituent elements? Besides, the absurdity of describing the smoke as air when, as Carneades points out, the main portion of it descends as soot, what an odd piece of reasoning it is which makes the appearance of flame during the combustion prove that fire is one of the principles of the wood.

In the succeeding discourses Carneades proceeds to apply his judgment to the other theories of the elements as well. He states that the so-called elements obtained by the chemists are not even pure. He is told that later Aristotelians have undertaken to further purify these supposed elements (salt, sulphur, and mercury). Very well, that does not alter the truth of what he has said as to the ordinary operations. "And as to the thing itself, I shall freely acknowledge to you that I love not to be forward in determining things to be impossible, till I know and have considered the means by which they are proposed to be effected. And therefore I shall not peremptorily deny either the possibility of what these artists promise, or my assent to any just inference, however destructive to my conjectures, that may be drawn from their performance. But give me leave to tell you withal, that, because such promises are wont (as experience has more than once informed me) to be much more easily made than made good by chemists, I must withhold my belief from their assertion till their experiments exact it, and must not be so easy as to expect beforehand an unlikely thing upon no stronger inducements than are yet given me."

The extreme and almost amusing caution of Carneades is sufficiently evident from the above quotations. He has begun to distrust the old theories and beliefs, but he is not prepared to dogmatically assert a new creed of his own. But in the course of the discussion it becomes more and more clear what definition of the "element" Carneades is inclined to favour. The modern view is here for the first time suggested, that an element is a body which by no known process can be split up into two or more different substances. It is a *simple* body. It is a whole made up of similar parts. If we find that we can, by some new analytical process, split up an apparently simple body, we cease to regard it as an element; and it is by no means improbable that we may in this way cease to regard as elements many of the substances now so-called.

Boyle was quite aware of the variability of the number of apparently elemental principles. He thinks "that it may as yet be doubted whether or no there be any determinate number of elements; or, if you please, whether or no all compound bodies do consist of the same number of elementary ingredients or material principles." Finally, in a sequel added to the discourses proper to the *Sceptical Chymist*, Carneades goes so far as to say: "I am content . . . . to tell you that . . . . though it may seem extravagant, yet it is not absurd, to doubt whether, for ought has been proved, there be a necessity to admit any elements or Hypostatical principles at all." Boyle had certainly penetrated far into the period of doubt.*

From these details we see the great credit due to Boyle for first openly distrusting the curiously vague and mystical notions, concerning the constitution of the various kinds of matter, which for so long had held in bondage the infant science. It was a strangely deep insight which led him to view the number of so-called elements as variable, and it may even be that his suggestion that, after all, there may be no such thing as a true element, may become the most acceptable hypothesis. Or it may be thought that all the elements enumerated in our tables are modifications and combinations of modifications of one primordial element. Oxygen, hydrogen, nitrogen, iron, copper, are well-known examples of substances now regarded as elements. It may well, however, be that, by spectroscopical or other mode of research, these substances may be found to be made up of still simpler bodies,

* See also the interesting Appendix to the *Sceptical Chymist, on the Producibleness of Chemical Principles*. In this Boyle discusses the want of uniformity among bodies supposed to be part of the same principle. Thus some oils, spirits, and brimstone, were all termed sulphurs, because inflammable. Boyle looks with disfavour upon so loose a notion, and thinks it more probable that "sulphur" itself is made up of the same universal matter as other bodies.

though of this at present not much can be said. We have even had suggestions as to the possible ways in which the elementary bodies may have come into existence and how also they may cease to be.* At present much of the work in this region must consist in speculation, but speculation is ever the forerunner of discovery.

Besides his really remarkable observations upon the nature of the elementary bodies, Boyle was the author of some pregnant work upon that great puzzle of chemists up to the time of Lavoisier, the phenomenon of combustion. We all of us now know that what happens when a candle burns, is that its carbon and hydrogen combine with the oxygen of the air thus forming carbonic acid gas and water vapour. But at the time of Boyle vague notions, such as that described by Themistius in the *Sceptical Chymist* were in vogue. The first step towards clearing up the difficulty was to find out whether the air had anything to do with the burning of combustible materials, and accordingly Boyle experimented with a view to finding whether they would burn under the exhausted receiver of his air-pump. There being under these conditions very little air present Boyle found that such combustibles as a candle, charcoal, sulphur, etc., would not light.

On the other hand gunpowder, if strongly heated under the receiver by means of a burning-glass,

* See the suggestive paper by Prof. Crookes in his presidential address to the Chemical Society (1888).

exploded, and from this it was concluded that the *nitre* in the gunpowder gave up something capable of acting as a substitute for air. Nitre, we now know, contains oxygen and readily parts with it to other combustible bodies. Boyle's conclusion was therefore perfectly correct. But in spite of such advance Boyle still believed in the material nature of flame, and, owing to bias of this kind, though he was aware that many metals when heated in air are altered with gain of weight, he ignored the true explanation. It seems strange that it should not have occurred to him that the metals had absorbed a ponderable constituent (oxygen) of the atmosphere. Instead of this he supposed them to weigh heavier, owing to addition of " igneous corpuscles."

To sum up Boyle's work, his discussion of the qualities proper to an element led to the views concerning those bodies at present entertained; he was the first to distinguish definitely between an element and a compound, and between a compound and a mixture; his work upon combustion was accompanied by very suggestive experiments; he seems to have introduced vegetable colour tests to distinguish acid and alkali,* and he developed the law of the compression of gases now so familiar by his name and so serviceable alike to chemists and physicists.

His style of writing, as may have been suggested by the quotations given, though quaintly interesting,

---

* The every-day test now in use is that of litmus, which is turned red by acid and blue by alkali.

136 THE BEGINNINGS OF SCIENCE.

is intolerably prolix, a characteristic in those days not uncommon.* But we readily forgive his defects when we find how earnestly painstaking he was.

* *The Life and Works of the Honourable Robert Boyle* were brought out in five volumes folio by Thomas Birch in 1744. A curious pamphlet, by Boyle, *An Historical Account of a Degradation of Gold made by an Anti-elixir,* not mentioned in the text, gives a description of the conversion of gold into a baser metal.

CHAPTER VIII.

FOURTH PERIOD: THE BEGINNINGS OF SCIENCE.
HOOKE: MAYOW: HALES.

THE next of those to be considered in this period is Robert Hooke (1635—1702). Hooke is naturally associated with Boyle, as he was for a considerable time his assistant and aided him in some important work. But his character is very much less attractive than that of his employer; he wanted the unambitious earnestness which had always characterized Robert Boyle.

Robert Hooke was born in the Isle of Wight and was originally intended for the Church, but he was of a weakly constitution, and much subject to headache, and owing to these causes the idea was finally abandoned. His leanings were first shown in a considerable aptitude, as a boy, for constructing mechanical toys. After his father's death Dr. Busby took him into his house and supported him while at Westminster School. After leaving school he went to Christ Church, Oxford, and, in 1655, he was introduced to the Philosophical Society. Here his talents were speedily discovered and he was employed to assist first Dr. Willis and then Mr. Boyle. In 1662 he was made curator of experiments to the Royal Society, and when this body was established by charter he was one of the first nominated to fellowship. He obtained several professional posts and in 1665 he published in folio his *Mierographia, or some physiological descriptions of minute bodies made by magnifying glasses, with observations and inquiries thereupon.* The work was dedicated to Charles II.

After the great fire of London Hooke was appointed one of the city surveyors, and in this capacity seems to have amassed a considerable sum of money which, after his death, was found locked up and untouched in a large iron chest. He seems to have had an ungovernable tendency to believe that all new discoveries had been anticipated by himself, and when Newton, in 1686, published his *Principia* Hooke claimed priority in the idea of gravitation. There was enough truth in this to cause Newton to allow the claim, but the fact is that the idea of gravitation is a very old one, and Newton's honour was to have made it a workable theory. When Hooke laid claim to having originated Newton's views as to gravitation Newton wrote to Dr. Halley: "I intended in this letter to let you understand the case fully, but, it being a frivolous business I shall content myself with giving you the heads of it." In a postscript he adds, "Since my writing this letter I am told by one who had it from another lately present at one of your meetings how Mr. Hooke should make a great stir, pretending that I had all from him . . . . This carriage towards me is very strange and undeserved . . . . he has published Borell's hypothesis in his own name . . . . Borell did something and wrote modestly. He has done nothing and yet written in such a way as if he knew and had sufficiently hinted all but what remained to be determined by the drudgery of calculation and observations . . . ."

But here Hooke was somewhat maligned by report. The facts were that at a meeting of the Royal Society a member remarked that Newton had done the work so thoroughly that no more was to be added. Sir John Hoskins, the Vice-President, was in the chair, and replied that the book was the more to be prized; the theory was both invented and perfected at the same time. This gave Hooke offence, "upon which," writes Halley, "they two who till then were the most inseparable cronies have since scarcely seen one another and are utterly fallen out." A spirit such as this would cause us to reluctantly withdraw our reverence from a worker of even the highest intellectual predominance. Hooke lived the life of a cynic and recluse, and on the death in 1687 of his niece, Mrs. Grace Hooke, with whom he lived, he became more cynical than ever. The tradition runs that for the two or three last years of his life he sat night and day at a table engrossed with his inventions and studies, and never went to bed or undressed. Wasted and emaciated by his strange mode of life, and by the denial to himself of comforts he could readily have gained, he died in 1702 and was buried in St. Helen's Church, Bishopsgate Street. He is described as penurious, melancholy, mistrustful, and jealous. We could more readily pity his melancholy had it not been so self-imposed. We must, however, admire his keen insight and penetrative power.

The main interest of Hooke's work centres in his *Micrographia* and probably the most remarkable words he ever uttered are contained, almost parenthetically, in a work where, from its title, we should have no expectation of finding the subject they deal with treated of at all.*

Hooke seems in the quietest and most unbiassed way to have set about observing the facts of combustion, and waited for these facts to work out in his

---

* To understand Hooke's work thoroughly, the pregnant preface to the *Micrographia* should be read. First of all Hooke implores the reader to observe great caution in accepting the conclusions there set forth. Caution is naturally the key-note of the period of doubt. But an over-caution often produces a tendency to cling to a hypothesis once accepted and an over-reluctance to accept the plunge into the stream of new ideas. Hooke avoids both Scylla and Chary The door of the senses, he says, must always be left open. The understanding "must watch the irregularities of the senses, but it must not go before them or prevent their information."

mind their natural conclusion. He arrives at the opinion that the combustion of a combustible, or, as he calls it, "sulphureous," body, for instance, charcoal, is due to the combination of part of it with a substance contained in the air, and also in saltpetre. This resulting body is volatile and flies off, and, of course, corresponds to carbonic acid gas, together with water vapour. Another portion of the body uniting with part of the air is supposed to form an unvolatile "coagulum" extractable from soot. Part of the combustible will often not combine with the air and is left behind as the ashes. The air is spoken of as the solvent of inflammable bodies, by a somewhat inaccurate analogy, so that when charcoal burns, it is viewed as an analogous action to that of dissolving a solid in alcohol. The air is viewed as containing but a little of the true solvent; a view quite correct, as four-fifths of the atmosphere consist of nitrogen; and the solvent is therefore easily exhausted. Thus, for instance, air must be continually admitted into a vessel in which we are burning a large piece of charcoal, or the charcoal will cease to burn. Just as heat is sometimes generated by dissolving substances in a liquid, so, says Hooke, heat is produced during the solution or combustion of a body in air, and this heat shows itself as flame, and is not an element, but a phenomenon resulting from the violent agitation of the particles of the burning body. Saltpetre contains more of this supporter of combustion and hence burns more rapidly. Altogether, this is a very wonderful anticipation of the present ideas about combustion. So far as it goes it is accurate, and if it could have been followed up farther in the same spirit, chemistry might have advanced more rapidly than it did. The passage from *Micrographia* above described is so interesting and deals with so immensely important a subject that we shall not hesitate here to quote at some length therefrom :—

"Thirdly, from the experiment of the charring of coals (whereby we see that notwithstanding the great heat, and the duration of it, the solid parts of the wood remain, whilst they are preserved from the free access of air, undissipated), we may learn that which has not, that I know of, been published or hinted, nay, not so much as thought of, by any ; and that, in short, is this.

"First, that the Air in which we live, move, and breathe, and which encompasses very many, and cherishes most bodies it encompasses, that this Air is the *menstruum*, or universal dissolvent of all sulphureous bodies.

"Secondly, that this action it performs not till the body be sufficiently heated, as we find requisite also to the dissolution of many other bodies by several other menstruums.

"Thirdly, that this action of dissolution produces or generates a very great heat, and that which we call fire ; and this is common also to many dissolutions of other bodies, made by *menstruums*, of which I could give multitudes of instances.

"Fourthly, that this action is performed with so great a violence and does so minutely act, and rapidly agitate the smallest parts of the *combustible* matter, that it produces in the diaphanous medium of the air the action or pulse of light, which what it is I have elsewhere already shown.

"Fifthly, that the dissolution of sulphureous bodies is made by a substance inherent and mixed with the air, that is like, *if not the very same with that which is fixed in saltpetre,** which by multitudes of experiments that may be made with saltpetre, will, I think, most evidently be demonstrated.

"Sixthly, that in this dissolution of bodies by the air *a certain part is united and mixed, or dissolved and turned into the air and made to fly up and down with it** in the same manner as a metalline or other body dissolved in any menstruum does follow the motions and progresses of that menstruum till it be precipitated.

"Seventhly, that as there is one part that is dissoluble by the air, so are there other parts with which the parts of the air uniting do make a coagulum or precipitation, as one may call it, which causes it to be separated from the air, but this precipitate is so light and in so small and rarefied or porous clusters that it is very voluble and is easily carried up by the motion of the air, though afterwards, when the heat and agitation that kept it rarefied ceases, it easily condenses and, commixt with other indissoluble

* Italics not in the original.

parts, it sticks and adheres to the next bodies it meets withal, and this is a certain salt that may be extracted out of soot.

"Eighthly, that many indissoluble parts being very apt and prompt to be rarefied and so, whilst they continue in that heat and agitation, are lighter than the ambient air, are thereby thrust and carried upwards with great violence and, by that means, carry along with them not only the saline concrete I mentioned before, but many terrestrial or indissoluble and irrarefiable parts, nay many parts also which are dissoluble but are not suffered to stay long enough in a sufficient heat to make them prompt and apt for that action. And therefore we find in soot, not only a part that being continued longer in a competent heat will be dissolved by the air or take fire and burn, but a part also which is fixed, terrestrial and irrarefiable.

"Ninthly, that as there are these several parts that will rarefy and fly or be driven up by the heat, so are there many others that, as they are indissoluble by the aerial menstruum, so are they of such sluggish and gross parts that they are not easily rarefied by heat and therefore cannot be raised by it; the volubility or fixtness of a body seeming to consist only in this, that the one is of a texture or has component parts that will be easily rarefied into the form of air, and the other that it has such as will not without much ado be brought to such a constitution; and this is that part which remains behind in a white body called ashes, which contains a substance or salt which chemists call alkali. What the particular nature of each of these bodies is I shall not here examine, intending it in another place, but shall rather add that this hypothesis does so exactly agree with all phenomena of fire and so genuinely explicate each particular circumstance that I have hitherto observed that it is more than probable that this cause which I have assigned is the true, adequate, real and only cause of those phenomena, and therefore I shall proceed a little further to show the nature and use of the air.

"Tenthly, therefore, the dissolving parts of the air are but few, that is it seems of the nature of those saline menstruums or spirits that have very much phlegm mixed with the spirit, and therefore a small parcel of it is quickly glutted, and will dissolve no more; and therefore unless some fresh part of this menstruum be applied to the body to be dissolved the action ceases and the body leaves to be dissolved and to shine, which is the indication of it, though placed or kept in the greatest heat; *whereas, saltpetre is a menstruum, when melted and red hot, that abounds more with those dissolvent particles*, and therefore as a small quantity of it will dissolve a great sulphureous body, so will the dissolution be very quick and violent.

"Therefore, in the eleventh place, it is observable that, as in other solutions, if a copious and quick supply of fresh menstruum, though but weak, be poured on or applied to the dissoluble body, it quickly consumes it: so this menstruum of the air, if by bellows or any such contrivance it be copiously applied to the shining body, is found to dissolve it as soon and as violently as the more strong menstruum of dissolved nitre.

"Therefore, twelfthly, it seems reasonable to think that *there is no such thing as an Element of fire* that should attract or draw up the flame, or towards which the flame should endeavour to ascend out of a desire or appetite of uniting with that as its homogeneal, primitive and generating Element; but that that shining transient body, which we call flame, is nothing but a mixture of air and volatile sulphureous parts of dissoluble or combustible bodies which are acting upon each other whilst they ascend; that is flame seems to be a mixture of air and the combustible volatile parts of any body, which parts the encompassing air does dissolve or work upon, which action, as it does intend the heat of the aerial parts of the dissolvent, so does it thereby further rarefy those parts that are acting or that are very near them, whereby they, growing much lighter than the heavy parts of that menstruum that are more remote, are thereby protruded and driven upward; and this may be easily observed also in dissolutions made by any other menstruum, especially such as either create heat or bubbles. Now this action of the menstruum or air on the dissoluble part is made with such violence or is such that it imparts such a motion or pulse to the diaphonous parts of the air as I have elsewhere shown is requisite to produce light."

This hypothesis, Hooke says, is the result of "an infinite of observations and experiments." He holds out the prospect of a much larger discourse on the same subject, "the air being a subject which (although all the world have hitherto lived and breathed in and been conversant about) has yet been so little truly examined or explained that a diligent inquirer will be able to find but very little information from what has been (till of late) written of it."

John Mayow (1645—1679) was born in Cornwall and became a student of medicine. He practised chiefly at Bath in the summer.

Mayow carried on investigations into the nature of combustion, published in 1674 in his *Tracts on various Philosophical Subjects*,* which, apparently unknown to himself, had been to some extent anticipated in Hooke's *Micrographia* (1665). He burned a candle under a bell-glass over water, observed that the air diminished in volume, and that the gas left was a little lighter than air and had no longer the power of supporting combustion or life. This gas was, of course, nitrogen, the other constituent of the atmosphere. The carbonic acid gas formed had been slowly absorbed by the water. He recognised that the portion of the air necessary to combustion and to life (*i.e.* oxygen) was contained also

---

* Mayow's first paper, however, *De Sale Nitro et Spiritu Nitro-aëreo*, was published in 1669.

in saltpetre (potassium nitrate, KNO^3). The nitre or saltpetre he said contains fire-air (oxygen) and no sulphureous (combustible) particles. For combustion he asserted that fire-air and sulphureous particles were needed.

Mayow seems to have been the first to use the pneumatic trough for collecting gases, and the use of this alone makes possible the examination of most gases. An example of it is given farther on in the sketch of Priestley's apparatus.

In the course of his investigations Mayow was, by his medical leanings, induced to consider the chemical meaning of breathing. He ascertained, as already stated, that one part only of the atmosphere is the supporter of life, but he did not wish to stop there. The idea of his time was that respiration cooled the blood. Mayow, on the other hand, seeing the part played by these "nitro-aërial particles" or oxygen in combustion, concluded that this gas was connected with the heating of the blood.* He showed the existence of gases in the blood by subjecting it to the action of the air-pump, which extracts them. Mayow was quite right in thinking that the "fire-air" had to do with supplying the heat of the blood.

On the subject of chemical affinity Mayow made remarks of some moment. It may be as well to explain here shortly what the term chemical affinity is supposed to convey. There is no doubt that

* *Chemisch physiologische Schriften.* Jena (1799).

strictly speaking affinity should mean similarity to or relation to; but the word has been diverted from its proper significance and is now generally used to denote the tendency exhibited by substances to combine with each other. Thus we say that phosphorus has a great affinity for oxygen, thereby intending to convey the fact that phosphorus and oxygen have a strong tendency to combine together. This is brought home to us by observing that phosphorus when exposed at ordinary temperatures to the air burns slowly away, without a distinct flame, but giving off light fumes of phosphorus pentoxide (anhydrous phosphoric acid) and emitting a pale glow when observed in the dark. If slightly heated, as, for instance, by the sudden pressure of a blow, the phosphorus at once bursts into flame. Again, if sufficiently finely divided the phosphorus will inflame, as we say, *spontaneously* and without application of heat. Thus if a small piece of white phosphorus be dissolved in some carbon disulphide (a highly refracting liquid usually possessing an atrocious smell) and a little of the solution be poured upon blotting paper, the volatile carbon disulphide very rapidly evaporates and leaves the phosphorus on the paper in a very fine state of division. Directly the paper has become thoroughly dry the outer edges of the phosphorus disc left by the carbon disulphide begin to fume strongly, the heat developed by the combination rapidly increases, the paper begins to char, and the next instant the whole mass bursts into flame.

Such facts as these teach us that phosphorus and oxygen are very eager to become united, and we express the general result of our observations in the statement that phosphorus and oxygen have a strong affinity for each other.

The cause of the luminosity of phosphorus when exposed to the air was not for some time decided. The obvious suggestion would be that the light arose from combination with the oxygen of the air. On the other hand it was stated that phosphorus became luminous when exposed in an atmosphere upon which it would exert no chemical action, for instance, hydrogen or nitrogen gas. The luminosity in these cases was, however, found to be due to the presence of traces of oxygen gas, and it seems at last decided that these phenomena of phosphorescence are to be seen only in the presence of oxygen gas. From these facts we should naturally expect phosphorus to be more luminous in pure oxygen than in air. But now comes a curious surprise for our expectations; in pure oxygen phosphorus exhibits no luminosity at all. If the temperature be raised or the gas be rarefied, the phenomenon of phosphorescence is observed, but below 20° C., and at atmospheric pressure, phosphorus may be preserved for many weeks in this gas without undergoing the slightest oxidation. If the oxygen be diluted with an indifferent gas, as hydrogen, or be rarefied, the luminosity is once more seen. If a stick of phosphorus be introduced into a tube filled with oxygen, closed above and connected below with a mercury reservoir, by raising or lowering the latter we may alternately increase or lower the pressure in the tube, and at the same time extinguish or revive the phosphorescence. Certain gases and vapours such as sulphuretted hydrogen, ether, turpentine, permanently put out the luminosity.

Robert Boyle had made some remarks upon these tendencies of bodies to combination, and held that combination consists of an approximation, a bringing close together of the smallest particles of matter. Previous to this time it was thought that the substances entering into a compound were annihilated by the act of combination. Mayow strongly combated this error. The views advocated by him would lead us to say that when phosphorus and oxygen combine, both bodies are still present in the compound, and could by suitable means be obtained from it. Mayow supported his argument by a somewhat ambiguous example; that of the combination between hydrochloric acid and ammonia. For although it may in a certain way be said that hydrochloric acid and ammonia exist together in sal-ammoniac, yet it by no means follows that each of them exists *as such*. Hydrochloric acid consists of hydrogen and chlorine combined together in a certain way; it is perfectly true that the hydrogen and the chlorine occur in the sal-ammoniac but probably not combined in the same way; there may, in the sal-ammoniac, be a re-arrangement of the constituents of the gas.

The phenomena of double decomposition were also

studied by Mayow. We may illustrate these by the action of sulphuric acid upon potassium nitrate (nitre) from which result nitric acid and potassium sulphate. In this case the group of elements attached to the hydrogen of the sulphuric acid exchange this bondage for a union with the potassium of the nitre, the group attached to the potassium combining at the same time with the hydrogen to form nitric acid. In chemical symbols this is expressed thus :—

$$2\ KNO^3 + H^2SO^4 = K^2SO^4 + 2\ HNO^3.$$
Nitre + sulphuric acid = potassium sulphate + nitric acid

Mayow's comments upon this reaction correctly express this exchange, though their explanation of *why* it occurs is somewhat erroneous.

Mayow, like the medical chemists of an earlier school, offers a timely warning to the physicians who may be ignorant of the mutual affinities and decompositions of bodies. He reminds them that the different substances in their prescriptions may act upon each other with surprising results; "one substance may destroy the efficacy of another, and something perfectly different from the original may result."

Mayow's work was almost wholly forgotten, as was the fate of so much other work previous to this time. At the close of the eighteenth century his fame was revived chiefly through the agency of Drs. Beddoes[*] and Yeats. There was indeed then a tendency to overrate his discoveries in the spirit of those who

[*] *Chemical Experiments, &c., from Mayow.* Edited by Beddoes. Oxford (1790).

are fond of exclaiming that there is nothing new under the sun. Beddoes attributed to Mayow the discovery of, "if not the whole, certainly many of those splendid truths which adorn the writings of Priestley, Scheele, Lavoisier, Crawford, Goodwin, and other philosophers."

Certainly Mayow was remarkably lucid and far-sighted in some of his expositions, but it must be allowed that such judgment as that quoted much overrates his achievements.

Before leaving this period of the science, mention may be made of Dr. Stephen Hales (1677—1761), an ingenious and able experimenter, though one who was too much engrossed in the details of his experiments to consider sufficiently their purpose.

He was the grandson of Sir Robert Hales, and, after leaving Cambridge, resided till the time of his death at Teddington. Offered a canonry at Windsor, he showed unusual wisdom by refusing it, preferring to continue to devote himself to the parochial duties and scientific pursuits engaged in which he felt perfectly content. He published in 1727 his *Statical Essays* . . . . *also a Specimen of an Attempt to analyse the Air, by a great variety of Chymico-Statical Experiments*. Hales made a number of experiments on the "air" produced by heating bodies, by fermentation, etc. He collected his gases in ingeniously-devised apparatus, but thinking they were all modifications of common air he appears never to have examined them systematically, and thus a whole series of discoveries eluded his grasp. He obtained "air" by distilling wood, and found it fatal to animals (carbonic acid), from nitre (oxygen), etc., and he details the amount of air obtained by distilling hogs' blood, tallow, sal-ammoniac, Indian wheat, peas, mustard seed, amber, tobacco, sugar, by fermenting sheeps' blood, by the action of vinegar on oyster shells, &c., but with the mass of undigested facts so obtained he seemed content. He found that iron filings and strong sulphuric acid produced scarcely any air, he observed that on adding water a gas is abundantly evolved. This gas was hydrogen, but including all gases as "air" he did not stop to examine it.

Dr. Hales also made a number of investigations into the movement of sap in vegetables. In his experiments, directed to ascertain the force with which trees imbibe moisture, he obtained some striking results. Thus, after cutting across the root of a pear-tree, the section being half an inch diameter, he cemented this into a tube, twenty-six inches long, filled with water, and dipping at its lower end into mercury. So vigorously was the water absorbed that in six minutes the mercury rose eight inches in the tube. The experiment was made in August. Eight inches of mercury would be about equal to 109 inches or about nine feet of water. Thus the absorption of the root would be sufficiently powerful to raise or support a column of water nine feet high.

FIFTH PERIOD.

CHAPTER IX.

FIFTH PERIOD: THE CHILDHOOD OF TRUTH. CULLEN, BLACK.

Y those readers acquainted with some of the chief characteristics of modern science it will have been observed that up to the date we have now reached very little notice had been taken of the quantitative aspect of phenomena. *Weight* was not yet considered an all-important factor in chemical investigations; and, indeed, it could not be so until, at least to some extent, the fact of the *indestructibility of matter* was recognised. It is true that in the directions given by such men as Basil Valentine and Glauber, for the preparation of various bodies, mention is often made of the *quantities* of the different ingredients intended to be mixed together. But there is no precise attempt to connect the quantity of the product with the quantities of the substances employed to produce it, nor to elucidate in this way its composition.

When we reflect how often a portion at least of the product of a reaction is gaseous and would therefore seem to be destroyed, we shall not wonder that the value of weight in chemical science was lost sight of. When a candle burns, all that we are directly aware of is that light is given out and the candle slowly disappears; and what more natural than to conclude that where there is disappearance there is destruction? As a matter of fact we now know that in this process no particle of the candle has ceased to exist; all the matter that composed it is there, but the *candle* is no longer there *as such*. But so long as chemists could not collect the carbon dioxide and measure or weigh it, what could they suggest, but that matter was now and again in the habit of evanescing, or, so to say, "going to coloured cob-web" and becoming inappreciable. While these views prevailed no great depths could be reached by science; it was held back, as it were, by the want of weight.

But we are now entering upon the period when quantitative chemistry really begins. It is true that many of the experiments of Dr. Hales included measurement of gases; but he was not sufficiently aware of any definite purpose in what he did. It has, indeed, been very shrewdly remarked that Hales had learnt how to question Nature, but not how to cross-examine her.* The cross-examination was to be conducted, in part, by the well-known chemist, Dr.

* F. H. Butler, *Encyc. Brit.* Art. *Chemistry*.

Black, and it has been continued with increasing skill and penetration to this day.

Before, however, we proceed to sketch Black's life and work it is only just that some reference should be made to his instructor, Dr. Cullen, of Edinburgh. Dr. Cullen was a man who engaged in remarkably little original work, and yet such was the charm of his character, and so wide-spread was the elevating influence of his enthusiasm, that, after we have got to know his life, we are almost glad that the brilliance of original achievement should not be there to distract us from the calm of his energy and the loving-kindness of his toil. Cullen* was essentially a man who influenced others. Not striving after his own fame he was content that others should reap the benefits of his knowledge, and that to them should pass the glory of penetrating those problems which his conscientious enthusiasm as a teacher left him no time to solve. He was an example of the few teachers who follow closely the mental unfolding of their pupils, and of the still fewer who aim at influence upon character as well as upon brain. He was uniformly attentive to his students, while his cordiality and warmth of heart took them by storm.

He made himself personally known to all his pupils. He used to invite them to his house, two, three, and sometimes four at a time, and he would place himself on terms of the easiest intimacy with those

* William Cullen, M.D., born at Hamilton in Scotland (1710—1790).

of whose character he formed high opinion. He would talk with them upon any topic to which they chose to refer, and by the complete confidence with which he spoke to them would win from them confession as to all their plans and difficulties in life. He became their friend, and by the individuality of his contact with them won a high place in their hearts. Caring little for the emoluments of office he succeeded by the most delicate tact in evading payment for his courses where he thought his students pecuniarily unable to afford it. In such a case, for instance, he might invite the student to attend certain lectures, as he would be glad of his opinion on certain parts of the course. Or, again, he would press books from his own library upon them. As persons in such positions are often peculiarly sensitive he was here again obliged to resort to little schemes in order to make the offer agreeable. He would point out some particular passage of importance in the book that he wished the student to borrow, and use his professional authority to desire him to take the book home at once and study this passage as a matter of immediate importance.

By such winning generosity and insight Cullen acquired a quite exceptional popularity with his pupils, and as a result a quite exceptional bitterness of jealousy on the part of his colleagues. But to this jealousy he gave no heed, and went on his way without appearing to hear the sneers uttered at his expense. As an instance of his deserved popularity it may be mentioned that when the professor of Materia Medica, Dr. Alston, died in 1763, Cullen was invited to continue his course. Alston had opened the lectures with ten students. When Cullen consented to continue them one hundred new students instantly enrolled themselves. That is sufficiently indicative of the position he had attained.

Among those thus taught by him was one pupil whose name was to be remembered for many long years as a true son of science, Dr. Joseph Black. It was well for Black to have obtained his instruction at the hands of such a man, for Cullen saw chemistry, not as a curious and useful art, but as a division of the vast science of nature.

Dr. Black* had, as a man, about him much of the charm that attached to Cullen. There is a quiet and dignified simplicity about his character that clings round his name to this day. He was so gentle, so unassuming, and so sincere, that it is reassuring to find that in this brawling world his voice could yet be heard above the tumult. Black obtained the chemical chair at Glasgow. Thomson says of him that he "constituted the most complete model of a chemical lecturer that I ever had an opportunity of witnessing." He was not a mere chemist but a cultivated man. He had considerable æsthetic taste, as shown in his love of music and painting. Even a retort or crucible was to his eye an example of beauty or deformity. He was also warm-hearted and affectionate, and with

* Joseph Black, 1728—1799.

Dr. Hutton he formed an unusually close friendship, imparting to him every one of his speculations and receiving the same confidence in return. The two friends were seldom asunder for two days together.

Black always suffered from delicate health, and towards the end of his life this became so pronounced that he had to give up all professional work. He did not attempt to achieve what his strength would not allow: "he spun his thread of life to the very last fibre." Careless of his own fame he did not torment himself by restlessness or eagerness, but happily resigned work which he felt himself unable to fulfil. Thus his life was always tranquil and at peace. The manner of his death was curiously sudden and calm. He was sitting alone at table with some bread, prunes, and milk before him. It seems that he had the cup of milk raised to his lips when, feeling some sensation of approaching weakness, he set it down on his knees and held it there between his two hands; and so, without a single tremor or struggle, he died. It might almost have been an experiment designed by him to show how quietly he could pass away, for the cup was not displaced nor was a drop of the milk spilt. His servant, coming in and seeing him sitting still in so easy an attitude, thought he had dropped into a doze. When the man had left the room, however, he had some unaccountable misgivings and went gently back into the room once more. Still, however, the pose seemed so easy and natural that he went out reassured. Coming back a third time, and finding Dr. Black still seated in the same posture, he at last went up to waken him and found him dead.

The two great pieces of work for which Black is renowned are his investigation of the alkalies and his discovery of latent heat. The former is contained in his *Experiments on Magnesia Alba*,* of which some account must now be given. The reader may here be reminded of the chemical reactions, called double decompositions, examined by Mayow. One of the first experiments that strike us in Black's paper has an interesting bearing on these reactions. He distilled together in a retort magnesium carbonate, ammonium chloride, and water, and found some magnesium chloride left behind in the retort. Magnesium chloride is, of course, made up out of the metal magnesium and the "negative" element chlorine, or, as it was then less accurately expressed, it contains a base and acid for its constituents. When ammonium hydrate† is added to its solution the ammonium combines with the chlorine to form ammonium chloride, whilst magnesium hydrate separates out as a white precipitate. This Black expressed by saying that "the attraction of the volatile alkali (ammonia) for acids is stronger than that of magnesia."

But the reaction observed by him in the experi-

* Edinburgh (1777).
† Ammonium hydrate is the ordinary ammonia solution expressed as a derivative of the *metallic radical* ammonium. The formula for the hydrate is $NH_4(OH)$, the NH_4 group being ammonium.

ment first referred to is the very reverse of this. The ammonia is already combined with the strong hydrochloric acid to form ammonium chloride, yet it gives up its "negative," or "acid," element which becomes combined with the magnesium. Thus Black remarks: "But it also appears that a gentle heat is capable of overcoming this superiority of attraction." The truth was beginning to appear that the final arrangement of the elements in a mixture of various bodies is not simply dependent upon *superiority of attraction;* for under different circumstances totally different arrangements will result. The view now generally held is that in a mixed solution all possible combinations of the negative and positive elements occur. Thus, suppose we have a mixture in solution of sodium carbonate and magnesium chloride. Then the following bodies will all actually at first occur: sodium carbonate, magnesium chloride, sodium chloride, and magnesium carbonate. But magnesium carbonate (the "magnesia alba" of Black) is insoluble, and hence is precipitated at once. Being thus withdrawn from solution it is at the same time withdrawn from the sphere of action of the other ingredients. Those ingredients now consist of sodium carbonate, magnesium chloride, and sodium chloride, and there being one possible combination now absent more magnesium carbonate is at once formed. This again goes out of solution, and so on until there is left in the solution sodium chloride, and the precipitate consists of magnesium carbonate. It is not that the magnesia has a superior attraction for carbonic acid, but it is simply the fact of the insolubility of the magnesium carbonate which brings about the reaction. Other considerations enter into the study of chemical reactions which we cannot go into now.

Before Black's time it was known that ordinary lime is *quickened* by heat. Black experimented with a view to finding out whether magnesia would form "a quicklime." An ounce of magnesia alba was heated for an hour to the melting point of copper. When it came out of the furnace it had lost seven-twelfths of its weight. After being thus treated Black found it would still dissolve in acids to form salts, but laid stress on the fact that it did so "without any the least degree of effervescence."

The question was, what had happened to the magnesia alba (magnesium carbonate) in this process of quickening? To elucidate this he distilled magnesia* in a retort, and, as it was evident from the previous experiment, that the magnesia lost something while being quickened, he expected to condense this volatile body in his receiver. To his surprise, however, all he could condense was a little water (a substance only present as an impurity in this reaction) the weight of which was not nearly equivalent to the loss of weight sustained by the magnesia. Now this use of weight to assist in unravelling the knots of the problem is exceedingly important. It might have

* In the course of this passage the term *magnesia* is used, as it was used by Black, to signify *magnesia alba*.

been thought that some matter had merely been destroyed in the reaction, but it does not seem to have occurred to Black to accept such a view of the matter as rational. His conclusion therefore was that something had gone off in a non-visible form, and the question now was—what?

His view was that the volatile matter lost in calcination was mostly air. He next calcined two drams of magnesia alba, dissolved the resulting quick magnesia in dilute sulphuric acid and reprecipitated the magnesia alba from this solution by means of a "mild" alkali. The weight of substance thus obtained was one dram fifty grains, from which it is seen that the magnesia had in this process very nearly recovered its original weight. Obviously part of the addition must be "air," that is gaseous matter, for it could be again driven off as "air" by heat. Furthermore this "air" must have come from the mild alkali by means of which the magnesia alba was reproduced.

Further Black's argument is this: Stephen Hales had already shown that the mild alkalies contain a large quantity of air which they emit when joined to an acid. Thus if ordinary washing soda be treated with hydrochloric acid there is copious effervescence and evolution of gas. In the case before us, when the quick magnesia dissolved by acids is reprecipitated as magnesia alba by alkali, the alkali, Black argues, really becomes joined to the acid to form a *salt*, but without visible emission of air. Yet the air is not retained by the alkali, for the alkaline *salt* obtained *is the same in quantity as if pure acid and not magnesium salt had been used to obtain it.* That is to say, the weight of sodium sulphate obtained by adding one ounce of sodium carbonate to magnesium sulphate is the same as that resulting from the solution of one ounce of sodium carbonate in sulphuric acid, no "air" having attached itself to the sodium sulphate in either case. What then has become of this air which was in the mild alkali to start with, and is there no longer?

Obviously, concludes Black, forced from the alkali by the acid this air has lodged itself in the magnesia, and *it is the presence of this air that distinguishes magnesia alba from quick or calcined magnesia.* In our way of stating it the first is magnesium carbonate, the second is magnesium oxide. Carbonic acid added to the latter produces the former.

The whole course of this inductive reasoning as pursued by Black is peculiarly thorough and scientific, and in itself would make him well worthy of the place he has won. He went on to apply these views to the calcareous earths (such as chalk) and the mild alkalies in general. They are distinguished from the calcined earths and the caustic alkalies by the presence of this air, which the latter tend to reabsorb.*
Previously to his time the causticity of quicklime was supposed to be occasioned by its combination with igneous particles.

* That is, in modern language, they are *carbonates.*

Black collected the gas evolved by treating magnesia alba with acid, and distinguished it from atmospheric and other " airs." In this he was repeating the discovery made by Van Helmont more than a century before, but then entirely forgotten. He distinguished this peculiar body by the name of *fixed air*.

Black's researches upon these subjects afford a very instructive example of work conducted in a truly scientific spirit. Certain phenomena afforded interesting matter for investigation, and Black proceeded by endeavouring first of all to multiply facts. The quickening of lime by heat was already known. Would other analogous bodies, such as magnesia alba, give similar results? These were found to occur, and the next point was to observe accurately and in detail what took place during the calcination. The observed facts were loss of weight and loss of power of effervescence with acid. Could these losses be restored? By the processes above described he found that they could, use being made of mild alkali which in the reaction lost its "air." In regaining its weight and power of effervescence the magnesia then has taken up "fixed air," a definite gas found to be common to the calcareous earths and the mild alkalies, and conspicuous by its absence from the calcined earths and the caustic alkalies. In these steps Black aimed consistently at the cross-examination of nature. He did not allow himself to be led astray by any preconceived theory or to be turned aside by any apparent improbability. This case is only illustrative of the singularly unbiassed character of Black's mind, for he was the only chemist of his day who, in the great phlogiston controversy which will be dealt with in the next chapter, definitely avowed his conversion to the Lavoisierian doctrine of combustion.

The other research of Black's, which must be briefly sketched in order to appreciate the later development of the science, was his discovery of *latent heat*.

It may not be out of place to here refer first to the construction of the ordinary thermometer. It consists of a glass tube of fine bore, having a bulb at one end. This bulb and part of the stem is filled with mercury, and before the fine end of the tube is sealed off all air is expelled by boiling the mercury. When the end is closed the mercury, as its temperature is lowered, falls in the table. To graduate the thermometer the bulb is plunged into melting ice when the mercury becomes stationary at a definite point, which is then marked by the scratch of a file on the glass. This "freezing-point" is 0° in the centigrade scale and 32° in Fahrenheit's scale. The next operation is to immerse the bulb and stem in steam at the boiling point of water. The mercury, of course, rises, and this time another mark is made where it becomes stationary. Two fixed points are thus obtained, and all that remains is to divide the interval into the required number of degrees. On the centigrade scale the melting point will be 0° and the boiling point 100°. On the Fahrenheit scale the melting point will be 32° and the boiling point 212°.

Now, the ascertainment of these points is only made possible by the fact that ice while melting and water while boiling remain at a uniform temperature. If some pounded ice be placed in a basin and a centigrade thermometer immersed therein it will be found to indicate a temperature of 0°. As time passes the ice gradually melts and a good deal of water collects in the basin, but the mercury still stands at 0°. Later on only a few pieces of ice are left floating on the water, but the thermometer still marks the melting point of ice. Moreover, suppose we apply heat to the vessel containing it; the ice melts faster but it does not grow any warmer; the temperature is still zero (32° F.). In the same way if water be boiled in an open vessel, the more heat is applied the faster the water boils, but its temperature remains at 100° C. (212° F.).

It was these phenomena which led Black to conclude that an amount of heat was used up or rendered *latent* in converting the ice into water and the water into steam. Thus, if we start with a vessel full of hard frozen ice at a temperature below the freezing point, and apply heat by means of a small flame, the mercury of a centigrade thermometer immersed in the ice will gradually rise up to 0° and then will come to a standstill. The first quantity of heat raises the temperature of the ice; when that has reached its melting point the whole of the rest of the heat is used in melting the ice. When the whole of the ice is melted the water so formed begins to rise in temperature once more till the boiling point is reached, when again the mercury becomes stationary. At this stage all the heat is used in converting the water into steam. The steam may be superheated to any desired temperature.

Black determined the latent heat of water to be 79·44, and in order to explain how this is done we must use some very simple mathematics. A certain weight of ice M at $0°$, is immersed in a weight of water m at a temperature $t°$ more than sufficient to melt the ice. As soon as the ice has melted the final temperature is noted, say $\theta°$. In cooling from $t°$ to $\theta°$ the water has parted with a quantity of heat, $m(t-\theta)$. If x be the latent heat of ice it absorbs in liquefying heat Mx, but besides this the water *formed from the ice* has risen to $\theta°$ and has thus absorbed the heat $M\theta$. We have:—

$$Mx + M\theta = m(t-\theta).$$

from which x, the latent heat of water, is deduced. It is about 79·2.

The latent heat of steam, arrived at in a very similar way, is about 538, that is to say, a pound of water at $100°$ C. absorbs during vaporisation enough heat to raise the temperature of 538 lbs. of water by $1°$ centigrade.

SIXTH PERIOD.

CHAPTER X.

SIXTH PERIOD: THE CONFLICT WITH ERROR.
THE BIRTH OF ERROR.

IT is now time to discuss the development and meaning of a theory which for many long years was the object of blind idolatry to the chemists of the time. In previous pages some examples have been given of the attempts made to conjecture (for it was little more than conjecture) the nature of the fundamental principles of matter. We have seen how salt, sulphur, and mercury had their turn with air, earth, water and fire, and how in the advanced writings of Robert Boyle all dogmatism regarding the elements was eyed askance. Among subsequent theories only two need be mentioned. The first was propounded by a German chemist, Becher (1635—1682), who held that the primary ingredients of matter were water and earth, and that from these were produced three earths—the fusible or strong, the fatty, and the fluid earths—improperly called salt, sulphur, and mercury. The second was the phlogiston theory of Stahl.

George Ernest Stahl was born at Anspach in 1660, and studied medicine at Jena.* In 1694 he was named second professor of medicine to the University of Halle to which post he was helped by Frederick Hoffmann. In 1716 he was made physician to the King of Prussia, and went to Berlin, where he died in 1734. In his medical views Stahl to some extent followed Van Helmont. "The body as such has no power to move itself, and it must always be put in motion by immaterial spirits; all movement is a spiritual act." His dissertations, pamphlets, etc., number four or five hundred. His theory of the elements lasted half a century.

Stahl developed the doctrines of Becher and enumerated four elements, viz: water, acid, earth, and phlogiston. Metals on heating for the most part become oxidised, and this *calcination* was explained by Becher on the supposition that they consisted of an earth and something of which they became deprived on ignition; the burning of brimstone (sulphur) was, in like manner, thought to be its

* Some account of Stahl is given in the *Biographie Universelle*, where his unbounded arrogance is commented upon. "La lecture attentive de ses écrits prouve une grande disposition à la melancolie, un orgueil sans bornes, et un profond mépris pour tous ceux qui ne pensaient pas comme lui."

resolution into an acid and a true sulphur, or that combustible part which was dispelled by heat. It was this supposed combustible body to which Stahl gave the name of phlogiston (φλογιστόν, combustible). The "phlogiston" of Stahl is in many ways analogous to the souls and spirits assigned to metals and salts by the alchymists, or to what Geber called the "humidity" and Cardan the "celestial heat" of metals.

To illustrate this curious theory let us take the simple case of the burning of a piece of coal. The question is, what is happening while the coal burns? We have seen how Hooke would have answered this question more than a hundred years before the overthrow of the Stahlian views. According to him a certain part of the coal unites with a part of the air and is "made to fly up and down with it," and moreover the part of the air causing this action is contained, "fixed," in saltpetre. This comes very near to an account of the production of carbonic acid during combustion, but owing to his unfortunate analogy between the action of the "substance inherent and mixed with the air" and the action of a liquid solvent there was a loophole of escape. Had his ideas been only a little more matured the victory of phlogiston might have been averted. His facts were good, so far as they went, and he did not allow his creeds to outrun his facts The Stahlians, on the contrary, took a different method with the undeniable gaps in the ranks of their facts. They filled up the vacancies with fictions. Their fictions were the creations of clever minds whose facile ingenuity only led them farther astray.

To the problem above propounded—viz., what is happening while coal burns—the Stahlian answer was that the combustion of the coal was due to the loss of phlogiston which was given up to the air. The more perfectly combustible a body was the greater the amount of phlogiston it contained, so that charcoal and lamp-black, and other reducing agents, came in time to be regarded as nearly pure phlogiston. When by carbon a metallic calx was reduced, or a compound containing sulphur was obtained from fused sodium sulphate, phlogiston was supposed to be absorbed from the charcoal. Incombustible bodies were supposed to have already parted with their phlogiston. As most combustible bodies were insoluble phlogiston itself came to be regarded as a dry and earthy body, capable of receiving a motion of great velocity—the *motus verticillaris*—manifested when ignition or flame was produced.*

Mayow had stated that the "nitre air" of the atmosphere caused fermentation and souring of wines, produced sulphuric acid from sulphur, and effected the calcination of metals.

As early as 1630, John Rey had noticed that metals grew heavier when calcined, as he thought, by the absorption of "thickened air," but they had given no general theory of combustion, nor

* *Encyc. Britannica*, art. "Stahl."

explained why some bodies grow lighter on heating. Boyle, also, had observed the increase in weight of metals, but attributed it to combination with heat particles or "igneous corpuscles."* The bearing of these observations upon the hypothesis of phlogiston was quickly perceived. If calcination results in the *loss* of a material principle, phlogiston, how, at the same time, can it be accompanied by a *gain* in weight? This was the apparently unanswerable paradox. But with exquisite ingenuity the Stahlians surmounted the difficulty and retorted that phlogiston was *the principle of levity or of negative weight.* Such slippery opponents could readily elude one's grasp.

Frederick Hoffmann (1660—1742), who contributed to analytical chemistry in Germany, held with Stahl that sulphur consisted of acid and phlogiston, and that combustible bodies contained a principle describable as phlogiston; but he thought it possible that the calces of metals were formed, not by the subtraction of phlogiston, but by the combination of the metals with an acid material. Boerhaave, too, cast doubt on the assumption of the existence of an earth and a combustible principle in metals. Neumann (1683—1737), J. H. Pott (1692—1777), Marggraf (1709—1782), and Macquer (1718—1784), the discoverer of arsenic acid, supported Stahl, and for many years his doctrine held its ground against all opponents.

Let us now examine a few chemical facts by the

* See *ante*, p. 135.

light of the phlogistic hypothesis and see what is the explanation it affords us.

When lead is heated it undergoes characteristic changes of colour, becoming first yellow and then red. What is happening to it? It is losing more and more phlogiston. The yellow substance (massicot) is the partially dephlogisticated calx of lead. When the metal is wholly deprived of phlogiston it is converted into the red substance (red lead). But the yellow substance weighs more than the metal. That is because the metal has been losing "the principle of levity." And the red substance weighs more than the yellow from which it is obtained. That, too, is because the yellow substance has been losing more of "the principle of levity."

But here is another fact for the Stahlians to explain. Some charcoal is mixed with a little massicot and the mixture heated. A malleable globule of metallic lead is formed. What has occurred? The charcoal has given up phlogiston to the partially phlogisticated calx, and this, by complete phlogistication has become converted into metal. So too red lead may be reduced to the metallic state, only more phlogiston is needed.

An interesting phenomenon observable in this experiment if carried on in a closed vessel is the evolution of a considerable amount of an incombustible gas. Does not this suggest that the calx has been losing something during reduction? So far the ingenuity of the Stahlians is fairly successful. But next let us ask them, how is it that lamp-black, consisting of very nearly pure phlogiston, weighs anything at all? Or at least, why is it not lighter than air? Probably they would reply that it does not contain enough phlogiston for that. There is no need to dwell on this trifle, so we will next point out an interesting experiment.

Here is a small porcelain crucible. The crucible on trial does not alter in weight after heating. A small piece of charcoal is placed in it, and crucible and charcoal are heated over a Bunsen burner. The charcoal enters upon a vigorous combustion. On withdrawing the flame the mass is seen to be losing its dense black colour, and presently there is left in the bottom of the crucible only a little grey ash. The charcoal has been in combustion; it has therefore been losing phlogiston; phlogiston is the principle of levity, therefore obviously the charcoal, since it contained so large a proportion of this principle, should now weigh *far more* than before it was burnt. Surely that is a correct Stahlian argument. Now let us weigh the crucible with the ash in it. To our astonishment it weighs much *less*. This loss is not due to the crucible, for that, we have already shown, is unchanged by heat, and if now cleaned and weighed will be found to have undergone no alteration. The loss, then, is due to the charcoal, and amounts to considerably more than 90 per cent. of its weight. How would the Stahlians answer that?

But it would be very easy to puzzle the Stahlians

with an examination of this kind, and perhaps it would be hardly fair to make use of our increased knowledge to do so.

The ideas of Scheele upon this subject illustrate the confusion of mind produced by these doctrines. He found that when air was phlogisticated by combustion the residual gas (nitrogen) occupied less bulk. Thinking it to be a compound of phlogiston with air he expected it to be heavier than common air. To his surprise he found it to be actually lighter. He concluded that one constituent of the air remained while another, united to phlogiston in some way, disappeared. In his endeavours to find out what had become of it, he finally came to the conclusion that the compound of air with phlogiston was heat or fire, which escaped through the glass. With these views present to his mind he heated nitre in a retort over a charcoal fire with sulphuric acid. In addition to a fuming acid he obtained a colourless air (oxygen). His explanation was that the charcoal in burning united with fire-air (oxygen) to form heat. This heat passed into the retort and was there decomposed, giving rise to red nitrous fumes and pure fire air.*

When Priestley discovered oxygen gas he tried to suit it to the phlogiston hypothesis. It supported combustion more readily than common air, that is it could take up more phlogiston. Thus in his opinion it contained less phlogiston than common air. It was therefore termed dephlogisticated air.

* Roscoe and Schorlemmer, *Treatise*, Hist. Introduction.

Nitrogen, not supporting combustion, was on the other hand termed phlogisticated air. It was already saturated with phlogiston and could not take up more. Hydrogen was looked upon as either pure phlogiston or phlogisticated water.

When we see such a man as Scheele drawn into fanciful assertions of the kind described above we can the better estimate the havoc played by the hypothesis of Stahl in the minds of his followers.

But it is inexpressibly strange to find such men as Priestley and Cavendish, the one clinging to this idea as though it were the soul of science, and the other unwilling to recognise its absurdity. That they might have been blinded to the meaning of their own discoveries we can to some extent understand, but that when this meaning was pointed out they should still have refused to see it, would be incredible were not the facts so certain. Priestley insisted that the effect of combustion was to load dephlogisticated air (oxygen) with the combustible principle phlogiston, in spite of Lavoisier's proof that the only product of the reaction was the incombustible gas—fixed air. Cavendish, more unaccountably still, in spite of his own accurate experiments, regarded it as most probable that inflammable air (hydrogen) was "phlogisticated water."

Harmful, however, as we cannot but think that the Stahlian hypothesis was, we must recognise that it contained in it at least an element of truth. The supposed loss of phlogiston was really a loss of potential energy. The attraction of oxygen for another element, so long as they are not combined, is capable of being converted into a certain amount of work or heat. Once the combination takes place the heat is evolved and the capacity for work is destroyed. The acting forces have been brought to a state of equilibrium. *The potential energy is lost.*

CHAPTER XI.

SIXTH PERIOD: THE CONFLICT WITH ERROR.

THE FIRST OF AUGUST, 1774.

"WITH this apparatus, after a variety of other experiments, an account of which will be found in its proper place, on the 1st of August, 1774, I endeavoured to extract air from *mercurius calcinatus per se* [*]; and I presently found that by means of this lens, air was expelled from it very readily. Having got about three or four times as much as the bulk of my materials I admitted water to it and found it was not imbibed by it. But what surprised me more than I can well express, was that a candle burned in this air with a remarkably vigorous flame, very much

---

[*] *I.e.* mercuric oxide (HgO) obtained by heating mercury in presence

like that enlarged flame with which a candle burns in nitrous air, exposed to iron or liver of sulphur; .... I was utterly at a loss to account for it."

In these words Priestley announces his discovery of oxygen gas. It may be said without qualification that here was the most important chemical fact discovered up to that time.

The rare cheerfulness which characterized Priestley's temperament had very serious difficulties to contend with in his early days. His father, Joseph Priestley, was a cloth-dresser by trade, living in Birstall, near Leeds. His son Joseph, the subject of this chapter, was born in 1733. As a boy, Priestley was of a weakly and consumptive habit, and his early education was, in consequence, somewhat desultory. His mother died early, and the strict Calvinism in which he was brought up by his aunt, Mrs. Keighley, of whom he speaks with much affection, threw an occasional deep gloom over his boyish life. "I felt occasionally such distress of mind as it is not in my power to describe, and which I still look back upon with horror." It must indeed have been a deep mental distress to be so vividly recalled in after life. His continued ill-health interfered for some time with his purpose of entering the ministry. But so inclined was Priestley to look at the bright side of all things that of these drawbacks he wrote: "I even think it an advantage to me, and I am truly thankful for it, that my health received the check that it did when I was young; since a muscular habit from high health and strong spirits are not, I think, in general, accompanied with that sensibility of mind which is both favourable to piety and to speculative pursuits." Eventually he went to the Dissenting Academy at Daventry and studied under Dr. Doddridge.

Priestley's first charge on leaving Daventry was Needham Market, in Surrey. He had a marked defect in his speech, and his stuttering manner not suiting his congregation they left him almost penniless. After resorting to many unsuccessful experiments for the purpose of earning his bread and cheese he was finally obliged to leave. Years after he came down to preach at the same chapel when better known. His delivery was much the same and the same congregation attended the chapel; but this time they flocked to hear him, and pretended to admire the utterance they had formerly despised. After other vicissitudes Priestley went, in 1761, to Warrington as "tutor in the languages" to a dissenting academy. Here he taught Latin, Greek, Hebrew, French, and Italian, and lectured on Logic, on Elocution, on the Theory of Language and Universal Grammar, on Oratory and Criticism, on History and General Policy, on Civil Law, and on Anatomy.*

Here also he found time to marry a daughter of Mr. Isaac Wilkinson, an ironmaster near Wrexham, in Wales. At Warrington, too, he got to know

---

* For a view of Priestley's versatility see the catalogue of his books published in 1794. An interesting lecture on Priestley was delivered at Manchester by Professor Thorpe, *Science Lectures* (Series 6).

Benjamin Franklin, but for whose influence most of Priestley's scientific work might have been left undone. It was about this time that he gave some attention to the study of Electricity and, in spite of all his other business, brought out a history of the subject, which was very favourably received. At the Academy he and the tutors lived together in unusual harmony. "We drank tea together every Saturday, and our conversation was equally instructive and pleasing."

In 1767 Priestley removed to Leeds. "At Leeds I continued six years very happy, with a liberal, friendly, and harmonious congregation." Here he made experiments on impregnating water with "fixed air" to prevent scurvy, and was to have accompanied an expedition, then sailing, as chaplain, but that his heretical tendencies were discovered in time. But the event at Leeds, of which he speaks with most warmth, is his meeting Thomas Lindsay, then of Catterick. "A correspondence and intimacy commenced, which has been the source of more real satisfaction to me than any other circumstance in my whole life."* His theological writings were never published without Lindsay's advice and approval. With Lindsay he kept up a very frequent and constant correspondence, while with other friends he corresponded very freely, though, as he remarks in a letter to Lindsay, his literary labours often obliged him to write till he could hardly hold the pen.

* In a much later letter to the same he says, "If I have been any use in the world you are the cause of it."

STATUE OF PRIESTLEY, AT BIRMINGHAM.

From Leeds Priestley went into the family of the Earl of Shelburne, afterwards Marquis of Lansdowne, who had his country seat at Bowood, in Wiltshire. His office was nominally that of librarian, for which he received a house and £250 a year, with a certain annuity for life. He had little employment, he says, attaching to his post, and was thus free to prosecute his own inquiries. When he went to his lordship he had materials for his volume, *Experiments and Observations on different Kinds of Air*, which he soon afterwards published.

In his winter residence in London, while with Shelburne, he saw much of Lindsay and of Franklin. This was just before the American war; and their conversation was chiefly of a political nature. Franklin was very pacifically inclined. He thought that if war broke out it would last ten years, and was sure that America would be finally victorious. As a fact the war lasted eight years, and she was victorious. In March, 1775, Franklin left England; his last day in the country he and Priestley spent together alone. They read some accounts of the reception of the Boston Port Bill in America, "and as he read the addresses to the inhabitants of Boston from the places in the neighbourhood the tears trickled down his cheeks."

With Shelburne Priestley continued for seven years, when a coolness sprang up between them, which, however, at a later date passed away. He was not very greatly pleased with this mode of life, and does not seem to have envied persons in high station. He believed much more happiness was to be found in the life of the middle classes. But he adds that wealth may be of immense value when in the hands of a good man, and that when a person is born to affluence and not hurt by it, "it produces a godlike character unattainable otherwise." After leaving Lord Shelburne he settled in Birmingham. Here, on 14th of July, 1791, riots in favour of "Church and King" broke out in consequence of a meeting to celebrate the anniversary of the French Revolution. Priestley's opinions being considered heretical and violent, the mob marched upon his house, where he was unsuspectingly sitting with his wife and family. Friends hastened to warn him; at first their news seemed to him incredible, but finally he consented to regard his own safety and left the house. He retired to Mr. Hawkes's in the neighbourhood, and from there saw his house, with library, manuscripts, and philosophical instruments, burnt to the ground. At this destruction of his property and labour he looked on with perfect calm, and afterwards fled in disguise to Worcester and thence to London. "Persons in the habit of *gentlemen*" were found secreting his papers with a view to discover incriminating details.* He was appointed successor to his friend Dr. Price at the dissenting meeting in Hackney, but still suspicion pursued him. His political opinions gave offence to

---

* Curry, *Life of Joseph Priestley*, a pamphlet. Birmingham (1804).

men in power, and he was finally obliged to quit the country.

He embarked in 1794, a victim to popular ignorance and ingratitude. Before leaving Priestley placed on record the following remarkable words :—"I cannot refrain from repeating again that I leave my native country with real regret, never expecting to find anywhere else society so suited to my disposition and habit, such friends as I have here (whose attachment has been more than an even balance to all the abuse I have met with from others), and especially to replace one particular Christian friend, in whose absence I shall, for some time at least, find all the world a blank. . . . . I can, however, truly say that I leave without resentment or ill-will. On the contrary, I sincerely wish my countrymen all happiness, and when the time for the reflection (which my absence may accelerate) shall come, they will, I am confident, do me more justice." It is hardly possible to do justice after a victim's death, but, so far as slow growth of somewhat wider views is equivalent to repentance for past narrowness, to that extent justice has tardily been done to Priestley, among others whose heroism was then considered no mitigation of their heresy. Heresy, not merely in religion but in political views and in social life, has ever been to the ordinary man the one unpardonable sin.

Priestley settled near his sons on the Susquehanna, and there died. His end was very calm. His mind was perfectly clear and tranquil. He dictated some last words, and then had the manuscript read to him. After making some needful corrections he said quietly, "That is right; I have done," and after a few hours he passed away.

He had reason, he said, to be thankful for a happy temperament of body and mind, and certainly a more cheerful mortal it is difficult to conceive of. His constitution had been far from robust, but with exquisite felicity he remarks, "excellently adapted to that studious life which has fallen to my lot." He always slept well, and, when fatigued, could sit down and sleep; "and whatever cause of anxiety I have had, I have almost always lost sight of it when I have got to bed, and I have generally fallen asleep as soon as I have been warm." His spirits after momentary depression always recovered their level, and, indeed, he had found that after trouble they would rise beyond their former height without any change in the circumstances.

He spoke of having a very failing memory which made his old writings, when re-read, seem perfectly new to him. One instance is mentioned by him in his autobiographical sketch, where his loss of memory went so far that he had serious fears of his mental powers totally failing. In writing a prefatory dissertation to one of his books he had occasion to refer to some point (he forgets what) connected with the Jewish passover. He had to consult and compare several writers, and he digested the results in a few paragraphs. For a fortnight his attention was drawn to other things, and at the end of this time it suddenly occurred to him that he had still to examine the point of the Jewish passover. Without any recollection that he had already done the work he proceeded to consult the same authorities, and to write out the opinions thus arrived at. He would never have remembered the former paper but that he accidentally discovered the manuscript, "which," says he, "I viewed with a degree of terror." Yet even this defect of memory he thought was, on the whole, probably a boon, being very likely compensated by greater inventive power.*

Priestley's manner of work was quiet and methodical. He could do nothing if hurried, but could work quickly if he felt that he had ample time. He wrote in the presence of wife and children, occasionally speaking to them; but could not write during reading aloud or uninterrupted conversation.

Certainly few characters afford us more varied and interesting material for study. Essentially, and from first to last, Priestley was a *brilliant* man, a man of splendid talents, wonderfully acute, and quick in perception, inventive and industrious. But his work was not that of a genius, it had hardly its ease or its accuracy. His versatility was amazing, but it was more the outcome of patience than of power, and to some extent he lacked the expansive capacity of a really great mind. In the latter part of his life, at least, he found it difficult to accommodate himself to

* J. T. Rutt, *Priestley's Life and Correspondence* (1831).

new ideas, and although his own discoveries were in themselves ruinous to the phlogistic theory yet he never could be got to see it. His last publication was *The Theory of Phlogiston Established*. We may say then that Priestley was a man of exceptional acuteness and versatility who made full use of his powers.

Such an estimate will fairly account for the work accomplished by his life. It is not necessary to say that he was a genius. Indeed, remarkably few scientific men would be worthy of such a title. The career has not as yet attracted many representatives of the highest order of mind. At the same time it will not do to lay too much stress upon Priestley's blunders over the phlogistic theory. We must bear in mind the great ascendency it had obtained over the minds of all chemists, and we must remember that only in rare cases is the scientific mind free from bias. Priestley's in this case was certainly not. The honour of acknowledging conversion belongs to Dr. Black, as we have already remarked. But the honour of a brilliant and eminently useful career, a life full of wide sympathies and noble unselfishness, a fame unsullied by jealousy or ambition, and a heart cheerfully hopeful through all misfortune belong to Joseph Priestley, whom the English people drove from their shores as their only tribute to his zeal.

The phlogiston theory is rather fully exemplified in some of the work undertaken by Priestley. When he found that a candle confined in a close vessel is

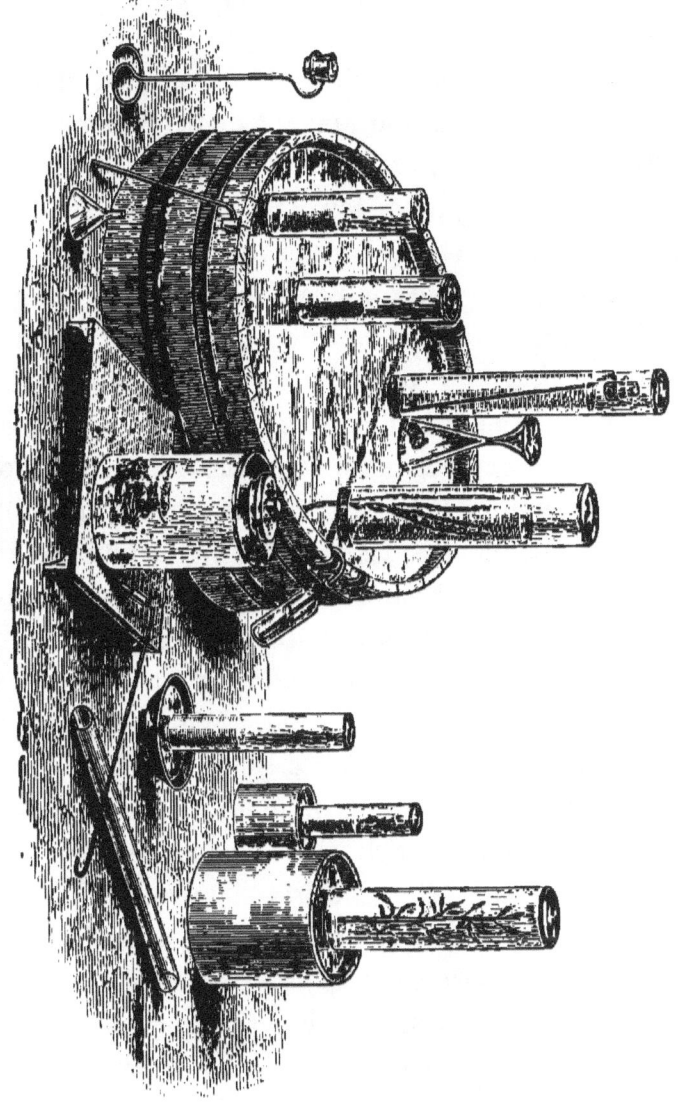

PRIESTLEY'S APPARATUS.
From an engraving in the *Observations on different Kinds of Air.*

after a while extinguished, he concluded that this was due to the limited amount of air becoming saturated with phlogiston. The candle burned while it could give off phlogiston, but the impulse to this evolution of phlogiston was to be found in the capacity the atmosphere had for combining with or absorbing phlogiston. As soon as this capacity was exhausted and the air could take up no more phlogiston the burning of the candle ceased.

Priestley experimented upon the action of hydrogen (rediscovered by his contemporary, Cavendish) on metallic calxes (oxides) heated by a burning-glass. The method was to heat the oxides in a cylinder of hydrogen inverted over water or mercury. In this way it was found that the hydrogen was absorbed and the calx converted into metal. We now know that what occurs in such a case is simply that the hydrogen abstracts the oxygen from the metallic oxide or "calx," combines with this oxygen to form water, and leaves the metal in a free state *reduced* from its oxide. Now Priestley observed that a small quantity of water was formed in these experiments, but he was bent upon explaining all things by means of phlogiston. He therefore neglected this item in the account and concluded that phlogiston was the same thing as inflammable air and existed in a combined state in metals; just as fixed air was contained in chalk and other calcareous substances, both being equally capable of being expelled again in the form of air.

Priestley seems to have been the first to substitute

mercury for water in the pneumatic trough, and thus succeeded in obtaining gases, the collection of which had baffled the endeavours of previous experimenters. Cavendish had tried to get "inflammable air" from a mixture of copper and "spirits of salt" (hydrochloric acid). He obtained an air that "lost its elasticity," that is, was absorbed on contact with water. Priestley was "exceedingly desirous" of becoming further acquainted with this gas. He therefore began the experiment, replacing the water by quicksilver, as, he says, he never failed to do where he suspected that a gas would be in any way affected by water. He in this way collected a gas which, he went on to show, was derived entirely from the acid, and might be equally well obtained by merely boiling common "spirit of salt" *per se*. In short Priestley obtained the true hydrochloric acid, which is a gas and had not before been isolated. Ordinary aqueous hydrochloric acid is merely a solution of this gas in water.*

This method of using quicksilver was of great service to Priestley; for by means of it too he showed that ordinary "spirits of hartshorn," or *spiritus volatilis salis ammoniaci*, is a solution of ammonia gas in water. Stephen Hales, in 1727, had heated lime with sal-ammoniac in a vessel closed by water, and he observed that no air was given out, but that, on the contrary, water was drawn into the apparatus. Using a mercury trough Priestley, by this same old method, obtained ammonia gas and showed that the

* *Observations on different Kinds of Air*, 1772.

ordinary aqueous ammonia, or "volatile spirit of sal-ammoniac," is a solution of this gas in water.* (1774.)

Priestley followed up these discoveries by endeavouring to obtain an "air" from oil of vitriol (sulphuric acid). He heated the acid for a long period without any result beyond the production of some white fumes which condensed in the upper part of his flask. The tube leading from the flask of course dipped under mercury. The end of this experiment is worth giving in his own words. "Despairing to get any air from the longer application of my candles I withdrew them; but before I could disengage the phial from the vessel of quicksilver a little of it passed through the tube into the hot acid;† when, instantly it was all filled with dense white fumes, a prodigious quantity of air was generated, the tube through which it was transmitted was broken into many pieces (I suppose by the heat that was suddenly produced), and part of the hot acid being spilled upon my hand, burned it terribly, so that the effect of it is visible to this day. The inside of the phial was coated with a white substance, and the smell that issued from it was extremely suffocating." In this way Priestley found out (1775) how to prepare pure sulphur dioxide. Stahl had shown that the fumes of burning sulphur are altogether different from sulphuric acid and are only partially on the

---

* *Observations on different Kinds of Air*, 1772.
† Being sucked up by the condensation.

way to it, but it was Priestley who first isolated the gas.

The next passage is characteristic both of Priestley's good spirits and of his obstinacy: "This accident taught me what I am surprised I should not have suspected before, viz.: that some metals will part with their phlogiston to hot oil of vitriol and thereby convert it into a permanent elastic air, producing the very same effect with oil, charcoal, or any other substance." The reaction may be most simply stated as follows:—taking copper, which is the metal usually employed, in place of mercury. First, the sulphuric acid is a compound of hydrogen, sulphur, and oxygen—hydrogen sulphate. The copper displaces the hydrogen of the acid, forming copper-sulphate and free hydrogen. This hydrogen is of course liberated in the presence of another portion of sulphuric acid which we may for convenience represent as composed of water and sulphur trioxide. The free hydrogen takes away a third of the oxygen from the trioxide, forming more water and sulphur dioxide, which is evolved as a gas.* Priestley was successful in producing this gas with copper, mercury, silver, iron, and sulphuric acid, the reaction being similar in the different cases. When carbon is used

---

* After reading the discussion of chemical symbols the reader may be able to appreciate this reaction when expressed in the more mathematical form of chemical equations:

(i.) $Cu + H^2SO^4 = Cu SO^3 + H^2$.
(ii.) $H^2O\ SO^3 + H^2 = 2H^2O + SO^2$.

carbon dioxide (the *fixed air* of Priestley and Black) is evolved.* Sulphur itself may be heated with sulphuric acid, the products in this case being only sulphur dioxide and water.† Priestley found that gold and sulphuric acid gave no result.

Sulphur dioxide is a colourless gas of suffocating odour like that of burning sulphur, and during this combustion it is formed. It will not support the combustion of a candle any more than will carbon dioxide. It combines with metallic oxides to form the salts termed *sulphites*. The moist gas bleaches vegetable colouring matter, such as litmus. The gas is readily soluble in water and its solution is known as *sulphurous acid*. The dry gas may be condensed to a liquid by being passed through a spiral tube surrounded by a freezing mixture.

Lastly we come to Priestley's supreme discovery, that of oxygen, or, as he termed it, *dephlogisticated air*. To some extent we may attribute such a discovery to chance; but chance as a rule will only assist men of rare intelligence and insight. Opportunities for good work of one kind or another occur continually to all, but the large majority of us are too blind to see them. Most good work is too near us for us to think it worth doing. All honour to those who have lent us their spectacles and shown us how *easy* their discoveries were!

Priestley was by no means definitely *in search of*

---

* $C + 2 H_2 SO_4 = 2 H_2O + CO_2 + 2 SO_2$.
† $S + 2 H_2 SO_4 = 3 SO_2 + 2 H_2O$.

oxygen when he found it. The conditions of scientific work then did not admit of such an attitude. Chemistry was not far enough on her uphill path to see the tracts of country crossed by her future advance. We can predict now what compounds and even what elements *ought* to occur in nature and can often tell how to search for them. If we do not always find them that is because either we or nature are not what we ought to be. In Priestley's time prediction in science, to have any chance of fulfilment, must be as vague as utterances of the Delphic sibyl. In most cases the only course was to "prospect around" and see what turned up. After showing, as he did by experiments with a candle similar to those employed by Mayow, that air would support only a limited amount of combustion, Priestley went on to prove that it could be renovated and made fit once more for respiration by the action of growing plants. Thus on the 17th of August, 1771, he first burned out a wax candle in a confined portion of air and then introduced into it a sprig of mint. On the 27th of the same month he found that another candle burned perfectly well in it. The mint had restored to the air its original virtues. To make assurance doubly sure he divided the used-up air into two parts. One he left standing alone over water; into the other he put the sprig of mint. After some days had elapsed he always found that a candle would burn in the latter but not in the former.

The true explanation of these phenomena is that the carbon dioxide formed by the combustion is absorbed by the plant and, in the presence of chlorophyll and sunlight, split up into carbon and oxygen, the plant retaining the carbon and giving the oxygen back to the air. Priestley did not recognise the full bearing of his discovery on the composition of the atmosphere. In 1772, however, Dr. Rutherford, Professor of Botany in the University of Edinburgh, showed definitely that common or atmospheric air contains a gas differing from fixed air, and yet, like it, incapable of supporting combustion. This he showed by treating air in which animals had breathed with caustic potash. The potash in this case absorbed the fixed air (forming the mild alkali or carbonate), yet when this absorption was complete a residual gas still remained and in this a candle would not burn. It was nitrogen gas.

In the same year Priestley found that combustion in a bell-glass over water gave rise to fixed air absorbable by milk of lime. The residual (phlogiscated) air, he found, would not support combustion, but he did not then consider it as a constituent of the atmosphere.* He showed that "nitrous gas" (nitrogen dioxide) when mixed with "phlogisticated air"

---

* At the time of the 1790 edition of his *Experiments and Observation*, Priestley seems to have been rather doubtful as to the correct way of regarding the composition of the air. He was inclined to regard air as a simple gas in a certain state of phlogistication, but the same nomenclature, he says, will suffice if it be regarded as composed of two distinct gases.

(nitrogen), occasioned no diminution in volume. If mixed with dephlogisticated air (oxygen), on the other hand, in due proportion, the whole of the resultant mixture was absorbed over water. This, indeed, was the method used by Priestley for the analysis of air, or of ascertaining what was termed the goodness of atmospheric air. The results of these analyses varied, and thus suggested the notion that the composition of the air varied, but this idea was exploded by Cavendish.

Interested as he became in his researches on gaseous bodies in general, Priestley proceeded somewhat as Hales had done before him, but with much more alertness of observation, to investigate the air obtainable from different bodies. In the course of these labours *mercurius calcinatus per se*, or mercuric oxide (red precipitate), was one of the bodies experimented on. From the important paper on this subject we may quote his own words: "For my own part I will frankly acknowledge that, at the commencement of the experiments recited in this section I was so far from having formed any hypothesis that led to the discoveries I made in pursuing them, that they would have appeared very improbable to me had I been told of them; and when the decisive facts did at length obtrude themselves upon my notice it was very slowly, and with great hesitation, that I yielded to the evidence of my senses. And yet, when I consider the matter, and compare my last discoveries relating to the constitution of the atmosphere with the first, I see the closest and easiest connection in the world between them, so as to wonder that I should not have been immediately led from the one to the other. That this was not the case I attribute to the force of prejudice, which, unknown to ourselves, biases, not only our *judgments*, properly so-called, but even the perceptions of our senses: for we may take a maxim so strongly for granted that the plainest evidence of sense will not entirely change, and often hardly modify, our persuasions; and the more ingenious a man is the more effectually he is entangled in his errors; his ingenuity only helping him to deceive himself by evading the force of truth."

How pointedly these latter remarks applied to Priestley himself it is scarcely necessary to say. Having discovered the supporter of combustion in oxygen gas, having seen its relation to combustion very fully discussed by others, how could he, except at the impulse of bias, continue fixed in his belief that combustion essentially means *loss* of phlogiston. He was aware that metals gained in weight by calcination, but still held to the idea that this gain was consistent with the *loss* of a constituent element. Lavoisier showed him that the only product resulting from combustion in dephlogisticated air was fixed air, but still Priestley held that the result of combustion was to load the air with phlogiston. And so, whatever difficulties and inconsistencies grew out of the Stahlian hypothesis, Priestley defended it, impervious to sense and reason. Yet the grim tyranny of a false idea is ever in the end overcome. "Nothing," said the old chemist, Glauber, "can extinquish truth; it may be prest, but cannot be overcome; like the sun's light it may be hidden, but not extinguished;" and when we see the distorting power of bias we need his faith to believe in the final vanquishing of error.

In the pursuit of his inquiries Priestley "proceeded to examine by the help of a burning-glass what kind of air a great variety of substances, natural and factitious, would yield, putting them in vessels filled with quicksilver and kept inverted in a basin of the same. . . . .

"With this apparatus, ... on the 1st of August, I endeavoured to extract air from *mercurius calcinatus per se:* and I presently found that, by means of this lens, air was expelled from it very readily." With true caution Priestley suspected that this result might be due to some peculiarity or impurity in his individual specimen of mercuric oxide. But other specimens obtained by him gave precisely similar results. He proceeded to test this gas with "nitrous air" (nitrogen dioxide), and, to his astonishment, found that it was better than common air, that is to say, the product was more completely absorbed by water. Now the nitrous air test is, according to Priestley's ideas, the fitness of air for respiration, and he naturally next experimented directly upon the respirability of the new gas. Placing a mouse in a jar of the dephlogisticated air he found that it would live for an hour. In the same bulk of atmospheric

PREPARATION OF OXYGEN FROM MERCURIC OXIDE.
t, receiver to condense the mercury vapour.

air it lived only a fourth of the time. He breathed it himself. "The feeling of it to my lungs was not sensibly different from that of common air;

but I fancied that my heart felt peculiarly light and easy for some time afterwards. Who can tell but that in time this pure air may become a fashionable article of luxury? Hitherto, only two mice and myself have had the privilege of breathing it."*

The conclusion deducible from the experiments related in the paper from which several extracts

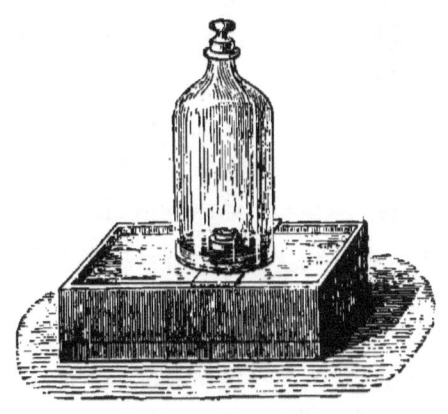

COMBUSTION OF PHOSPHORUS IN OXYGEN.

above are made is, that the atmosphere is, on an average, made up of four volumes of phlogisticated air (nitrogen) to one volume of this new gas, dephlogisticated air, or, as Lavoisier termed it, oxygen, Priestley, however, did not directly assert these conclusions himself, though we may so interpret his experiments. The analyses made by him and others of air gave somewhat varying results, and it was thought

* *Experiments and Observations on different Kinds of Air.* London (1774-75), 2 vols. Another edition in 3 vols. was published at Birmingham in 1790.

o

that the proportion of the two chief constituent gases was actually different at different places and seasons. It was left to Cavendish to show that this was not the case, but that the proportion of these constituents was, on the other hand, remarkably constant.

We have glanced rapidly at the more striking of Priestley's discoveries, and we can readily see that they were interesting and important. He had an admirable knack of finding out new things; but he hardly ever followed up sufficiently the discoveries he had made. Others had to show the bearing of his work upon the general theory of chemistry and to draw from his experiments conclusions he would not stop to deduce. Happily there was at least one man then living fit for the task, pre-eminent in the power of combining scattered ideas into an orderly whole, a man in intellectual power and grip surpassing any chemist before his time. That man was the great French chemist, Lavoisier. Before proceeding to the discussion of his work we must say something about the accurate and acute English worker, Cavendish. Next we shall pass on to Lavoisier, and with him the dawn of *modern* chemistry begins.

CHAPTER XII.

SIXTH PERIOD: THE CONFLICT WITH ERROR.
TRUTH IN DISGUISE.

AFTER Priestley's work the material, at least, for the solution of great chemical problems was at hand. The solution of one of the principal of these was afforded by Cavendish, whose other work also threw much light upon the path of chemical progress, though his eyes were too blinded by the dust of the phlogiston theory to fully discern what lay before him.

As a man Cavendish was certainly one of the most extraordinary of the chemists with whom we have had to deal. In fact, in no real or full significance of the word, was Cavendish a man at all. He was a well-arranged intellectual machine, a thing without enthusiasm, sympathy, or happiness. The questions coming before him were apparently answered with absence of emotion as complete as that of the logical machine invented by Professor Jevons when it draws conclusions from data which are given it. To use this machine a key is pressed for each term of the propositions forming the data from which conclusions are to be drawn. The proper series of keys having been pressed the correct deductions from those data are at once presented to view. This is apparently representative of the action of Cavendish's mind. Various facts struck different keys in his mind, and in consequence of its internal mechanical construction these facts were at once sorted out and arranged so as to make evident the conclusions derivable from them. He was more wonderful than the machine, in that he was able to vary the relations of external facts; he was less wonderful than it, in that his conclusions were not wholly accurate. Mechanical as he was, he was not free from bias.

Cavendish's family traces back its origin to Sir John Cavendish, Lord Chief Justice of the King's Bench in the reign of Edward III., while other genealogists have carried it back to Robert de Gernon, a famous Norman who assisted William the Conqueror in his invasion. The Honourable Henry Cavendish, son of Lord Charles Cavendish, was born at Nice, on the 10th of October, 1731. His mother died when he was about two years old, and of his early years nothing is known. In 1749 he went to Cambridge and remained there till 1753, but did not graduate.

For the next ten years his history is a blank. His intellect was gathering strength. His first contribution to the Royal Society was made in 1766, *On Factitious Airs.* Cavendish had training in many sciences, electricity, geology, chemistry and mathematics. His chief work was purely chemical. He was not at all eager to publish his researches. Two lengthy investigations, *Experiments on Arsenic* and *Experiments on Heat,* were written before 1766 and discovered for the first time after his death. They were apparently written out for some friend whose name never transpired, and the reason of their remaining unpublished was never known. His *Experiments on Air* were published in the *Philosophical Transactions* for 1784.

His father, Lord Charles Cavendish, allowed his son £500 a year during his lifetime, and it was argued, but with not much appearance of truth, that the smallness of this allowance led Cavendish into the too economical habits afterwards characteristic of him. Cuvier states that Cavendish was left a very large fortune by his uncle about the year 1773. At his father's death, in 1783, he also had a fortune left him. The details as to how he came by his wealth are somewhat contradictory, but however that may be, he died in 1810, leaving £700,000 in the funds and a landed estate producing an income of £6,000 a year. None of this great wealth went to the help of science.

Cavendish's London residence was close to the

British Museum, at the corner of Montague Place and Gower Street. Those who passed its portals reported that books and apparatus were its chief furniture. Latterly he had a separate house for books in Dean Street, Soho. It is one of the few indications that he might have been capable of interest in human affairs that he allowed books from this library to be lent to scientific men on recommendation. It is characteristic also of the extremes to which he carried his methodical habits that when he thus took a book from his own library he entered his name as an ordinary borrower. His favourite residence was a suburban house at Clapham, afterwards known as Cavendish House, the drawing-room of which was converted into a laboratory.

Many stories are told illustrative of Cavendish's extreme reserve, and his apparent freedom from all human sympathy.* He constantly attended the meetings of the Royal Society, and as a rule avoided all conversation. An F.R.S. wrote: "We used to dine at the Crown and Anchor and Cavendish often dined with us. He came slouching in, one hand behind his back, and, taking off his hat (which by-the-bye he always hung up on one particular peg) he sat down without taking notice of anybody. If you attempted to draw him into conversation he always fought shy. Dr. Wollaston's directions I found to succeed best. He said, 'The way to talk to Cavendish is never to look at him, but to talk as it

* See G. Wilson: *Life of the Honourable H. C. Cavendish* (1848).

were into vacancy, and then it is not unlikely but you may set him going.'" T. G. Children relates how, when he first became a member of the Crown and Anchor club he saw Cavendish talking very earnestly to Marsden, Davy and Hatchett. Children went up and joined the group. His eye caught that of Cavendish and the latter instantly became silent and would not say another word. He had seen a strange face.

Lord Brougham remarks : " He entered diffidently into any conversation and then seemed to dislike being spoken to. He would often leave the place when he was addressed, and leave it abruptly with a kind of cry or ejaculation, as if scared and disturbed." On one occasion, it is related, Cavendish was present at some reception when a foreigner was introduced to him. The latter began expatiating upon his talents to Cavendish's great annoyance. Growing more and more embarrassed he at length darted from the room and left the house.

His horror of females was extreme. He ordered his dinner by a note left on the hall table, and would not allow any maidservant to show herself on pain of instant dismissal. The person whom he had made his heir he saw only once a year, and then for about ten minutes. He lived by himself and no one was known to be his friend. One single letter written to him, and discovered after his death, signed " Your most affectionate," brings Cavendish nearer to ordinary human sympathies than anything else in his career.

In the journals kept by him of his travels about the country there is, except in one solitary spot, no reference to the beauties of scenery passed through, no suggestion that he was capable of being cheered by nature's brightness or made pensive by her gloom. In the one exceptional passage referred to he does mention the bald fact that from a certain place a fine view of the surrounding country is to be obtained. Otherwise the pages are untinged, in their dreary preciseness, by the warmth of a single emotion. It should, however, be stated that according to the journal recording his visit to his rival Watt at Birmingham in 1785, he seems to have felt quite a considerable interest in his inventions, if not in the man. Numerous references occur to the explanations Watt had given him.

For scientific purposes Cavendish would very occasionally invite Fellows of the Royal Society to his house, and his few guests were always treated to a leg of mutton. An F.R.S. is responsible for the following statement :—" Cavendish seldom has company at his house ; but, on one occasion, three or four scientific men were to dine with him, and when his housekeeper came to ask what was to be got for dinner he said 'a leg of mutton.' 'Sir, that will not be enough for five.' 'Well, then, get two,' was the reply."

In spite of his wealth Cavendish hardly ever gave pecuniary aid to science. It is amusing to find him, when an enlarged voltaic battery was desired at the

Royal Institution, joining in the complaints of illiberality in the patrons and himself doing nothing. He had apparently an objection to be considered liberal, or rather, perhaps, he was not sufficiently awake to the ordinary affairs of life to recollect that a liberal course was open to him. On one occasion he was induced to allow a gentleman of small means and considerable talents to reside in his London library in order to rearrange it. The man finished this work and left London. Some time after, when Cavendish was dining at the Royal Society's Club, the gentleman's name was mentioned. "Ah! poor fellow," said Cavendish, "how does he do, how does he get on?" "I fear very indifferently." "I am sorry for it." "We had hoped you would have done something for him, sir." "Me, me, me? what could I do?" "A little annuity for his life; he is not in the best of health." "Well, well, well, a cheque for ten thousand pounds, would that do?" "Oh, sir, more than sufficient, more than sufficient." And the cheque was accordingly written.

In person Cavendish was tall and rather thin, his face in the portrait prefixed to his life looking wizened and pinched. His dress was old-fashioned and sometimes a little neglected.

This is almost all that can be said of Cavendish apart from his scientific work. Occasional gleams of wider sympathy suggest that his nature held within it possibilities of a far higher order; there was a spark of fire buried deep in the ice. But no influence he encountered had power to develop the possibilities, or break down the ice-barriers. And so at last he became what we have seen him to be, a passively selfish cynic, aware only of monotonous existence, not of life, ignorant of laughter and of tears. Morally his character was a blank. There was not apparently a human soul with which he had relations other than those of business and science. He was interested in no one and in nothing outside his scientific work. His life was, in regard to all human sympathy, one of the most sadly wasted that history records. Through it all he was alone. For him no human face was rich in the beauty of affection, no voice was welcomed with gladness, no caress could soothe pain. To him was unknown the power of unselfish sympathy, the joy of helpful pity, or exultation in the redress of wrong. To him life brought only its morning of labour and its night of sleep, work without happiness, quiescence without rest. To him sky and earth were silent, and heaven was without hope. He understood the voices neither of joy nor sorrow. Life to him was an ashen desert of speculation and proof. Through it all he was loveless and alone. It is a saddening life to contemplate, and still sadder is it to think of what can have induced so chilling a frost. Whether definite sorrow and disappointment, or only absence of surrounding warmth of sympathy was its cause, it will now never be possible to say. With his sorrows, if his heart ever felt human pain, and with his errors, his life has passed out into the darkness, and of him there is left with us the best that he could leave us, the germ of nobleness that was in him, the work, in these latter days, so full in fruit.

The work done by Cavendish was small in amount, but what remains of it is excellent. Considering the power shown in what he did accomplish and the advantages he possessed it is only surprising that he did not do more. We are tempted to wonder how his time was employed. But when we recollect how withdrawn he was from the impulse of every-day contact with other men, a stimulus quickening and invigorating alike to heart and brain, we can readily believe that much of his intellectual life must have lain dormant and never wakened into activity of thought.

The first communication made by Cavendish to the Royal Society was, as already mentioned, in 1766, under the title of *Factitious Airs*. The research is divided into four papers and deals with hydrogen, carbon dioxide, and the gases evolved by fermentation, putrefaction, and destructive distillation. It is true that hydrogen had been obtained so far back as the time of Paracelsus, that Mayow had collected it, and that Hales had shown it to be combustible; but the phenomena of its production and its properties were first distinctly studied and clearly set forth by Cavendish. He showed that different metals yield different quantities of the gas, but that the same weight of the same metal evolved a like amount of gas from different acids.* He observed that, though itself inflammable, hydrogen extinguished flame and also destroyed life. He also proved it to be lighter than air, and as a result of this the gas was subsequently used in balloons instead of heated air.

In the same papers referred to above Cavendish

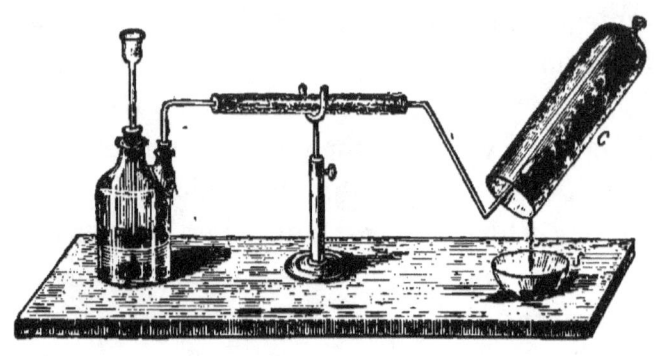

COMBUSTION OF HYDROGEN.

C, vessel in which the water vapour formed is condensed.
S, dish to receive the water.

discussed the properties of carbon dioxide, or fixed air, more fully than had previously been done, and showed the fixed air obtained from marble to be identical with the air produced during fermentation. His next paper (1767) consists merely of an analysis of the water in Rathbone Place. It is interesting as showing the results obtainable at that time. In the same paper he seems to have been the first to notice

---

* The suggestiveness of this discovery will appear in the sequel, when we see that a certain weight of any metal is *equivalent* to a definite quantity of hydrogen, and will therefore always replace and set free the same amount of it in any acid.

that the lime, existing in water as carbonate, is, though insoluble in pure water, held in solution by the excess of free carbon dioxide present. This carbonic acid can be removed by boiling the water, whereupon the calcium carbonate is deposited as the fur lining kettles and boilers.

In 1781 Cavendish accurately investigated by Priestley's method the composition of atmospheric air. Contrary to previous ideas he showed it to be of unvarying composition.

The paper, *Experiments on Air*, in the *Philosophical Transactions* for 1784,[*] contains his greatest work. He here relates experiments made on exploding together air and hydrogen "to find out what becomes of the air lost by phlogistication." According to some observations of Priestley's friend, Waltire, it appeared that this explosion was accompanied by loss of weight. Cavendish repeated these experiments with the result that in most cases there was no loss of weight and it never exceeded the fifth of a grain, an amount ascribable to errors of experiment. Waltire and Priestley had observed the production of water during the experiment, but, just as Priestley had done before in the case of the reduction of metallic calxes, they neglected it, and it was left for Cavendish to discover its meaning.

In his paper, *Experiments on Air*, in the *Philosophical Transactions* for 1784, we find the following epoch-making passage.

[*] *Philosophical Transactions*, 1784, p. 719.

"From the fourth experiment it appears that 423 measures of inflammable air are nearly sufficient to completely phlogisticate 1,000 of common air, and that the bulk of the air remaining after the explosion is then very little more than four-fifths of the common air employed, so that, as common air cannot be reduced to a much less bulk than that by any method of phlogistication, we may safely conclude that when they are mixed in this proportion and exploded, almost all the inflammable air and about one-fifth part of the common air lose their elasticity *and are condensed into the dew which lines the glass.*"

Now, 1,000 volumes of air actually contain 210 volumes of oxygen, and these need 420 volumes of hydrogen to combine with them. Cavendish's experiments, therefore, for that date, were remarkably exact.

The next point was to ascertain without doubt what was the nature of the "dew" so obtained. To this end he led oxygen and hydrogen gases into a long cylinder measuring eight feet by three-quarters of an inch, and there burnt them together. The dew condensed in the further part of the tube. "By this means upwards of 135 grains of water were condensed in the cylinder, which had no taste nor smell, and which left no sensible sediment when evaporated to dryness, neither did it yield any pungent smell during the evaporation; in short, it seemed pure water."

His conclusions are set forth in the following sentence :—

"By the experiments with the globe it appeared that when inflammable and common air are exploded in a proportion, almost all the inflammable air, and near one-fifth of the common air, lose their elasticity and are condensed into dew. And by this experiment it appears that this dew is plain water, and, consequently that almost all the inflammable air, and about one-fifth of the common air, are turned into pure water."

In another experiment Cavendish admitted the gases mixed in proper proportion into a vacuous globe, exploded them and found that the condensation was complete, so that repeated charges were admitted into the globe without any need for re-exhaustion.

The paper appearing in 1785 is also of great importance as containing the first account of the composition of nitric acid. Priestley had observed that some nitric acid was always present in the water obtained by the union of its constituent gases. Cavendish made a long and very careful series of experiments with the object of explaining the occurrence of this acid. After much trouble he was able to show that pure dephlogisticated air (oxygen), when combined with pure inflammable air (hydrogen), formed only pure water. He found that the addition of phlogisticated air (nitrogen) increased the amount of nitric acid formed, and finally concluded that its formation in ordinary cases was due to the presence of traces of atmospheric air, the phlogisticated air (nitrogen) of which went to form the acid.

In spite of the prolonged and accurate attention given by Cavendish to the composition of water he seems to have never clearly conceived that it was a compound of dephlogisticated and inflammable airs. It is strange, considering how obvious and simple a solution this afforded of the phenomenon that the two gases when exploded together produce water, that this plain notion should never have found favour with him. James Watt, the engineer, had already, in 1783, in a letter to Black thrown out the suggestion that "water is composed of dephlogisticated and inflammable air." In this opinion he anticipated and made a distinct advance upon Cavendish, and much has been written as to their rival claims to be considered as discoverers of the composition of water. Cavendish certainly first established the facts proving its composition, although he was so blind to their meaning as to write in 1784 the following words:—

"From what has been said there seems the utmost reason to think that dephlogisticated air is only water deprived of its phlogiston, and that inflammable air, as was before said, is either phlogisticated water or else pure phlogiston, but in all probability the former."

But although Cavendish remained to the last a believer in phlogiston, and was thus, like Priestley, precluded from seeing the full importance of his own work, yet he was by no means so bigoted in his partisanship as the latter chemist. He recognised in a passage not sufficiently noticed that many facts could be explained as well by the Lavoisierian method,* and although he never became a convert he was not an ungracious opponent. His aberration on the subject of phlogiston should not detract much from our opinion of his intellectual power, when we recognise how universal a sway that notion possessed over the minds of men. It is indeed an annoyance to find his acute and accurate papers reduced sometimes by its means, like all the work of his day, to an incoherence not unworthy of the jargon of the early alchemists; but our appreciation of his merit becomes more unalloyed as we become accustomed to the peculiar intellectual atmosphere in which he lived. And considering the power of one false idea over the minds of that day we gain an increased appreciation of the singular fairness and freedom from bias of Dr. Joseph Black, the one chemist who was converted to truth. But though Cavendish could not discern the widening dawn, his work did much to produce its light.

Two Swiss chemists of renown, Bergman and Scheele, were at work about this time. Bergman (1735—1784) was one of the pioneers of analytical chemistry, but of his work it is impossible to speak here in detail. Scheele (1742—1786) is famous as the discoverer of chlorine and as one of the first workers in the field of organic chemistry. Another discovery redounds much to his credit, though in it he had

* See p 246.

probably been anticipated by Priestley—the discovery of oxygen. Scheele obtained the gas by the decomposition of nitric acid by heat, and gave it the name of empyreal air. His discovery of chlorine gas was made in 1774, and this element was termed by him dephlogisticated marine acid gas.* He prepared it

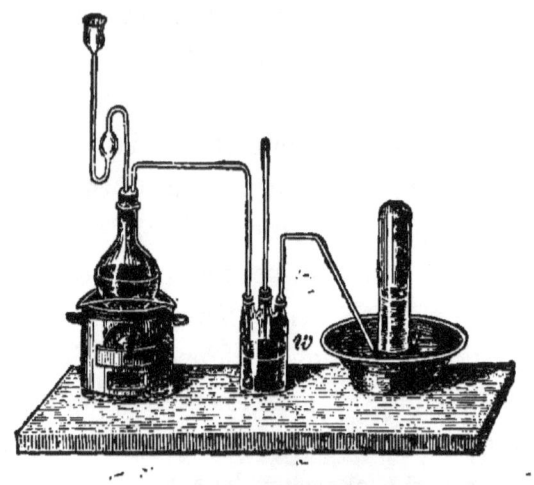

PREPARATION OF CHLORINE.
w, wash-bottle containing water.

by the action of hydrochloric acid upon manganese dioxide. On mixing the black oxide with the acid a greenish mass is obtained which rapidly begins to evolve chlorine. The first part of the operation may be conducted at the ordinary temperature of the air, unless the weather is very cold, but heat is needed to drive off the latter portions of the gas. This is passed through a small wash-bottle containing water to remove hydrochloric acid, and if needed dry is

* Marine acid = muriatic acid = hydrochloric acid.

further passed through sulphuric acid or other reagent capable of absorbing its water.

It seems also that Scheele was the first to carefully investigate sulphuretted hydrogen, a gas invaluable to the analytical chemist, as by its means different metals are under different conditions thrown out of solution as insoluble sulphides by the action of the gas. Furthermore it was Scheele's announcement of the existence of calcium phosphate in bones (a discovery made first by Gahn in 1769), which led to the manufacture of phosphorus from bone-ash, a source from which all the phosphorus of commerce is still obtained.*

Scheele's investigations of Prussian blue led him to the discovery of prussic acid which he made in 1782. This substance is still prepared by his process of acting on potassium ferrocyanide (yellow prussiate of potash) with sulphuric acid. The pure acid is a mobile liquid and one of the most powerful of known poisons. A few drops produce death in a dog in thirty seconds.

He first showed baryta to be a distinct earth, and proved the separate existence of molybdic and tungstic acids.

Some of Scheele's best-known discoveries lay in the domain of organic chemistry. A number of organic acids—tartaric, oxalic, citric, malic, gallic, uric, lactic, and mucic—were either first prepared or first identi-

---

* Phosphorus was probably first prepared by the alchemist Brand, of Hamburg, in the 17th century.

fied by him. But even this does not complete the long list of his discoveries, for he was the first to obtain the valuable substance glycerine, to which he gave the name of "the sweet principle of fats," and which afterwards bore the name of Scheele's sweet principle or oil-sugar. Scheele obtained his glycerine by the action of litharge on olive oil. Oils and fats contain glycerine or, more strictly, "glyceryl," combined with acids. If these be heated with potash or litharge the metal takes the acid and glycerine is set free. The name glycerine was first given to the body by Chevreul in his "Recherches sur les Corps gras," etc. He also determined its composition. Many workers were engaged upon this body before an accurate knowledge of its constitution was obtained, and these include Pelouze, Berzelius, Liebig, Berthelot, De Luca, and Wurtz.

The number of Scheele's discoveries is surprising, and he was the first to pay any accurate attention to the phenomena of organic chemistry. He, too, was blinded by his bias on the phlogiston theory, but his work contributed greatly to the building up of the modern science.*

* Some of Scheele's papers are translated by Beddoes under the title of Scheele's *Chemical Essays* (1786).

SEVENTH PERIOD.

CHAPTER XIII.

SEVENTH PERIOD: THE TRIUMPH OF TRUTH.
LAVOISIER.

THE greater chemists of this period represented three different types of mind; Priestley, brilliant and rapid in discovery, but somewhat inaccurate in experiment, and insufficient in theoretical grasp; Cavendish, slow but thorough in discovery, accurate and painstaking in experiment, but not directly influencing the theoretical ideas of his time: Lavoisier, who discovered no new fact, but was original and exact in his experiments, and exerted, by his marvellous intellectual grasp, incalculable influence upon the theoretical progress of his science. He was not one who dealt with isolated facts, his mind had something of the philosopher's taste for classification and general principles. There is, perhaps, some tendency in experimental work to arrest the imagination, to deter from speculation, to dull the worker's appreciation of what is not presentable to sense. But this tendency is indulged at the peril of the worker and his science. It produces a conservatism often delaying scientific advance. The conservative tendency was strong in Lavoisier's time, but he escaped it and rescued his science from its grasp.

Antoine Laurent Lavoisier (1743—1794) was born at Paris in 1743. His father, a wealthy tradesman, educated him at the College Mazarin, and encouraged him in his scientific tendencies. Lavoisier was relieved from the necessity of earning his bread, and was thus able to devote his time and energy to science. On leaving college he worked with extraordinary ardour, and a devotion greater than most would have exhibited had their work been forced upon them by want. His latter work was for the most part devoted to science for its own sake, but among his early experiments were some made in the hope of a prize offered for the best mode of lighting the streets of Paris. He experimented with various lamps, and it is indicative of the depth of his enthusiasm that, to increase the sensitiveness of his eyes while thus engaged, he lived for six weeks in a room deprived of all light and hung with black. Not long after this he refuted the belief, entertained by many, that water by distillation could be converted into earth.

Lavoisier availed himself, as much as possible, of

the benefits of discussion and criticism. One day a week he threw open his laboratory to a select company of friends, communicated his results, and invited comment or criticism.

In 1772 he recorded the results of his experiments on the calcination of metals. These led him to abandon the theories of the phlogiston school. In 1778 he broached his theory that oxygen was the universal acidifying or oxygenizing principle. In 1783 he completed the proof of the composition of water. In 1792 the Lavoisierian doctrines received recognition in Berlin, and in 1789 he published his remarkable *Traité élémentaire de Chimie*.

Lavoisier's abandonment of the old chemical creed brought upon him much obloquy and odium. At the height of his unpopularity he was burnt in effigy at Berlin on account of his antiphlogistic ideas; yet Berlin only a few years later was converted to his views. But it was not his independence as a chemist which was to cause his ruin. His overflowing energy had engaged him also in political work. He was a prominent member of the body of "Farmers-General" of the revenue, and in this administrative capacity is said to have done some good work. "Lavoisier," said Lalande, "was to be found everywhere."*

* François de Fourcroy speaks indignantly of Lavoisier's fate. "L'homme qui auroit illustré son siècle par ses talens, qui auroit répandu ses lumières sur la société, dont les travaux auroient eu pour but d'instruire, de rendre meilleurs et plus heureux les hommes, seroit placé dans un même tombeau avec celui qui en auroit fait le tourment ou qui en auroit été la honte!"—*Notice sur la vie de Lavoisier*. Paris (1796). Lalande's notice is given by Scherer in his *Nachträge*.

But in May, 1792, the year 2 of the Republic and at the height of the revolution, the arrest of all the Farmers-General was ordered. All were to give account of their moneys and incomings, and die " for putting water in the tobacco they sold." The charges were brought against the whole body on the 2nd of May by Dupin, a member of the Convention. Lavoisier found a hiding-place in the deserted rooms of the Academy. Hearing, however, that his action would tend to prejudice his colleagues he gave himself up and awaited his fate. He expected the confiscation of his property, and announced his intention if this sentence was passed of earning his bread as an apothecary, the trade most nearly suited to his tastes. But on the 6th of May he, with twenty-seven others, was condemned to the guillotine.

The death of a man of such peaceful eminence did not pass without some protest. Petitions for commutation of the sentence, in consideration of his high services to knowledge and the state, were presented in vain. He himself looked on calmly, and might have met his death without a word had he not been interrupted in some investigations. But to be snatched away just before an interesting research was completed, just when nature was in a mood to bring him more confidences—that, at its best, was annoying. So he petitioned for a fortnight's delay to get done with his experiments; *then* he would be at their service. But the petitions were all alike refused. The Republic had "no need of *savants*." And on the 4th of May, with the experiments unfinished, the guillotine receiv in him one of her most illustrious victims. We can only be thankful that his doom did not descend in time to rob us of the work, the results of which we are still permitted to inherit.

It is a very unfortunate circumstance that our admiration for Lavoisier is to some extent restricted by the too clearly proved fact that he laid claim to discoveries to which he had no right. His *Opuscules Physiques et Chymiques* contain discoveries of Joseph Black, put forward as if they were his own, while his claim to the simultaneous discovery of oxygen has been the occasion of many disputes, finally ending by an invalidation of the claim. It is much to be regretted that our warm admiration for the splendid talents and services of so great a worker should have to encounter the chill of disappointment we must experience in the character of the man.

Lavoisier claims our attention chiefly on account of his being the first to distinctly and clearly enunciate the great principle of the *indestructibility of matter*.* The belief in this pervades, and indeed alone makes possible, the whole of his work. He showed that chemistry could not exist without the chemical balance.

It is true that quantitative experiments in the

---

* As a philosophic principle this had been taught ages before: *e.g.* by Lucretius, who followed Greek masters. But as a scientific truth it had never been proved, and indeed was not generally held.

science had already been performed, and that Black and Cavendish had raised these to a high degree of exactitude. There was necessarily in these experiments a tacit assumption that at least in the case under investigation matter was not expected to be destroyed. If he had expected the destruction of matter how could Black have inferred that because magnesia alba lost weight on heating some *thing* was given off, and when he found out that the thing could not be condensed, further concluded that it was a gas? Or how could Cavendish have determined the relative amounts of oxygen and hydrogen condensing to form water, had he thought that during the explosion some of either gas might cease to exist? Clearly these experiments had an underlying disbelief in the destruction of matter in the course of these particular experiments. But such vague previsions were widely different from any assertion of a general law. It is the difference between the unscientific industry of his contemporaries and the far-sighted precision of Lavoisier. According to him every chemical change is accompanied only by transfer and exchange of matter, not by destruction. His doctrine is, "Rien ne se crée, rien ne se perde de la nature." The total weight of the reacting bodies remains the same from beginning to end of the reaction. We see here the first attempt at a chemical equation.

The theory was propounded in regard to fermentation, Lavoisier having tried to make out what became of the sugar during the process. After investigating the matter he came to the conclusion that, starting with a certain weight of sugar, there were obtained as a result of the fermentation certain weights of alcohol and carbonic acid gas, which together were equal to the weight of sugar present when the reaction began. Nothing, said Lavoisier, is lost; but instead of our sugar we have an equivalent quantity of carbonic acid and alcohol.

Strangely enough this argument, forming one of the bases of the great theory, was founded upon an experimental error. The carbonic acid and alcohol produced by the fermentation are *not* together equal in weight to the sugar made use of. What then is the final conclusion? Not that matter has been destroyed, but that, as shown by the eminent Frenchman, Pasteur, other substances besides alcohol and carbonic acid are formed. What Lavoisier said was quite true for about 95 per cent. of the sugar used, but the remaining 5 per cent., or thereabouts, is converted partly into glycerine and succinic acid, and partly used up for developing the growth of the ferment. But even this is not a full list of the products which include other "alcohols" differing from common alcohol (higher homologues of it, as they are called), organic acids of the fatty series and ethereal salts, from which the spirit derives a peculiar smell. All these bodies have a higher boiling point than common alcohol, and are classed together under the name of *fusel-oil*. The fusel-oil is got rid of by rectification, and if present forms a very deleterious impurity.*

Lavoisier then was not quite accurate in the example most immediately connected with his brilliant thought. But the theory need happily never be wanting in support. All the thousands of operations carried on daily in the laboratories eastward from San Francisco to Pekin are so many confirmations of its truth. The balance is the first requisite of the laboratory, and did we not believe in the indestructibility of matter the use of the balance would be meaningless and absurd.

It may be as well here to illustrate from everyday life the full force and truth of this great idea. When a candle has burnt out what has become of it? This is the chemist's riddle, and like most riddles we must give it up and ask our questioner for the answer. First of all the riddle was asked by nature and the chemist *had* to find out the answer for himself; for nature is not so lenient as the chemist, and would not allow us to give it up. The chemist knows her principles in these matters well, so that he at once sets to work to puzzle the matter out, and, as the result of his puzzling, this is what he would tell us to do, to find out what has happened to the candle.

We have already been introduced to many of the

---

* The reader wishing to follow the interesting subject of fermentation in more detail should consult Schützenberger's admirable book *On Fermentation*, Intern. Scientific Series.

facts destined to overthrow the Stahlian hypothesis, and need not therefore start from the beginning in our reasoning. Suppose we burn a candle under a glass jar* as Priestley did long ago. Its flame is soon extinguished, and after any fumes may have subsided a clear gas is left in the bell-jar not differing in sight from ordinary atmospheric air. Now let us light another candle and plunge it, as the chemists say, into this innocent-looking gas. The flame at once goes out, and if we were cruel enough to put a mouse into the jar the flame of its life would go out too. Evidently something is now in the air which was not there before.

If our gas-jar is appropriately constructed, open at both ends with the lower end placed in water and the neck closed by a wide glass stopper, we may do something further with the gas we have got. If we introduce some caustic potash into the water in which the jar is standing we shall soon have evidence that the potash is taking up or absorbing some of the gas in the jar, for the level of the water in it will rise. Repeating this experiment with the potash with a jar of air in which a candle has not been burnt we shall obtain no alteration of level; there is nothing here absorbable by the potash.† Evidently the combustion of the candle has produced a gas absorbable by potash.

* Any common glass bottle with a neck wide enough to admit a candle may serve for this purpose.
† Of course a little carbonic acid gas is present in ordinary air, but it will be very much too little to be, in this way, perceived,

If we repeat these experiments with a jar filled with pure oxygen instead of air we should obtain the following results. With the unaltered gas potash would effect no absorption. After the combustion of a candle therein potash would effect far more absorption than in the same circumstances with common air. Any gas left after absorption will be either nitrogen, an impurity derived from atmospheric air, or unused oxygen gas further reducible by repeated combustion. From these experiments we may conclude that part of the candle (its carbon) combines with part of the air (its oxygen) to form a gas (carbon dioxide) not supporting combustion and absorbable by caustic potash. The presence of carbon dioxide may be readily and simply shown by merely pouring a little clear limewater into a glass bottle in which a candle has been burnt. The limewater is at once turned milky. This phenomenon will not occur with ordinary air and is characteristic of carbon dioxide, the "fixed air" of Black.

One product of the combustion, then, is carbon dioxide. That another product results may be very readily shown by merely holding a common tumbler over a burning candle. A misty appearance is at once seen on the interior of the glass, soon gathering into drops of dew. If instead of using such primitive apparatus we suck the products of combustion through a cooled tube or *condenser*, we may collect enough of the drops formed to find out that they are pure water. We should find that it was tasteless, boiled at 100° C., and evaporated without leaving any residue.

The products of the combustion of a candle then are carbonic acid and water. The carbonic acid is derived from the carbon contained in a combined form in the candle. We may obtain the same gas by the combustion of charcoal, and, as Lavoisier showed, by the combustion of the diamond. The water must be obtained from the hydrogen of the candle, for as the facts of Cavendish showed, water is composed of hydrogen and oxygen. The matter of the candle has not, then, been wholly destroyed as appearances would at first suggest. By appropriate arrangements we may show that the products of combustion actually weigh *more* than did the candle itself or the part of it that has been burnt away.

A wide tube is suspended from one arm of a balance. A cork having a candle fixed upon its upper surface and pierced with holes to admit of the passage of a current of air, is fitted into the lower end of the tube. Its upper end is connected by a piece of caoutchouc tubing with a second glass tube bent into the form of a U. The bent tube is filled with fragments of solid caustic potash, a substance, as we just now learned, capable of absorbing carbonic acid gas, and at the same time very hygroscopic, or taking up water with great activity. The two tubes having been exactly counterpoised on the balance, are connected finally with an aspirator. By allowing the water to flow out from this last a current of air is drawn through the whole apparatus. The candle being lighted the aspirator is set to work, care being taken that the current is not too rapid, lest some carbonic acid or water vapour should be drawn past the caustic potash unabsorbed. When an appreciable amount of the candle has been burnt the apparatus is disconnected from the aspirator and the balance once more allowed to vibrate freely. It will now be found that the index point oscillates farther on the side of the counterpoise than on the side of the tubes.

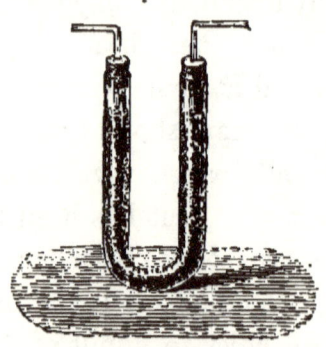

U-TUBE.

The tubes now weigh more than the counterpoise. But when the experiment began the tubes and their counterpoise were equivalent. They have therefore gained in weight. Thus in spite of the apparent disappearance of some of the matter composing the candle, not only has none of it been destroyed but it has actually *gained* in weight, owing to the addition to it of oxygen from the air during the process of combustion.

We have thus been able to catch the invisible

products of the combustion and render their existence evident to the eye.. We may further show that the amount of carbon and hydrogen in the products is just the same amount as that contained in the burnt portion of the candle, but the inquiry here would be somewhat more complicated. We know the proportions of hydrogen and oxygen in water, we know also the proportions of oxygen and carbon in carbonic acid, we know lastly, from individual experiments and by reason of the law of constant proportions first definitely recognised by Lavoisier, that the composition of these compounds is constant. If then we know the amount of water and carbonic acid generated we could calculate the amount of carbon and hydrogen in the candle. But to do this we must collect the water and carbonic acid *separately*.

Let us make use of a pure paraffin candle containing nothing but hydrogen and carbon. Let us pass its products of combustion first through a U tube, containing fragments of pumice soaked in sulphuric acid. This will absorb the water. The carbonic acid escaping from this tube may then be collected by passing the gases through bulbs containing caustic potash solution. We have thus got the means of collecting the two products separately. But, if we are to be at all accurate, we must make further provision against error; for water vapour and carbonic acid are present in the common air used to burn our candle, and will, of course, add their weight to the result. To obviate this, we may first pass the air through soda-lime and sulphuric acid to free it from carbonic acid and water, and then over the burning candle. If we were to weigh the tube containing the candle before and after the experiment, the loss of weight would give us the weight of candle burnt. The gain in weight of the U tube containing sulphuric acid, would give us the weight of water formed, while the gain in the potash bulbs would represent the carbonic acid evolved. Knowing the composition of water and carbonic acid, we could calculate the weight of hydrogen and carbon these gains respectively represented. Added together, we should find these very nearly the same as the weight of candle burnt. None of the matter composing it is lost during combustion. We might thus account for the matter composing the candle, and determine its composition.

The method is not quite the same as that at present in use for determinations of carbon and hydrogen in organic bodies, but it is substantially that used by Lavoisier in some of his attempts at organic analysis made by him just before his execution. We may refer to these experiments again in a chapter on the development of organic chemistry, a subject which can only, in a work of this kind, be very briefly sketched, and is more conveniently treated separately.

Finally, we must remember that the doctrine of the indestructibility of matter includes also a disbelief of its creatability. Just as it cannot be destroyed, so neither can it be created. The products of a reaction contain the *same* amount of matter as the substances taking part in it. They do not contain less, and they do not contain more. This belief is distinctly contained in Lavoisier's own words on the subject of fermentation: " We may consider the substances submitted to fermentation and the products resulting from that operation as forming an algebraic equation, and, by successively supposing each of the elements in this equation unknown, we can calculate their values in succession, and then verify our experiments by calculation, and our calculations by experiment, reciprocally. I have often successfully employed this method for correcting the first results of my experiments, and so to direct me in the proper road for repeating them with advantage."[*]

Lavoisier, in his mission of evolving order from incoherence, was also the first to openly acknowledge the law of combination in constant proportions. Bergman (1735—1784) tacitly acknowledged the truth in his numerous analytical researches. For what is the use of analysing a compound, if different specimens of it have varying composition? How can its composition be stated if it be indefinite? But this is not the first time in the history of science in which a great principle has been acted on before it was realised. Lavoisier distinctly stated that in

[*] Lavoisier: *Elements of Chemistry* (1787). Kerr's Translation, p. 197.

every oxide and every acid, the relation of oxygen to the metal is constant. He also refers to the different oxides of nitrogen exhibiting different, but in each individual compound definite, degrees of oxidation. He had, indeed, only just escaped discovering the law of multiple proportions. Had not his execution terminated his career, he might have followed up this among several others of his uncompleted trains of thought.

His first important research (1770) depended upon the use of the balance, and thus early indicated the tendency of his mind. In it he refuted the notion, at the time a moot point, that water, by being heated, may be converted into earth. He found that previous observers had been deceived by the use of impure water, or by the water having taken up some matter from the vessel in which it was heated.

Lavoisier's work on combustion and his combat with the Stahlian hypothesis began with some experiments first recorded in 1772, and not published till 1774, on the calcinations of the metals. His open rejection of phlogiston was not announced till 1777, and it is interesting to note that before this date, at least one other worker had seen reason to distrust the theory. Bayen, in 1774, had supposed calcination due to the absorption of an aerial fluid. He had found that calx of mercury (mercuric oxide) on heating loses weight, evolving a gas equal in weight to what is lost. From this he concluded that either the phlogiston theory was incorrect, or that this particular calx could be reduced without addition of phlogiston. But the phlogistians with their principles of levity and the like, were well capable of preventing these simple facts from dispelling the clouds which befogged the minds of the chemists in 1774.

Lavoisier's conclusions on the subject of the calcination of metals were first placed in the hands of the French Academy as a sealed paper in 1772, the final publication not taking place till 1774. His reason for first depositing the inquiry in its unfinished state in the hands of the Academy, was the desire to have proof of priority should another worker anticipate him before his investigation was complete. "I was young, I had just entered upon the career of science, I was eager for glory, and I believed I ought to take some care to protect the ownership of my discovery." In his first work on the subject Lavoisier finds that sulphur and phosphorus not only do not lose but actually *gain* in weight. His attention is thus directed to the calcination of metals with the idea that the combustion has in the previous cases been accompanied by an absorption of air, and that similar results may be expected from calcination. To elucidate his point he reduces the calx of lead or litharge with charcoal, and finds that a large quantity of gas is liberated. We see at once the point at which this meets the phlogistic theory. According to this last the addition of phlogiston to the calx was alone needed to produce the metal. But Lavoisier did not grasp these relations at once, though he saw that the discovery was important. "Experience has entirely justified my suspicions; I have effected the reduction of litharge in closed vessels with the apparatus of Hales, and I have observed that at the moment of the transition of calx into metal a large quantity of air was set free, and that this air had a volume at least a thousand times that of the litharge used. This discovery appears to me one of the most interesting made since Stahl, and I have thought it right to secure my property in it."

In 1774 Lavoisier made experiments on the calcination of lead and tin. These metals he, like Boyle, heated in closed glass globes. The globes did not alter in weight, proving that the amount of air absorbed was the same as that taken up by the metal. When the globes were opened air rushed in and the weight increased. In a paper on calcination, first read before the Academy in 1775, occurs his first reference to oxygen gas under the name of *l'air pur* or *l'air vital*.

In 1777 Lavoisier combated Priestley's assertion that combustion loaded air with phlogiston. He showed that air, after the combustion of a candle in it, contained "fixed air," and, moreover, that if for common atmospheric air *dephlogisticated air* (oxygen) were substituted, the gas left after combustion was almost wholly composed of fixed air. The phlogiston war was now raging, and in 1778 he broached his theory that *oxygen* (as he now called the gas : ὀξύς, sour, and γεννάω, I produce) was the universal acidifying or *oxygenizing* principle.

Two memoirs contain the chief portion of Lavoisier's views on combustion, one read before the Academy in 1775, *Sur la Combustion en général*, and another, *Réflexions sur le Phlogistique*, published by the Academy in 1783. The second paper contains the full development of his theory, and in it he denies the existence of phlogiston, upholds the elementary character of the metals and such substances as carbon, sulphur, etc., and states emphatically that when these bodies are burnt all that occurs is their combination with oxygen.* The simple truth of these views was possessed of a resistless force which in the end carried all before it.

After Cavendish's experiments in 1783 Lavoisier completed the proof that water was a compound of oxygen and hydrogen. He repeated, in conjunction with Laplace, the experiments of Cavendish and added a further confirmation of his own. In this case water was allowed to drop slowly into a gun-barrel heated to redness in a furnace. Here part of the water was decomposed, any that escaped being condensed in a worm through which the gases passed after leaving the furnace. The oxygen combined with the metallic iron in the gun-barrel, and the gas finally collected under the bell-jar was found to be pure hydrogen. This completed the proof now resting upon both

---

* Lavoisier was thus the first to ascertain the composition of "fixed air" or carbonic acid, as also of sulphur dioxide.

analytical and synthetical foundations. The exact composition of water has since been most accurately determined both by endiometric synthesis or explosion of the mixed gases in a carefully graduated tube, and by gravimetric synthesis by passing perfectly pure hydrogen over a known weight of copper oxide.

Lavoisier was not slow to appreciate the full import of these discoveries. Kopp has concisely set

LAVOISIER'S APPARATUS FOR THE ANALYSIS OF WATER.

forth the steps leading to a clear knowledge of the composition of water; Cavendish first ascertained the facts; Watt first argued from them as to the compound nature of water; Lavoisier first clearly recognised its compound nature and the nature and amounts of its components.

Before closing the account of Lavoisier's work mention must be made of his very remarkable *Traité Elémentaire de Chimie*. It is a work remarkable for its arrangement and lucidity, for scientific accuracy, and for the originality of the ideas it contains.

"It is a very constant principle, and one of which the general application is well recognised in mathematics as in all kinds of sciences, that we can, for our instruction, proceed only from the known to the unknown. . . . . When we enter for the first time upon the study of a science we are, with regard to this science, in a state very similar to that in which children are, and the course that we have to follow is precisely that which nature follows in the formation of their ideas. Just as in the child the idea is the result of sensation, and it is sensation which causes the idea, in the same way too, for him who begins to devote himself to the study of the physical sciences, ideas should only be a consequence, an immediate result of an experiment or of an observation." *

It is in his "Traité" that he gives the very clear proof devised by him of the presence of oxygen in the air. He heated mercury in a retort connected by its bent neck with air confined under a bell glass over mercury. After heating for twelve days the air had been reduced from 50 to 42 or 43 cubic inches, while red particles appeared on the surface of the mercury. These last, which consisted of mercuric oxide, were carefully collected, and on heating yielded $41\frac{1}{2}$ grains of mercury, and 7 to 8 cubic inches of pure oxygen. The whole of the oxygen was thus recovered from the mercury.

* *Œuvres de Lavoisier* (1862), tom. i. Introduction to the *Traité*.

He gives a table of thirty-three simple substances, among which he still includes heat or caloric and light. He also gives tables of the combinations of the various elements, and in these he looks upon the gaseous elements as combinations of a ponderable substance, the true element, with heat. Thus the combination of "l'hydrogène avec le calorique = gas hydrogène."* So too the combination of sulphur with caloric gives rise to sulphur gas. After all, though incorrect, these views only veil a great truth, for in these gases heat is *rendered latent*. Black, the discoverer of latent heat, had himself regarded the phenomenon as an act of combination. Of combustion Lavoisier here remarks,† "Combustion is nothing but the decomposition of oxygen gas acted upon by a combustible body. The oxygen which forms the base of this gas is absorbed, the caloric and light become free and are liberated (*deviennent libres et se dégagent*). All combustion then carries with it the idea of oxygenation. . . ."

The view of combustion here set forth is now, perhaps, somewhat modified, and combustion is regarded as "an act of chemical union accompanied by the evolution of light and heat."

This same work contains a prediction of the compound nature of the alkaline earths (soda and potash) previously thought to be simple bodies. From their ready combination with acids he concludes that "they may very possibly be metallic oxides with

* *Œuvres*, tom. i.   † *Œuvres*, i. 338.

which oxygen has a stronger affinity than with carbon, and consequently are not reducible by any known means." This was a prediction of Sir Humphrey Davy's discoveries on this point.

Quite enough has been said to account for the enormous and resistless influence exerted by Lavoisier on the progress of the science, but one more achievement must be recorded of him, and that is, that he entirely revised its nomenclature. He devised the term *oxide* for those combinations of oxygen which

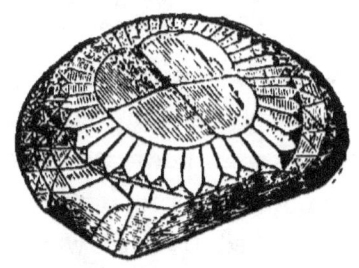

SPECIMEN OF DIAMOND. THE KOH-I-NOOR.

were not acids. When more than one oxide or acid was known the one containing less oxygen was distinguished by the termination *ous*, as *nitrous* oxide, the one containing more by *ic*, as *nitric* oxide. He devised the term *hydrogen* (ὕδωρ, water; γεννάω, I produce) in place of inflammable air, and *carbonic acid* as a substitute for fixed air. The meaning of the term *acid* has somewhat changed since Lavoisier's day, and it is now used for substances containing hydrogen *replaceable by a metal*. Lavoisier was the first to show that the combustion of diamond gives rise to carbonic acid, and thus to show the identity of the diamond with common charcoal. The diamond may readily be burnt when heated in air or oxygen. The formation of carbonic acid in the process may be readily shown by igniting a diamond, encircled in platinum wire, by means of an electric current from a few Grove's cells. A little lime-water contained in the jar will, after the combustion, become turbid.

It is difficult to over-estimate the influence of Lavoisier, and after seeing for ourselves what he did, and what precision and simplicity he introduced where so much before was only inaccuracy and incoherence, time would be wasted in panegyric.

Liebig's summary of his achievements is as follows: "He discovered no new body, no new property, no new natural phenomenon previously unknown; but all the facts established by him were the necessary consequences of the labours of those who preceded him. His merit, his immortal glory, consisted in this—that he infused into the body of science a new spirit."*

* *Letters on Chemistry*, ii.

EIGHTH PERIOD.

CHAPTER XIV.

EIGHTH PERIOD: THE ATOMIC THEORY. DALTON'S IDEA.

BY the atomic theory the older chemistry has been transformed into the modern science. It will be our business in the two succeeding chapters to trace its growth. Lavoisier had asserted the law of constant proportions. He recognised that, for example, a given weight of mercuric oxide always contained the same weights of mercury and of oxygen. This was a great advance upon the older ideas of chemical combinations. But so simple and true a doctrine was not to remain uncontested. It was assailed by Berthollet, a pupil of Lavoisier's, in a memoir read before the Egyptian Institute at Cairo. Berthollet ascribed the composition of compounds to *physical* causes.

He showed that varying results could be obtained in the neutralisation of an acid by a base. S. L. Proust enlisted himself on the side of the Lavoisierian theory, and the battle was converted into a duel between these two opponents. The contest was continued for a period of seven years with varying fortune, but Proust finally came off victor. He had rendered a lasting service to science. "The discussion," says Wurtz, "was maintained on both sides with a power of reasoning, and a respect for truth and propriety, which have never been surpassed."*

Proust found that on dissolving carbonate of copper in acid and reprecipitating by alkaline carbonate, the same weight of carbonate as that originally dissolved was obtained. This is an example of his work, and by it he was led to conclude that copper carbonate was of unvarying composition. Subsequent work led to similar conclusions about other compounds. The varying composition attributed by Berthollet to salts was explained by showing that although two or more salts may be formed by different quantitative combinations between a given acid and given base, yet *for these salts* the proportions are constant. Thus mercury forms two different chlorides, one containing twice as much chlorine as the other. There is only a difference in the proportion of chlorine present, yet the properties of the two substances are wholly distinct,

* *The Atomic Theory* (International Scientific Series); to which book is owing much of the material of these chapters. Those who wish to follow more closely the development of the theory cannot do better than consult this very ably and lucidly written work.

and for each of the two salts the composition is constant. The lower chloride, mercurous chloride ($Hg^2 Cl^2$), is a white insoluble powder, used as a non-poisonous medicine, and, in this capacity, known as *calomel*.*

The next step was the discovery of the law of definite proportions by the German chemist, J. D. Richter, of Berlin. He was much possessed with the idea of applying mathematics to chemistry. He followed his hobby too far, and by many ingenious manœuvres attempted to show that the quantities of bases saturating a given weight of acid represent the terms of an arithmetical progression, while the quantities of acids combining with a given weight of base, form the terms of a geometrical progression. His reasoning on these points broke down, but he did succeed in showing† that definite, but different, amounts of bases are needed to saturate and neutralise a given weight of a given acid. The weights of bases saturating a given amount of a given acid bear to each other a definite ratio. Thus 60 grammes of acetic acid are saturated by 40 grammes of caustic soda, and by 56 grammes of caustic potash, the proportions being as 5 to 7. Further, a certain weight, 36·5 grammes, of hydrochloric acid will be neutralised by exactly these same weights of soda and potash, they have the same relative capability of saturating the two

* From καλομελας, a fine black colour, because it turns black when acted upon by an alkali.

† *Anfangsgründe der Stöchiometrie, oder Messkunst chemischer Elemente*.

different acids. Considerations such as these led Richter to draw up a table showing the *equivalent* quantities of different bases saturating 1000 parts of different acids. The numbers, though of course inaccurate, contained a great truth more clearly exhibited by G. E. Fischer, in a note to his translation of Berthollet's *Chemical Statics*.

The following is part of Fischer's table, and it shows at a glance the equivalent quantities of bases and acids. Thus it states that 859 parts of soda are equivalent in neutralising power to 1,605 parts of potash; further, that 712 parts of muriatic acid (hydrochloric) are equivalent to 1,480 parts of acetic acid. It also contains the assertion that 859 parts of soda will neutralise 712 parts of muriatic acid, or 1,480 parts of acetic acid, and that 1,605 parts of potash, the equivalent of the foregoing amount of soda, will neutralize the same weights of these acids.

BASES.		ACIDS.	
Alumina	525	Fluoric acid	427
Magnesia	415	Carbonic ,,	577
Ammonia	572	Muriatic ,,	712
Lime	793	Oxalic ,,	755
Soda	859	Phosphoric,,	979
Strontia	1,329	Sulphuric ,,	1,000
Potash	1,605	Nitric ,,	1,405
Baryta	2,222	Acetic ,,	1,480
		Citric ,,	1,583

The precise bearing of these results upon the atomic theory will be presently seen. Had the weights here given been those of elements, instead of acids and bases, they would be analogous to the *chemical equivalents* of a later date.

We have said that with Lavoisier came the triumph of truth over fanciful error. But it was a hard-won fight, and her fit weapons had yet to be forged. The evil power had been driven from her own land, but she had need of added strength before attempting the conquest of his kingdom. Her trustiest sword was to be forged by John Dalton and tempered by the workers that came after him.

John Dalton was born in 1766, at Eaglesfield, two miles and three-quarters south-west of Cockermouth, in Cumberland.

"The township of Eaglesfield, situated on the undulating limestone formation of West Cumberland, previous to the enclosure of the waste lands and the introduction of good husbandry, about half a century ago, would offer little more than herbage for rough kine, and hard lines of life to the scattered inhabitants. Bucolic life of the boorish[*] sort prevailed in the hamlet, in which farmers of small holdings, their clodhopping service, and common craftsmen, laboured for a subsistence of a vegetative or earthy sort. The village consisted, and its features are not much altered to-day, of old-fashioned grey-stone dwellings, regular in their irregularity of position, and in structure dilapidated; straggling manure heaps, a bit of dirty common or village green, and dirtier duck-pond, backed

---

[*] Boorish is perhaps an unfortunate word. The race that produced Dalton can hardly have been boorish.

by a dingy 'smiddy,' to which the loungers with their gossip and tittle-tattle daily gravitated to discuss the news of the district . . . . . Eaglesfield folk were a stiff race of countrymen, presenting stalwart forms in a coarse woollen garb of home-make, and the horny hands and sweating brows of labour, rejoicing in hamlet isolation, and heedless of the contentions and turmoil of the world."*

This vivid description helps us to clearly realise the surroundings of Dalton's early life. The one light of the village was quakerism, and this the Daltons well represented.

"The house in which Dalton was born has been altered and much improved since his days; its low thatched roof has been raised and slated; the partially boarded loft converted into upper rooms; its small leaden windows displaced by large panes of glass; and the grey-stone facing of the building whitewashed. Still the general features of the interior of the humble dwelling remain pretty much as when occupied by weaver Joseph Dalton and his active spouse Deborah."

"By a small porch, showing quaint recesses for pots and pans, you enter the kitchen or general sitting and business room of the family, where probably, Joseph had his loom placed; from this apartment, by a narrow passage, you reach a smaller room immediately adjacent, in height and width six feet, and in length fifteen feet. The recess to the left of the

* Lonsdale's *Life of Dalton* [Cumberland Worthies].

doorway was occupied by a chaff bed, upon which Joseph and Deborah slept, and there John Dalton, the chemist, first saw the light of day, on or about September 6th, 1766." When Dalton afterwards showed friends his birthplace he used to point with a smile to the corner cupboard, where, in his early boyhood, the sweets were kept. Having a great longing for these, when his mother was one day out, he tried to reach the door-handle, but was too small. To effect his purpose he, regardless of consequences, kicked a hole in the plaster of the wall below the cupboard, and in this way gained a footing. Detection was, alas, inevitably certain, and his feat was followed by an interview with an angry mother terminated by a sound whipping.

All Dalton's ancestors were real "sons of toil," but some of them must surely have had latent intellectual power, or else whence did his wonderful insight arise. His father, Joseph, showed no special ability, or at least none is recorded of him. He earned small wages by his shuttle, and had six children, three of whom, Jonathan, Mary, and John, grew to maturity. No record occurs of John's birth, and the date of it is a matter of hearsay and guesswork. He was sent to Pardshaw Hall school, two and a half miles off, and placed under Mr. John Fletcher. John was by no means a quick boy, either at work or play. But he was steady-going and thoughtful, and fond of his books. At ten or eleven years old, Dalton delivered his first lecture to some of his schoolfellows from the top of a hedge. The audience was enthusiastic, and received his demonstrations with loud applause. Mr. Fletcher was wise enough to discern the boy's latent power, and led him to begin the study of mathematics. Later on, Elihu Robinson, a Quaker gentleman of the neighbourhood, helped him in his studies. Another youth, Alderson, and he would puzzle together over a problem. Alderson was more ready to seek Robinson's help than was Dalton. "Yan med deu't,"* John would say. Such a dialogue as the following would sometimes take place between Robinson and Dalton:—

"Well, John, hast thou done that question?"

"No; yan med deu't," and then later, "I can't deu't to-neet, but mebby to-morn I will."

In 1785 he, with his cousin and brother, became joint-managers of a school at Kendal. The school was not a great success. He continued at Kendal till 1793, when he obtained a post of teacher of mathematics and natural philosophy at New College, Mosley Street, Manchester. In 1792 he made his first visit to London, "a surprising place," but "the most disagreeable place on earth for one of a contemplative turn of mind." In 1794 he first described colour-blindness, being himself an instance of it. His discovery of his own defect arose through the purchase of a pair of stockings as a present for his mother. His mother was somewhat startled by their appearance, their colour being a brilliant red, unfit for any

* "One might do it."

Quaker to wear. To Dalton they seemed a bluish dark drab.

New College was removed in 1799 to York and, unwilling to leave Manchester, where he evidently formed close associations, Dalton became a private tutor. In 1805 he took up his abode with the Rev. W. Johns, and lived with him in a very delightful harmony. The way in which it came about was characteristic of Dalton's childlike simplicity. Johns' wife met Dalton one morning:

"Mr. Dalton, how is it that you so seldom come to see us?"

"Why, I don't know, but I have a mind to come and live with you."

At first the wife doubted whether he was serious, but finding that he was so, she consulted with her husband who had a true attachment for Dalton, and the arrangements were made. Dalton came and remained with them for the following twenty-six years. "During the long period," says Johns' daughter, "he and my father never, on any occasion, exchanged one angry word."

Dalton was robust and muscular, and of a simple and open countenance, his profile in old age striking us with a certain strange beauty of enduring patience. He stooped slightly, his height being about five feet seven inches. His health, compared with that of most of the chemists of whom we have spoken, was exceptionally good. It is related that on one occasion, when he had an attack of catarrh, his physician prescribed James's powder. Next day, finding Dalton better, he naturally put the cure down to his medicine. "I do not well see how that can be," said Dalton, "as I kept the powder until I could have an opportunity of analysing it." In general company Dalton was silent, and on religious topics extremely reticent. He was fond of tobacco, and of Davy he said, "the principal failing in his character as a philosopher is that he does not smoke." He did not marry; he had never, he said, had time. The truth of this statement may be doubted, but possibly the smallness of his pecuniary resources may have helped to prevent it. With growing age his capacity to receive new truths seems to have become somewhat narrowed, but he always preserved the genuine simplicity of heart which lends an added charm to his name.

It was in 1802 that Dalton conceived his theory. The facts influencing him were such as these. He noticed that nitric oxide would combine with two different amounts of oxygen to form two distinct more highly oxygenated compounds. These two distinct compounds could be formed by combining the nitric oxide (or nitrous air, as it was still called) with a lesser or greater amount of oxygen. But between these no definite compound could be obtained. A compound of nitric oxide with either one volume or two volumes of oxygen gas could be got, but not between nitric oxide and one and a half volumes of oxygen or one and three-quarters.

Again Dalton observed that marsh gas* contains just double as much hydrogen as olefiant gas.† It was these facts, as we learn from Thomson in his *History of Chemistry*, which formed the foundations of Dalton's theory. Meditating upon such facts as these, Dalton asked himself why nitrogen will combine with oxygen only in quantities which are simple multiples of a certain number? or why carbon will similarly combine with hydrogen only in like definite proportions? Then came the brilliant hypothesis won from this apparently barren fact.

It had been supposed by others long before Dalton's time, by Democritus, Epicurus, and Lucretius, that matter is made up of minute *indivisible* particles or atoms. Just before Dalton's hypothesis was developed, Kirwan (**1783**) and Higgins (**1789**) had suggested that chemical combination is due to the approximation of these unlike particles. Higgins represented certain compounds as formed by the union of particles or atoms of the same weight, but united in different proportions. So far had speculation gone before Dalton's turn came, and so far speculation was barren.

In spite of the efforts of other workers the conception remained until Dalton's time, wanting in cohe-

* Marsh gas is a hydrocarbon given off, as its name implies, in marshes and forming the fire-damp of mines. It is evolved with petroleum in petroleum springs, and the gas of the mud volcanoes at Bulganak, in the Crimea, consists, according to Bunsen, of pure marsh gas or methane. It exists in large quantities in coal gas.

† Bicarburetted hydrogen, olefiant gas, or ethylene, is formed by the action of sulphuric acid on common alcohol.

rence and consistency. But Dalton's keen intuitive insight readily saw where the error lay. The hypothesis was reasonable enough, but one fatal mistake deprived it of influence upon science. The atoms of different elements are *not* of equal weight, and Dalton set about weighing them. It is not certain how in some cases his results were arrived at. His first table of atomic weights is introduced casually at the close of a paper read before the Manchester Literary and Philosophical Society, October 23rd, 1803, on the absorption of gases by liquids. He applies his theory, and wrongly, to the particular subject in hand.

"The inquiry," he says, "into the relative weights of the ultimate particles of bodies is a subject, as far as I know, entirely new; I have lately been prosecucuting this inquiry with remarkable success. The principle cannot be entered upon in this paper, but I shall subjoin the results, as far as they appear, ascertained by my experiments." He then gives a table of the relative weights of atoms, starting with hydrogen as unity. It is of special interest as being the first table of atomic weights; but as a table given at a later date is less inaccurate, we shall quote that instead.

Before, however, proceeding farther we must notice that three distinct ideas lie embedded in this atomic theory of Dalton's. It includes the law of constant proportions of Lavoisier and Proust, the law of definite proportions of Richter[*] and others, and the law

---

[*] Wurtz terms Richter's law the law of proportionality.

of multiple proportions of Thomson, Wollaston, and Dalton himself. Let us briefly consider what each of these laws states.

The law of constant proportions asserts that in every individual compound there is a fixed relation between the weights of the elements composing it. Thus. 216 grammes of mercuric oxide always contains 200 grammes of mercury and 16 grammes of oxygen. It has a constant composition.

The law of definite proportions asserts something more than this. It asserts that there is a definable relation between the proportions in which different bodies unite. It is really a law of equivalence. As an illustration we may take the following facts:—

One part by weight of hydrogen combines with 35·5 parts of chlorine, with 80 parts of bromine with 126·5 of iodine, or with 19 parts of fluorine.*

Now 39 parts of potassium combine with 35·5 parts of chlorine to form potassium chloride. 39 parts of potassium therefore combine with the same amount of chlorine as does 1 part of hydrogen. We naturally inquire farther, with how many parts of the other elements just named will this quantity of potassium combine?

We find that—

39 parts by weight of potassium combine with 35·5 parts of chlorine, with 80 parts of bromine, with 126·5 parts of iodine, and with 19 parts of fluorine.

39 parts of potassium therefore combine with the same amount of chlorine, bromine, iodine, or fluorine, as does 1 part of hydrogen.

* To form the corresponding acids, hydrochloric, hydrobromic acids, &o.

This is a striking relation. From these statements it appears that 39 parts of potassium are *equivalent* to 1 part of hydrogen. If we suppose the compounds formed to be, in Dalton's nomenclature, *binary* compounds, containing one atom of each element, one of hydrogen to one of chlorine, one of potassium to one of chlorine, and so on, we must conclude that the atom of potassium is equivalent in combining power to the atom of hydrogen, but *weighs 39 times as much*. As a matter of fact the modern *atomic weight* of potassium is approximately 39.

The law of multiple proportions contains an additional truth. It asserts that in a series of compounds of the same elements, these are always combined together in the proportion of simple multiples of certain definite weights, the combining weights of the elements combined. Thus, to take an example in the series of hydro-carbons known as the paraffins, we observe the following relations:—

In the first of the series methane or marsh gas—

12 parts of carbon are combined with $4 \times 1 = 4$ parts of hydrogen.

In the second, ethane—

$2 \times 12 = 24$ parts of carbon are combined with $6 \times 1 = 6$ parts of hydrogen.

In the third, propane—

$3 \times 12 = 36$ parts of carbon are combined with $8 \times 1 = 8$ parts of hydrogen.

In the fourth, butane—

$4 \times 12 = 48$ parts of carbon are combined with $10 \times 1 = 10$ parts of hydrogen.

Starting with 16 parts of methane we cannot add

less than 12 parts of carbon* to get the next higher compound. We could not, for instance, obtain a compound containing 20 parts of carbon to 5½ parts of hydrogen.

Again, in the case of the nitrogen oxides, already united, we have a series of five compounds—

The first containing 28 parts of nitrogen to 16 of oxygen (nitrous oxide).
The second containing 28 parts of nitrogen to $2 \times 16 = 32$ of oxygen (nitric oxide).
The third containing 28 parts of nitrogen to $3 \times 16 = 48$ of oxygen (nitrogen trioxide).
The fourth containing 28 parts of nitrogen to $4 \times 16 = 64$ of oxygen (nitric peroxide).
The fifth containing 28 parts of nitrogen to $5 \times 16 = 80$ of oxygen (nitrogen pentoxide).†

Now, if we consider these facts in the light of the atomic theory how can we explain them? Very simply; thus: we cannot add less than 12 parts of carbon at a time, because we cannot add less than one atom of carbon at a time. The atom of carbon we have reason to believe weighs twelve times as much as the atom of hydrogen. In the first compound one atom of carbon weighing 12 combines with four atoms of hydrogen, weighing altogether 4, to form a *molecule* of methane. The composition of the whole volume of the gas is of course the same as the composition of each molecule, 12 parts of carbon to 4 of hydrogen. To get the next higher compound we add

* The reader must understand that the addition of carbon cannot be made directly; all that is meant is that no intermediate compound is obtainable.
† The older formulæ for these gases are, for present convenience, adopted.

one atom of carbon to each molecule of methane, and the atom being indivisible we cannot add less. We also add two atoms of hydrogen. Each molecule of the gas (ethane) will now contain two atoms of carbon to six atoms of hydrogen, that is 24 parts by weight of carbon to 6 of hydrogen, and the gas as a whole, possessing the composition of each of its own molecules, contains 24 parts of carbon to 6 of hydrogen. In the case of the nitrogen oxides we may picture the relation as simpler still, one atom of oxygen being added at each step. Unfortunately, however, matters are here somewhat complicated by other changes.

The law of combination in multiple proportions may now be more shortly stated thus : *The elements unite in the proportion of simple multiples of certain definite weights, called their combining weights.*

It is easy to see how readily these laws fall into their places under the atomic theory. Indeed, it would be impossible to fully express them without its aid. In the cruder form assumed by them in Dalton's day, they led him to his great conception. He conceived of each element as made up of minute indivisible particles or atoms. These atoms for each element had a definite weight of their own. How did he arrive at this weight? To answer this question we must form some idea of the different kinds of combination possible among these atoms. In Dalton's *New System of Chemical Philosophy* we find the following :—

"If there are two bodies, A and B, which are disposed to combine, the following is the order in which the combinations may take place, beginning with the most simple, namely :

    1 atom of A + 1 atom of B = 1 atom of C, binary.*
    1 ,,   + 2 ,, = 1 ,, D, ternary.
    2 ,,   + 1 ,, = 1 ,, E, ternary.
    1 ,,   + 3 ,, = 1 ,, F, quaternary."

and so on. The left hand side of the equation represents the elements combining, the right hand side the compound formed. Dalton applied the term atom to the smallest particles of the resulting combination where we now should use the word molecule. Having formed this conception of the possible combinations, Dalton was further guided by the following set of arbitrary rules.†

"1st. When only one combination of two bodies can be obtained, it must be presumed to be a *binary* one, unless some cause appear to the contrary.

"2nd. When two combinations are observed they must be presumed to be a *binary* and a *ternary*.

"3rd. When three combinations are obtained we may expect one to be a *binary* and the other two *ternary*.

"4th. When four combinations are observed we should expect one *binary*, two *ternary*, and one *quarternary*.

"5th. A *binary* compound should be specifically heavier than the mere mixture of its two ingredients.

"6th. A *ternary* compound should be specifically heavier than the mixture of a binary, and a simple, which would, if combined, constitute it.

"7th. The above rules and observations equally apply when two bodies, such as C and D, D and E, &c., are combined."

---

* That is, containing one atom of each element ; a ternary compound contains two atoms of one element, one of the other.
† *New System of Chemical Philosophy*, pt. i.

From rule 1, Dalton deduced that water was a binary compound. Water thus contained, according to Dalton, one atom of hydrogen to every atom of oxygen. Further, it contained, by weight, he said, 1 part of hydrogen to 7 parts of oxygen. Taking the hydrogen atom as the unit of weight this meant that the oxygen atom weighed seven times as much as the hydrogen atom, the *atomic weight* of oxygen was 7. In his assumption that water was a binary compound Dalton was wrong, but it was the best possible assumption under the circumstances. Moreover, the proportion of oxygen to hydrogen is not 7 to 1, but very nearly 8 to 1; but this inaccuracy was necessary to the determinations of that time. Ammonia, Dalton also supposed to be binary, containing one atom of nitrogen to every atom of hydrogen. By weight it consisted, according to him, of 1 part of hydrogen to 5 of nitrogen. This meant that the nitrogen atom weighed five times as much as the hydrogen atom, the *atomic weight* of nitrogen was 5. "Nitrous gas" (nitric oxide) he considered to be binary, containing one atom of nitrogen to one of oxygen, 5 parts by weight of nitrogen to 7 of oxygen, in accordance with the atomic weights.

By steps such as these Dalton arrived at his table of the atomic weights of the elements. Moreover, he adopted a characteristic symbol for the atom of each element, and combined these to symbolise the "atom" of compounds. A few of his atomic weights are here given. Had his determinations been correct they should have been simple submultiples of the weights now in use. The numbers he would have obtained by accurate experiment appear in the second column.

Elements.	Dalton's atomic weights.	Corrected numbers.	Symbol.
Hydrogen	1	1	☉
Nitrogen	5	4·66	⊕
Carbon	5	6	●
Oxygen	7	8	○
Iron	38	28	Ⓘ
Silver	100	108	Ⓢ

OF COMPOUNDS.

Compound.	Dalton's atomic weights.	Corrected numbers.	Symbol.
Water	8	9	☉○
Carbonic oxide	12	14	○●
Carbon dioxide	19	22	○●○

In Dalton's first table there are some curious inaccuracies which it is difficult to explain. Thus the "atomic" weight of nitric oxide should be the sum of the weights of nitrogen and oxygen; these in the first table, are 4·2 and 5·5, giving 9·7. But 9·3 is the number in the table. These discrepancies are difficult of explanation.[*]

The symbols adopted at a somewhat later date were analogous to those now in use. For these in

[*] See Roscoe on Dalton's first table of atomic weights, *Nature*, 1874.

most cases the first letter of the name of the element is taken to represent the atom. Thus on the Daltonian hypothesis that water is a binary compound, containing one atom of hydrogen to one of oxygen, its symbol will be HO, H representing the hydrogen atom and O the oxygen atom. Ammonia will be NH, sulphuretted hydrogen HS, olefiant gas HC, carbonic oxide CO, and carbonic acid CO^2.

One word more must be said before closing this account of Dalton's work. The fact of the inaccuracy of his determinations should not be allowed to detract from the grandeur of his conception. It should rather enhance and elevate our admiration for his talent, that with means so imperfect he could achieve so much. It is easy from our modern laboratories to look back with a smile upon the crude methods in use at Dalton's time. It is easy to suggest that determinations so inaccurate could never alone have given the atomic weights their true value and position in the science. That may be, but it was Dalton's intuitive penetration and patient thought which transformed the old atomic theory from a baseless fancy into a resistless truth.*

---

* It is legitimate to term the atomic theory a truth, and one of a high order, so long as we regard it as only expressing an analogy between the actual constitution of matter and our conception of it. It was by sifting the truth of the conception from the falsehood that the theory became capable of serving its science.

CHAPTER XV.

EIGHTH PERIOD: THE ATOMIC THEORY.
THE DEVELOPMENT OF DALTON'S IDEA.

WHEN we wish to estimate the quantity of anything we describe it in measures of weight or of volume. Dalton described the quantity of his individual atoms by weight. The introduction of their measure by volume was to complete the power of the atomic theory as a weapon of science.

Gay-Lussac found that the relations existing between the volume of one gas and that of another with which it will combine, and that of the compound formed, are very simple. The starting-point was the determination of the volumetric composition of water by Gay-Lussac and Humboldt in 1805.

2 volumes of hydrogen unite with 1 volume of oxygen to form 2 volumes of aqueous vapour.

2 volumes of nitrogen unite with one volume of oxygen to form 2 volumes of nitrogen protoxide.

1 volume of chlorine unites with 1 volume of hydrogen to form 2 volumes of hydrochloric acid.

1 volume of nitrogen unites with 3 volumes of hydrogen to form 2 volumes of ammonia.

1 volume of carbonic oxide unites with 2 volumes of chlorine to form 2 volumes of carbonyl chloride.*

Carbonic oxide is a compound gas, and therefore not on quite the same footing as the rest of the bodies mentioned in this table.

In 1808 Gay-Lussac stated his general law of gaseous volumes: *The weights of the combining volumes of the gaseous elements bear a simple ratio to their atomic weights.* He suggested that the relative weights of the gaseous volumes entering into combination exactly represent the relative weight of the atoms. The specific gravities of the elementary gases, *i.e.* their weight in terms of the weight of an equal volume of hydrogen as unity, are therefore the same as their atomic weights. Thus, taking the unit volume of hydrogen to weigh 1, we find that the unit volume of nitrogen weighs fourteen times as much ;† the specific gravity of nitrogen is 14 and its atomic weight is 14. This is the outcome of Gay-Lussac's theory, and establishes an intimate relation between the volumes of the elementary gases and their atomic weights.

* $CO + Cl^2 = COCl^2$.
† According to modern determinations.

THE ATOMIC THEORY. 279

The Italian chemist, Amedeo Avogadro, in 1811, explained the relation between the volumes and the combining weights by the supposition of a simple relation between the volumes of gases and the number of ultimate particles they contain. The hypothesis put forward by Avogadro was that equal volumes of all gases contain always equal numbers of these ultimate particles.*

Let us consider the case of a compound, and, to choose a simple case, take water. The volume of the atom is necessarily taken as the unit volume. Now, to use the language of the chemists of Gay-Lussac's time : 2 volumes of hydrogen, *i.e.* 2 atoms of hydrogen, unite with 1 volume of oxygen, *i.e.* 1 atom of oxygen, to form 2 volumes of water, *i.e.* two *atoms* of water. 2 volumes of water thus contain 2 volumes of hydrogen and 1 volume of oxygen. Then comes the difficulty, for it follows from this that 1 volume of water, *i.e.* 1 atom of water, must contain 1 volume of hydrogen, *i.e.* 1 atom of hydrogen and $\frac{1}{2}$ volume of oxygen, *i.e.* $\frac{1}{2}$ atom of oxygen. By similar reasoning we should find that 1 atom of hydrochloric acid gas contains $\frac{1}{2}$ atom of hydrogen and $\frac{1}{2}$ atom of chlorine. Obviously as we have started with the atom as the ultimate particle and the indivisible unit, it is a contradiction of our own theory to introduce $\frac{1}{2}$ atoms into it.

This difficulty was seen by Avogadro, and it seemed

---

* What these ultimate particles are will appear in the sequel. Also see p. 271.

likely to invalidate his hypothesis about the relation between the number of the ultimate particles and the volumes of the gases. If the atom of water vapour occupied twice the volume occupied by the atom of oxygen the relation became less simple. But Avogadro brought a subtle and, the same time, essential distinction to the aid of the theory. The ultimate particle of water occupies the same volume as two atoms of oxygen or of hydrogen, &c. The ultimate particle of water consists of more than one atom. It becomes in the end most simple to assume that there similarly exists an ultimate particle of oxygen gas made up of more than one atom. This it is which occupies the same volume as the smallest particle of water, and in modern language we call it a *molecule*. But the molecule of water occupies the same volume as two atoms of oxygen.

The *molecule* of oxygen is thus composed of two *atoms*.

The chemical definition of an atom is:—

An atom is the smallest portion of matter which can enter into a chemical compound.

A molecule is the smallest quantity of an element or of a compound which can exist in the free state.

To illustrate these definitions, the smallest portion of oxygen, represented by the symbol O, can be transferred from one compound to another, but cannot exist alone. Directly the atom is set free it tends to combine with another atom either of its own kind or not. The molecule of oxygen, consisting of two atoms, and represented by the symbol O_2, can exist free.

In the production of water by the combination of oxygen and hydrogen, each molecule of oxygen is acted on by two molecules of hydrogen. We may represent this as an equation by the use of chemical symbols. The first letter of the name is taken to represent the atom of the element, thus O represents an atom of oxygen occupying 1 volume and weighing 16.* To represent two atoms a small numeral is placed below or above the symbol, O_2. The molecule of water composed of two atoms of hydrogen to one atom of oxygen, or of two volumes of hydrogen to one volume of oxygen, or of two parts by weight of hydrogen to 16 parts by weight of oxygen, is represented by the symbol H^2O; two molecules of water will be represented by $2H^2O$. Now we are ready to express symbolically the formation of two molecules of water from one molecule of oxygen and two molecules of hydrogen.

$$O_2 + 2H_2 = 2H_2O.$$

In this reaction the molecule of oxygen is separated into its two constituent atoms, one of which goes to each molecule of water. The atom of oxygen can exist in the compound, water, but cannot exist by itself.

Having now got some idea of what is the chemist's

* That is 16 times the weight of an atom of hydrogen, the atom of hydrogen, the lightest element known, being always taken as unity.

conception of atom and molecule we can give a clear and concise statement of Avogadro's law :*—

Equal volumes of gases and vapours at equal temperature and under the same pressure, contain the same number of molecules, and consequently the relative weights of these molecules are proportional to the densities of the gases or vapours.

This is often termed the law of Avogadro and Ampère, for the latter, in 1814, propounded ideas similar to those of the Italian chemist. He drew a distinction between *particles* and *molecules*, the molecule of Ampère corresponding to the modern atom. According to Ampère the distances between the individual "particles" of gases, or, as we should say, their molecules, "depends entire upon the heat to which the gas is subjected." Under equal pressure and temperature the molecules of all gases are equidistant from each other. From these suppositions the fact, already noticed, of the equal expansibility of all gases by equal rise of temperature or fall of pressure follows as a simple deduction. The fact that all gases have the same co-efficient of expansion as air was first discovered by Charles. This co-efficient is independent of pressure. These two laws were arrived at independently by Dalton and Gay-Lussac, and it was the latter chemist who first accurately determined the co-efficient of expansion of gases. They are in complete harmony with the hypothesis of Avogadro and Ampère.

* *Journal de Physique,* xxxiii. 58.

The great achievement of Avogadro and Ampère was not, however, well received by chemists. Its simplifying power was not acknowledged, and other and more confused ideas were for many years preferred to it. This is only one of the many instances of a great scientific truth being ignored by the men of science themselves. Contradictions were found to occur in the rigorous application of the hypothesis, and it was too readily concluded that a speculation not immediately and in every detail commendable to the average scientific mind must for ever remain barren. The simplicity and truth of Avogadro's hypothesis were indeed too far in advance of the time.

The great Swedish chemist, Berzelius, attempted a union between the atomic hypothesis and the law of volumes. His views were first stated in 1813, but were more perfectly presented in 1818. He conceived that equal volumes of the simple gases contain not only, as Avogadro and Ampère had stated, equal numbers of *molecules*, but equal numbers of *atoms*, so that to compare densities was to determine not merely the relative weights of the molecules but the relative weights of the atoms. Thus if we find that a litre of chlorine weighs 35·5 times as much as a litre of hydrogen, we may, according to Avogadro, conclude that the molecule of chlorine is 35·5 times as heavy as the molecule of hydrogen. But if the molecules of hydrogen and of chlorine may contain any numbers of atoms, this tells us nothing about the *atomic* weight. Now if we suppose that each molecule of hydrogen contains two atoms, and each molecule of chlorine the same number, the comparison of molecules comes to the same thing as the comparison of atoms. 35·5 may now be taken as the *atomic weight* of chlorine.

This was the view taken by Berzelius. In general it holds good, but in some cases there are marked exceptions. Thus the vapours of liquids at a temperature not far removed from their boiling points often exhibit very anomalous densities. Taking the atomic weight of sulphur as 32, its vapour density, 96, not far above its boiling point, shows that the molecule at that temperature must consist of six atoms.* Above 860° its vapour density (32) corresponds to its atomic weight. The molecule of six atoms is broken up into 3 molecules of two atoms each.

The hypothesis of Prout was set forth about this time (1816), to the effect that the atomic weights of the elements were integral multiples of that of hydrogen. One of the advantages claimed for such a system of weights was that it would enable us to conceive of hydrogen as the primordial element, from which the others were formed by successive condensations. The ½ or ¼ of the atomic weight of hydrogen has been suggested as the atomic weight of this fundamental element, but even then the weights cannot be reduced to integral multiples of it. The

---

* Sulphur boils, according to Regnault, under normal pressure at 448°·4 centigrade, its vapour density being, according to Dumas, 35·55 at 524°.

suggested hypothesis of a single primordial element is not, however, to be lightly set aside. It is a profound speculation, and viewed rightly, may afford valuable guidance to future research.

Two important principles were at this time formulated and incorporated by Berzelius in his table of atomic weights. The first was the law of specific heats of Dulong and Petit. We must first offer some explanation of what is to be understood by the term *specific heat*. Shortly, then, it is found that equal weights of different bodies require different amounts of heat to raise them through the same number of degrees of temperature. The unit of heat or thermal unit may be taken as the quantity of heat necessary to raise 1 gram of water through 1° centigrade. It takes less heat to raise a gram of nickel one degree than to raise a gram of water through the same temperature.

Now a body will give out on cooling through a certain number of degrees the same amount of heat as would be needed to raise it through the same number of degrees. To find how much is needed we may therefore mix a certain weight of the heated substance with a certain weight of cold water. Thus suppose we mix 100 grams of metallic nickel at 100° C. with 100 grams of water at 10° C. When the heat of the nickel has become equally diffused through the water we find the temperature to have risen to 18·9°. The nickel has cooled through 81·1°, and has in so doing heated an equal weight of water through 8·9°. 100 grams of nickel thus requires 890 units of heat to raise it through 81·1°. But 100 grams of water requires 8110 units of heat to raise it through 81·1°, since 1 gram needs 1 unit to raise it through 1°. Thus the 100 grams of nickel takes $\frac{890}{8110}$ times as much heat to raise it through a given temperature as does the same quantity of of water. Its *specific heat* is $\frac{890}{8110}$ = ·1097. The quantity of heat which would raise the temperature of a given weight of nickel through 1° C. would raise the temperature of a given weight of water through only ·1097° C. In actual experiments of the kind just described, the specific heat of the calorimeter or vessel in which the water is contained must be taken into account. It of course becomes heated at the same time as the water, but to understand the bearing of Dulong and Petit's law, it is unnecessary here to enter into further detail.

In 1819 these chemists gave the specific heats of many solid bodies, particularly metals, and made the observation that in most cases they were inversely proportional to the atomic weights. The specific heat gives the capacity of each gram of the substance for heat. If we multiply this number therefore by the atomic weights we shall get the *capacities of the atoms for heat*, or, as it is termed, the atomic heat of the elements. On performing this multiplication we see that with the greater number of the solid elements the atomic heat is a nearly constant quantity. The atomic heats of most of the elements are found to lie near 6·4. Dulong and Petit's law then states that *the atomic heat of the elements is a constant quantity;* or that *the atoms of all simple bodies have precisely the same capacity for heat.**

It is readily seen that this generalisation must be of great service in controlling the atomic weights. In the case of these metals a very close adherence to the law is observed, so that Dulong and Petit corrected by its means the atomic weights of zinc, iron, nickel, copper, lead, tin, and gold. In the case of these metals the atomic weight attributed by Berzelius had been just double that which was in accordance with the law of specific heats. Their weight was therefore halved and the formulæ of the oxides changed from ZnO_2, FeO_2, NiO_2, CuO_2, &c., to ZnO, FeO, NiO, CuO, &c.†

A few of the specific and atomic heats are given below:

Element.	Specific heat.	Temperature of observation.	Atomic weight.	Atomic heat.
Zinc	0·0955	+ 55°	64·9	6·2
Cadmium	0·0567	+ 55	111·6	6·3
Lead	0·0315	+ 34	206·4	6·5
Mercury	0·0319	− 59	199·8	6·4
Iron	0·1140	+ 58	55·9	6·4

Among the non-metals carbon has an atomic heat which is far too low. In the form of diamond its atomic heat at 45° is 1·8. It is found, however, that

* *Annales de Chimie*, 1819.
† Fe = iron (*ferrum*), Cu = copper (*cuprum*), Zn = zinc.

its atomic heat rises with the temperature and at 985° is 5·51.

Another generalisation destined to exercise considerable influence upon the development of the atomic theory was the law of isomorphism made known by the German chemist, Mitscherlich, in December, 1819. Mitscherlich observed that similarity of constitution in salts tended to produce similarity of crystalline form. Thus potassium chloride is isomorphous with sodium chloride; magnesium sulphate is isomorphous* with the sulphate of zinc and nickel. Ordinary sodium phosphate is isomorphous with the corresponding sodium arsenate. The similarity of constitution is exhibited in the following formulæ, the water of crystallization being united by a plus sign to the formula of the salt. Ordinary sodium phosphate is phosphoric acid, H^3PO^4, in which 2 atoms of hydrogen are replaced by sodium, Na^2HPO^4; and it crystallizes with 12 molecules of water, $Na^2HPO^4 + 12H^2O$. The corresponding arsenate is similarly derived from arsenic acid, H^3AsO^4, and is thus represented by the formula $Na^2HAsO^4 + 12H^2O$.† As a last instance we may take the case of sodium nitrate isomorphous with calc-spar (calcium carbonate), the formulæ being respectively $NaNO^3$ and $CaCO^3$. Upon the older view of the constitution of metallic salts, the view held down to the time of Gerhardt,

---

* *i.e.* built up or constructed on the same lines; from *isos*, equal; and *morphe*, shape.

† For explanation of any of these symbols see the table of modern atomic weights given below.

that they were formed by the union of an acid with a basic oxide, the formulæ of these salts would become $N^2O^5 + Na^2O$ and $CO^2 + CaO$; the similarity of constitution would be obscured and the fact of their isomorphism remain unexplained.

Mitscherlich's law of isomorphism was stated by him as follows :—The same number of elementary atoms, combined in the same manner, produce the same crystalline form, and this form is independent of the chemical nature of the atoms, and determined solely by their number and arrangement. The statement so made is somewhat too wide, and important restrictions and exceptions have to be allowed. Nevertheless, the law is an important one, and had considerable influence with Berzelius in his determination of atomic weights. Chromium oxide being Cr^2O^3 the isomorphism of chrome alum and iron alum led to the adoption of Fe^2O^3 as formula for ferric oxide and FeO for ferrous oxide. The adoption of the last formula led, by chemical analogy and isomorphism, to similar formulæ for lime (calcium oxide), magnesia (magnesium oxide), and zinc oxide. Thus this law as well as the law of specific heats could only be recognised by halving the atomic weights of a number of metals, and the weights were accordingly halved.

Guided by these considerations Berzelius adopted the atomic weights given by him in 1826. His weights are referred to oxygen as 100. On calculating them for the atomic weight of hydrogen as the

T

unit we are struck by the very remarkable accuracy of the results he had arrived at. All the accurate appliances of modern chemistry and the labour of workers of unexampled patience and skill have only in the more important cases succeeded in effecting alterations in the decimal places of his atomic weights. A few examples from his table may here be given.

Element.	Symbol.	Atomic weights referred to Oxygen as 100.	Atomic weights referred to Hydrogen as 1.	Modern atomic weights.
Oxygen	O	100	16·02	15·96
Carbon	C	76·44	12·26	11·97
Phosphorus	P	196·14	31·44	30·96
Sulphur	S	201·17	32·24	31·98
Selenium	Se	494·58	79·26	79·0
Iodine	I	789·75	126·56	126·53
Chlorine	Cl	221·33	35·48	35·37
Calcium	Ca	256·02	41·04	39·9
Aluminium	Al	171·17	27·44	27·3
Zinc	Zn	403·23	64·62	64·9

Up to this point the atomic theory had progressed rapidly, but the chemists began to repent of their rapid adoption of the new ideas. Atomic weights had at their first start been regarded as expressive of what quantities of the different elements were *equivalent* to each other. Upon this idea the theory had been founded, it was difficult to change its foundations, it was difficult to admit that additional facts must be contained in the formulæ adopted. Gay-Lussac, Wollaston, and Gmelin used their influence in favour of atomic weights founded only upon equivalence, and

Berzelius was obliged in some points to give way. He did not, however, readily yield, and, driven back to the older formulæ, he adopted H̶O, H̶C̶l̶ and H̶₃N̶, as formulæ for water, hydrochloric acid and ammonia, regarding H̶ as a double atom of hydrogen representing the *equivalent* of other chemists.

Any inaccuracies in the conceptions of Berzelius now came rapidly to light. We have seen how he considered the vapour densities of the elements, where obtainable, as identical with their atomic weight. Avogadro had stated that equal volumes of gases or vapours contained equal numbers of *molecules*. Berzelius, in the case of the elements at least, held that they contained equal numbers of *atoms*. In some cases this idea proved to be erroneous. Thus we are obliged to adopt 200 as the atomic weight of mercury. The laws of Dulong and Petit, the vapour densities of its volatile compounds, and purely chemical considerations necessitate the adoption of this weight. But, as first pointed out by the French chemist Dumas, the vapour density of mercury vapour compared with that of hydrogen is very nearly 100. It is only half what, according to the ideas of Berzelius, it should be. There is not the same number of atoms in a litre of hydrogen and of mercury vapour. The atom of mercury occupies twice the space that the atom of hydrogen does. If the molecule of hydrogen consists of two atoms, the molecule of mercury vapour consists of one. Anomalous vapour densities were also found by

Dumas, in 1832, in the cases of phosphorus and sulphur. In the case of sulphur the molecule is disintegrated at a high temperature, but phosphorus preserves a four-atom molecule at 1040° (*Deville and Troost*), while the molecule of arsenic consists of four atoms at 860° (*Deville and Troost*).

In consequence of this and other actual or supposed flaws in the theory of Berzelius the system of chemical equivalents, as distinguished from the true atomic weights, gradually gained ground. The attempt to represent as equivalent molecules not really comparable led to great complication and difficulty. Into this labyrinth it is unnecessary here to attempt to follow chemical theory. An emergence began with the work of Laurent and Gerhardt* but the influence of these chemists like that of Avogadro was unrecognised and unrewarded till they passed beyond gratitude or condemnation.

* For the work of these two chemists Laurent's *Chemical Method* (Cavendish Society) may be consulted.

CHAPTER XVI.

EIGHTH PERIOD: THE ATOMIC THEORY.
THE ATOMIC THEORY OF TO-DAY.

THERE are a number of reactions in organic chemistry as a result of which carbonic acid, water, or ammonia is produced. Gerhardt noticed a curious point with regard to these reactions when written out as equations in the formulæ in use in his day. The equations were observed never to contain formulæ for *single* molecules of water or carbonic acid, while they did contain single molecules of ammonia. The acute mind of Gerhardt sought for a cause of this strange fact. Representing the molecules of carbonic acid and water by CO^2 and HO, never less than two molecules of either occurred in the representation of these reactions. It appeared to Gerhardt an unwarrantable supposition to conclude that these substances were never liberated in less than two molecules at a time. For example, let us take oxidation of alcohol to aldehyde. On the old system of atomic weights this is formulated :—

$$C^4H^6O^2 + O^2 = 2HO + C^4H^4O^2$$

alcohol + oxygen = water + aldehyde.

Again, take the action of any acid upon alcohol :—

$$C^4H^6O^2 + HCl = C^4H^5Cl + 2HO.$$

We here see two molecules of water always liberated, and on this system it was possible always to represent the water taking part in a reaction as a whole multiple of H^2O^2. The use of the formula HO seemed to Gerhardt to be therefore in a large measure gone. So too with the formula CO^2, and both were accordingly doubled, becoming H^2O^2 and C^2O^4. These formulæ were the true *equivalents* of the formulæ then in use for ammonia, NH^3. So too S^2O^4 and C^2O^2 represented, according to Gerhardt's equivalents of sulphur, dioxide and carbonic oxide.* The same equivalent, might, however, be obtained by simpler means, and instead of using these double formulæ, Gerhardt concluded that the atomic weights of carbon, sulphur, and oxygen should be doubled. The school of equivalent chemists had assigned to these elements the weights 6, 16, and 8; Gerhardt adopted the atomic weights 12, 32, and 16. C^2, representing two atoms of carbon weighing 12 times as much as the atom hydrogen, is thus replaced by C representing one atom weighing the same amount. In this way the double formulæ are halved and become CO^2, H^2O, SO^2, and CO. These

* The molecules represented by these formulæ would occupy *four* volumes, if the molecule of hydrogen, H^2, be taken as occupying two.

formulæ possess the great advantage of being in accordance with Avagadro's law of volumes. The older formulæ were not comparable in this respect. Thus the molecule of ether vapour, C^4H^5O, would occupy two volumes, while that of alcohol vapour, $C^4H^6O^2$, would occupy four. Williamson showed, by purely chemical reasoning, that the old formula of ether must be doubled. It then becomes simpler to use the new atomic weights, and the molecular formulæ of ether and alcohol then become $C^4H^{10}O$ and C^2H^6O, each occupying two volumes.

After adopting the new atomic weights, Gerhardt saw that it would be necessary to halve the organic formulæ so obtained, if single molecules of water or carbonic acid were to appear in the equations, and if the formulæ were to be brought into accordance with the law of volumes. But here he was met by a difficulty. Silver acetate under his new system had the formula $C^4H^6AgO^4$. How could this be halved, seeing that it contained only one atom of silver? Gerhardt solved this problem by halving the atomic weight of silver. The formula then became $C^4H^6Ag^2O^4$, and when halved, $C^2H^3O^2Ag$. Oxide of silver then became Ag^2O, analogous to water H^2O. In following out his analogy, Gerhardt halved the atomic weights of a number of metals. He went too far, but in many cases the idea was a correct one.

The reforms of Gerhardt necessitated a change in the conception of the constitution of *salts*. Previously salts were considered as combinations of an acid oxide with a basic oxide. Silver nitrate was, for instance, regarded as a combination of silver oxide with nitrogen pentoxide, $AgO.NO^5$. Under the new régime such formulæ became simplified, and silver nitrate became $Ag^2N^2O^6$ and thus $AgNO^3$. The old ideas as to the constitution of salts thus became untenable, and we now define a salt as an acid having the whole or part of its hydrogen replaced by a metal.

Laurent adopted and extended the notions of Gerhardt. He pointed out that the hydrates cannot be considered as compounds of oxide and water, any more than the salts could be considered as compounds of oxide with oxide. A hydrate, said Laurent, is an intermediate stage between water and oxide.

Water is H^2O; when one hydrogen atom is replaced by potassium it becomes KHO, caustic potash; when two atoms are replaced it becomes K^2O, potassium oxide. There is a close analogy here between the organic and inorganic compounds. Replacing one hydrogen atom by the *organic radical* ethyl (C^2H^5) we obtain ordinary *alcohol*. Replacing both hydrogen atoms we obtain ordinary *ether*.

H^2O, water.
KHO, potassium hydrate.
K^2O, potassium oxide.

H^2O, water.
(C^2H^5) HO, alcohol.
($C^2H^5)^2$ O, ether.

Cannizzaro (1858) doubled the atomic weight of a number of metals once more in accordance with the law of specific heats, and by a series of gradually narrowing oscillations the opinions of chemists at length gravitated to an almost stationary point, and the table of atomic weights and system of formulæ now adopted is the result of their agreement.

THE ATOMIC THEORY.

The following is a table of the atomic weights now in use.*

Element.	Atomic Weight.	Symbol.	Element.	Atomic Weight.	Symbol.
Aluminium	27·3	Al	Molybdenum	95·8	Mo
Antimony	120·0	Sb	Nickel	58·6	Ni
Arsenic	74·9	As	Niobium	94·0	Nb
Barium	136·8	Ba	*Nitrogen*	14·01	N
Beryllium	9·2	Be	Osmium	198·6	Os
Bismuth	210·0	Bi	*Oxygen*	15·96	O
Boron	11·0	B	Palladium	106·2	Pd
Bromine	79.75	Br	*Phosphorus*	30·96	P
Cadmium	111·6	Cd	Platinum	196·7	Pt
Cæsium	132·5	Cs	Potassium	39·04	K
Calcium	39·9	Ca	Rhodium	104·1	Rh
Carbon	11·97	C	Rubidium	85·2	Rb
Chlorine	35·37	Cl	Ruthenium	103·5	Ru
Cerium	141·2	Ce	Scandium	44·0	Sc
Chromium	52·4	Cr	*Selenium*	79·0	Se
Cobalt	58·6	Co	Silver	107·66	Ag
Copper	63·1	Cu	*Silicon*	28·0	Si
Didymium	147·0	Di	Sodium	22·99	Na
Erbium	169·0	Er	Strontium	87·2	Sr
Fluorine	19·1	F	*Sulphur*	31·98	S
Gallium	69.8	Ga	Tantalum	182·0	Ta
Gold	196·2	Au	*Tellurium*	128·0	Te
Hydrogen	1·0	H	Terbium	148·5	Tr
Indium	113·4	In	Thallium	203·6	Tl
Iodine	126·53	I	Thorium	231·5	Th
Iridium	192·7	Ir	Tin	117·8	Sn
Iron	55·9	Fe	Titanium	48·0	Ti
Lanthanum	139·0	La	Tungsten	183·5	W
Lead	206·4	Pb	Uranium	240·0	U
Lithium	7·01	Li	Vanadium	51·2	V
Magnesium	23·91	Mg	Yttrium	92·5	Y
Manganese	54·8	Mn	Zinc	64·9	Zn
Mercury	199·8	Hg	Zirconium	90·0	Zr

* Some of the symbols are derived from the Latin names of the elements, *e.g.*, Potassium, K (*Kalium*); Silver, Ag (*Argentum*); Sodium, Na (*Natrium*); Mercury, Hg (*Hydrargyrum*), &c.

In the above table the non-metallic elements are printed in italics. The distinction between metals and non-metals is a convenient one, but the two classes are not sharply separated from each other. It is in Geber's writing that the first definition of a metal occurs: "Metallum est corpus miscibile, fusibile, et sub malleo ex omni dimensione extendibile."* The discovery of the brittle metals (antimony, bismuth, and zinc) destroyed the completeness of this definition. There is no attempt now at a sharply drawn distinction, but the metals are, as a rule, distinguished by their peculiar lustre. The metals are also characterized by the formation of basic oxides. These basic oxides unite with acid oxides, the oxides of the non-metallic elements, to form salts. Thus copper oxide, CuO, unites with sulphur trioxide, SO_3, to form copper sulphate, $CuSO_4$. If now an electric current be passed through a solution of this salt it is decomposed, and the copper is deposited at the negative pole. Copper is thus positive as compared with the other group SO_4, and its oxide is termed positive or basic. The non-metals have a special tendency to form negative oxides. Thus sulphur forms two oxides, SO_2 and SO_3; both are negative, and combined with water form respectively sulphurous and sulphuric acids, H_2SO_3 and H_2SO_4. The hydrogen in these acids may be replaced by a metal to form a salt, and, indeed, the acids themselves may be re-

* "A metal is a fusible body susceptible to combination, and which may be extended in all directions under the hammer."

garded as *hydrogen salts* (hydrogen sulphite and sulphate), and hydrogen itself considered as a metal owing to its numerous chemical resemblances to that class of bodies. We already know a liquid metal, and there is no *à priori* objection to the existence of one which is gaseous at ordinary temperatures. On January 10th, 1878, Raoul Pictet, of Geneva, succeeded in liquefying hydrogen under a pressure of 650 atmospheres and at a temperature of $-140°$. When the stopcock was opened a *steel-blue* coloured, opaque jet of liquid hydrogen rushed out, and particles of solid hydrogen fell with a rattle upon the floor. If this solid hydrogen could be examined it would perhaps agree with ordinary ideas of a metal.

This table of the atomic weights is based upon the great laws of the atomic theory already discussed. It is founded on the laws of constant, definite, and multiple proportions. Its supporting pillars are the laws of volume, of specific heat, and of isomorphism.

Take the symbol of any individual element and ask what does it tell us? O is the symbol for the atom of oxygen weighing 15·96 and occupying one volume. Further, as in most cases the density of a gaseous element corresponds with its atomic weight, we learn that the density of oxygen as compared with hydrogen at the same temperature and pressure is about 16. But this is not all; if we express the atomic weight in grams instead of in hydrogen units 15·96 grams of oxygen occupy 11·2 litres, and in the same way 1 gram of hydrogen occupies 11·2 litres. All this is contained in the symbol O.

Take now the symbol of a metal, lead, Pb. This represents an atom of lead weighing 206·4, and if this atomic weight be correct we must assume that this amount of lead in the gaseous state would occupy one volume. We also know that the atomic weight multiplied by the specific heat of lead must give a result approximating to 6·4, and we can thus calculate the approximate specific heat of the metal.

Let us now pass to the case of compounds. What do we learn from the symbol CO^2? It represents one molecule of carbon dioxide containing 1 atom of carbon and 2 atoms of oxygen, that is 12 parts of carbon[*] and $2 \times 16 = 32$ parts of oxygen. This molecule we know will occupy 2 volumes, and contains its own volume of oxygen. It occupies the same volume as 2 atoms of hydrogen, weighing 2. Its density compared with hydrogen is therefore $\frac{32 + 12}{2} = 22$, or *half its molecular weight*. If the molecular weight of carbon dioxide were unknown we could deduce it from its density. The molecular weight of a gaseous compound is always equal to twice its specific gravity compared with hydrogen. If the molecular weight of carbon dioxide be expressed in grams we see that 44 grams of the gas occupy 22·4 litres (*i.e.* $2 \times 11·2$), and contain 22·4 litres of oxygen.

[*] In ordinary use decimal places in the atomic weights smaller or greater than ·5 may be disregarded.

When a substance, as ordinary quick-lime (calcium oxide), CaO, cannot be volatilised, we cannot definitely say that the true molecular formula has been determined. Indeed, it is probable that in the solid state most bodies have complicated molecules consisting of aggregations of many molecules of the same substance when gaseous.

Lastly, let us see what is contained in an ordinary chemical equation,

$$2 H_2 + O_2 = 2H_2O.$$

Interpreted, this means that two molecules of hydrogen, weighing 4 and occupying 4 volumes, combine with one molecule of oxygen, weighing 32 and occupying 2 volumes, to form two molecules of water weighing $2 \times 18 = 36$ and occupying 4 volumes. Also we see that 4 grams of hydrogen, occupying $4 \times 11\cdot 2 = 44\cdot 8$ litres, combine with $2 \times 16 = 32$ grams of oxygen, occupying $22\cdot 4$ litres, to form 36 grams of water vapour occupying $22\cdot 4$ litres.

Other equations representing interchanges may be similarly interpreted, though in many cases the volume relations cannot be so fully given. As a case take the following:

$$BaCl_2 + CuSO_4 = BaSO_4 + CuCl_2.$$

If we add a solution of barium chloride to one of copper sulphate a precipitate of baric sulphate is obtained, and cupric chloride remains in solution. The chlorine is here transferred from the barium to the copper, and the SO_4 group from the copper to the qarium. By consulting the table of atomic weights the reader may follow out this reaction quantitatively.

It will not be difficult now to see the immense advantage conferred upon chemistry by this concise and accurate method of recording and generalising its facts. The coping-stone has yet, however, to be put in place. This is the idea of *valency* or *atomicity* developed by the aid of a large number of workers, among whom were Dumas, Williamson, Odling, Kekulé, and many others. We have seen that a certain school of chemists, disdaining the use of Avogadro's hypothesis or Dulong and Petit's law, wished to restrict chemical symbols to a representation of the *equivalent* weights of the elements, or those quantities which were of the same value. When the real atomic weights came to be adopted it was, however, seen that the true atoms of the elements were not really equivalent to each other, they had not all the same capacity for combination. Some elements would combine together only in single atoms, one with one; they were termed monads, and said to be *monovalent*. Other elements could combine with two atoms of a monad element, and were thus termed diads, or said to be divalent or diatomic. As an illustration, hydrogen, chlorine, bromine, iodine, fluorine, potassium, sodium, are taken to be monovalent. Their atoms combine together in pairs, one atom of hydrogen with one of chlorine, forming a molecule of hydrochloric acid, and so on. The fact that the molecule of hydrogen consists of two atoms explains why the molecular weight of a

THE ATOMIC THEORY.

compound is equal to *twice* its vapour density compared with hydrogen. Taking hydrogen, fluorine, chlorine, bromine, iodine, as monovalent, we gain insight into the valency of other elements from a survey of the following compounds:

$HgCl^2$; HgI^2; OH^2, OCl^2; SH^2; SeH^2; $ZnCl^2$; NH^3; PCl^3; AsH^3, $AsCl^3$, AsI^3; CH^4, CCl^4; SiF^4; PF^5; $NbCl^5$; WCl^5; WCl^6.

Oxygen is here seen to be divalent (OH^2), arsenic trivalent (AsH^3), and carbon tretravalent (CH^4).* The valency of an element was formerly regarded as definitely fixed. As a matter of fact, however, many elements are capable of exhibiting different valencies in different compounds. Thus, phosphorus is trivalent in the trichloride, PCl^3, and pentavalent in the pentafluoride, PF^5.

Combining power runs parallel to replacing power. An element capable of combining with two monovalent atoms will be capable of replacing two also. Each zinc atom combines with two chlorine atoms in the chloride, $ZnCl^2$; each zinc atom replaces two hydrogen atoms of sulphuric acid, H^2SO^4, in the sulphate, $ZnSO^4$.

Valency or "atomicity" is variable, but the conception does not on this account lose its significance. In some elements it is much more strictly marked than in others, and the very variability of it is characteristic of certain elements (*e.g.* tungsten) and therefore useful. What has yet to be done is to find out

---

* The prefixes mono, di, tri, tetra, penta, sex, hepta, octo, must be understood to stand respectively for one, two, three, four, five, six, seven, eight.

the laws of the variation of valency, to determine the conditions under which it varies.

While upon the subject of valency a word must be said with regard to the *structural* formulæ of compounds, a subject now of the highest importance. Can we tell in what manner the atoms are combined together in the molecule? Take such a simple case as water, H^2O. How are the atoms combined together? In the molecule of free hydrogen, H^2, we must suppose each hydrogen atom directly united to the other, and, representing direct union by a straight line, our structural formula becomes H—H. Similarly the molecule of hydrochloric acid, where monovalent hydrogen is combined with monovalent chlorine, is H—Cl, and the most natural conclusion is that the structural formula for the molecule of water, where monovalent hydrogen is combined with divalent oxygen, is H—O—H. This formula is entirely supported by chemical facts. The two hydrogen atoms in this molecule being similarly united to the oxygen atom would be expected to play a similar rôle, and this is actually found to be the case. The compound obtained by replacing one hydrogen atom by potassium is always the same substance. But if the two hydrogen atoms were differently combined we should expect them to play different parts, and to give rise to two distinct compounds according as one or the other was replaced by potassium or other metal. Furthermore *both* atoms may be so replaced, a common property further accentuating their similarity. In the same way either or both atoms may be replaced by an organic radical, as in alcohol C^2H^5OH and ether $C^2H^5.O.C^2H^5$, and we thus become convinced of the similarity of the two hydrogen atoms in water which we consider as each directly united to the oxygen atom. Other and far more complicated structural formulæ are built up by similar reasoning. It is obvious that in building up such formulæ considerations of valency will often be useful, enabling us to detect which arrangement is in accordance with the prevalent valency of the elements, and therefore which arrangement is most probable.

It may be asked what purpose do such structural formulæ serve? They enable us, in the first place, to express the internal molecular structure of a compound, so that we may see at a glance what are its chief observed chemical properties and relationships, what is the way of obtaining it, and how it may be named; in the second place, they enable us to predict what *will* be the chemical properties which have not yet been observed. In most cases we may condense these structural formulæ, writing together the atoms forming a group or radical which acts as a whole. Thus the full structural formula of sulphuric acid may be written $\begin{smallmatrix} O\diagdown & \diagup O-H \\ & S \\ O\diagup & \diagdown O-H \end{smallmatrix}$ but this may be advantageously condensed to $SO^2\diagdown_{OH}^{OH}$. The use of structural formulæ is at present most markedly evident in the region of organic chemistry* but as an inorganic

* See p. 369.

example of it we may take the formula of pyrophosphoric acid, $H^4P^2O^7$. From this *empirical* formula we learn very little. We cannot even tell how many hydrogen atoms of the acid are replaceable by a metal, for usually in oxygen acids only those hydrogens occurring as hydroxyl (OH) can be so replaced. But if we expand the formula the properties and relationships of the acid appear at once. So expanded the formula becomes $O{=}P{<}^{OH}_{OH}{>}O{<}^{HO}_{HO}{>}P{=}O$, and we see that the acid contains four hydroxylic hydrogens, that is four hydrogen atoms replaceable by a metal, and further that it is obviously obtained from orthophosphoric acid $O{=}P{\lower1pt\hbox{$\scriptstyle<$}}{OH \atop OH}^{OH}$ by the withdrawal of water from two of its molecules thus:—

$$O{=}P{<}^{OH}_{OH}{-}OH + HO{-}P{>}^{HO}_{HO}{=}O = H^2O + O{=}P{<}^{OH}_{\ }{>}O{<}^{HO}_{\ }{>}P{=}O.$$

Two molecules of phosphoric acid = water + one molecule of pyrophosphoric acid.

In these formulæ phosphorus is represented as pentavalent, the union with the divalent oxygen atom being represented by a double line. This is merely a convention, and is not to be taken as implying a stronger union. The two "units of saturation" of the oxygen atom are supposed to be satisfied by the two "units of saturation" of the phosphorus atom.*

---

* W. Lossen would do away with these double bonds and any adherence to the idea of distinct valencies for each element. He regards the valency of an element in any particular compound as represented by the *number of atoms* with which each atom of the

The following table gives the valency of a number of elements :—

Monovalent.	Divalent.	Trivalent.	Tetravalent.	Pentavalent.	Hexavalent.
Bromine	Barium	Antimony	Carbon	Antimony	Platinum
Chlorine	Calcium	Arsenic	Chromium	Arsenic	Tungsten
Gold	Carbon	Bismuth	Iron	Bismuth	
Hydrogen	Chromium	Gold	Molybdenum	Molybdenum	
Iodine	Iron	Nitrogen	Platinum	Nitrogen	
Lithium	Magnesium	Phosphorus	Selenium	Phosphorus	
Potassium	Manganese	Potassium	Silicon	Tungsten	
Silver	Molybdenum	Silver	Sulphur		
Sodium	Oxygen	Sodium	Tellurium		
Thallium	Platinum	Thallium	Tin		
	Selenium		Titanium		
	Sulphur		Tungsten		
	Tellurium		Zirconium		
	Tin				
	Titanium				
	Tungsten				
	Zinc				
	Zirconium				

element is in that compound combined. Thus he would regard carbon in carbonic oxide, CO, as monovalent [C-O] and in carbon dioxide, CO_2, as divalent, being combined with two oxygen atoms [O-C-O or O-C-O]. There is direct action and reaction between the carbon atom and one oxygen atom in the first case, and between the carbon atom and two oxygen atoms in the second. Lossen's views are the outcome of an attempt to give greater precision to our conceptions of valency. The desirability of such an attempt cannot be exaggerated, and Lossen's ideas are important and suggestive. It must, however, be remembered that, in the present state of our knowledge the conceptions of valency cannot by any ingenuity be made very precise, and that theories in a state of unperfected evolution must lose their possibilities of development with loss of mobility. (*Ueber die Vertheilung der Atome in der Molekel; Annalen der chemie*, cciv. 265.) His reasoning is followed and adopted by Pattison Muir in his *Principles of Chemistry* (1884).

The question as to whether the valency of chlorine, bromine, and iodine varies has yet to be solved. Thus, one of the compounds discovered by Prinvault, PCl^6I, may be represented as $\begin{smallmatrix} Cl \searrow & \swarrow Cl \\ & P{-}I{=}Cl^2 \\ Cl \nearrow & \nwarrow Cl \end{smallmatrix}$ where phosphorus is pentavalent and iodine trivalent. Platinum must be supposed to be octovalent in the double chloride $(KCl)^2PtCl^4$, unless we allow that this is a molecular as distinguished from an atomic compound.

The present system of atomic weights has received much confirmation from the views developed by Newlands and Mendelejeff. These chemists found that the elements may be arranged in periods according to their atomic weight, each period repeating the gradation of properties observed in each of them to accompany the rise of their atomic weights. This generalisation was first made by Newlands, and independently originated by the Russian chemist, Mendelejeff, who more developed the theory which is known as the *periodic law*.

That there is a relation between atomic weight and chemical properties is readily seen by a study of the following table. It gives some of the principal properties of the Nitrogen family of the fifth natural group of the elements.

$N=14.01$	$P=30.96$	$As=74.9$	$Sb=122$	$Bi=210$
Physical State gas	M.P.*44.3°. B.P. 290°.	Sublimes abt. 180°.	M.P. 425°	M.P. 270° B. white heat.
Specific gravity of Solid ?	1.83	5.73	6.75	9.82
Atomic Volume ?	16.92	13.07	18.07	21.33
Metallic Properties unmetallic —	unmetallic brittle	feebly metallic brittle	decidedly metallic brittle	very perfect metal. brittle
Hydrogen Compounds NH^3 NH^3, ammonia, is a very stable body. It is only with great difficulty decomposed by heat.	PH^3 PH^3, phosphuretted hydrogen, is stable, but more readily decomposed by the electric spark.	AsH^3 AsH^3, arseniuretted hydrogen, is readily decomposed by heat. Is always obtained mixed with hydrogen.	SbH^3 Antimoniuretted hydrogen decomposes with great case. Is only obtained mixed with 96 per cent. of H.	— BiH^3 is unknown.
It has strongly basic properties.	Less strongly basic.	No basic properties.	—	—
It burns with difficulty.	Burns above 100°.	Readily inflammable.	Very readily inflammable.	
Oxygen Compounds N^2O is the most stable. N^2O^3 is unstable, as is N^2O^5. Both N^2O^3 and N^2O^5 have strongly acid propreties.	P^2O^3 and P^2O^5 are very stable and form well-defined phosphorous and phosphoric acids.	As^2O^3 and As^2O^5 are both stable. As^2O^3 is less acid than P^2O^3 but As^2O^5 is strongly acid.	Sb^2O^3 has very feeble acid properties. It is also basic. Sb^2O^5 is somewhat more strongly acid.	Bi^2O^3 is strongly basic. Bi^2O^5 is very unstable and only very feebly acid.

* M.P.=melting point; B.P.=boiling point.

In the above table we see a very well-marked gradation of properties as the atomic weights of the elements rise. Beginning with unmetallic nitrogen, we end with perfectly metallic bismuth; and beginning with very stable and strongly basic ammonia, we end with very unstable and non-basic antimoniuretted hydrogen, and finally with the unknown bismuthamine. There is also much similarity among the different members of the family, as is shown by the formation of analogous hydrides and oxides.

The following is Mendelejeff's table. The vertical column (Roman numerals) constitutes a *group*, each group corresponding, for the most part, with a natural family. The horizontal column (Arabic numerals) constitutes a *series*. In the groups the members present striking similarities, in the series they present still more striking gradations. The properties of any member of a series may be taken as standing between those of the members immediately preceding and succeeding it.

THE ATOMIC THEORY.

	I.	II.	III.	IV.	V.	VI.	VII.	VIII.
				Typical Oxides.				
	R^2O	R^2O^{2} *	R^2O^3	R^2O^{4} *	R^2O^5	R^2O^5 *	R^2O^7	
1	H = 1							
2	Li = 7	Be = 9	B = 11	C = 12	N = 14	O = 16	F = 19	
3	Na = 23	Mg = 24	Al = 27	Si = 28	P = 31	S = 32	Cl = 35·5	
4	K = 39	Ca = 40	Sc = 44	Ti = 48	V = 51	Cr = 52	Mn = 55	Fe = 56, Ni = 58·6, Co = 58·6
5	Cu = 63	Zn = 65	Ga = 69	Ge = 72	As = 75	Se = 79	Br = 80	
6	Rb = 85	Sr = 87	Y = 89	Zr = 90	Nb = 94	Mo = 96	?	Rh = 104, Ru = 104·5, Pd = 106
7	Ag = 108	Cd = 112	In = 114	Sn = 118	Sb = 120	Te = 126 ?	I = 127	
8	Cs = 133	Ba = 137	La = 139	Ce = 141	Di = 144			
9					Er = 166			
10			Sb = 173		Ta = 182	W = 184		Ir = 192·5, Os = 193, Pt = 194·5
11	Au = 196	Hg = 200	Tl = 204	Pb = 206·5	Bi = 209			
12				Th = 232·5		U = 240		
13								

* These formulæ are doubled to exhibit the gradation more clearly.

In the horizontal series of the elements thus arranged we observe periodical gradations of properties. The periodicity may be shown by reference to the densities of third series of elements which increase towards the centre of the series and diminish towards the ends. The *atomic volume*, on the contrary, that is, the specific gravity divided by atomic weight, diminishes towards the centre and increases towards the ends.

	Na	Mg	Al	Si	P	S	Cl
Densities	0·97	1·75	2·67	2·42	1·84	2·06	1·38
Atomic Volumes . .	24	14	10	11	16	16	27

The capacity of combination with monovalent elements or the valency also undergoes modification. Thus, taking the first two series we have :—

$LiCl$ $BeCl_2$ BCl_3 CCl_4 ; CH_4 NH_3 OH_2 FH
$NaCl$ $MgCl_2$ $AlCl_3$ $SiCl_4$; SiH_4 PH_3 SH_2 ClH

What we now observe is that the second series *repeats* the changes observed in the first, so that the elements in the vertical groups are closely connected in their properties.

When we come to the fourth series a certain change in this arrangement, so far as physical properties are concerned, is observed. From potassium the specific gravity increases steadily up to nickel and decreases again down to rubidium, the oscillation in this case including two groups. The atomic volume, on the contrary, decreases down to nickel and rises again up to rubidium. If we arrange the elements upon a curve which rises and falls according to increase and decrease of atomic volume, as was done by Lothar Meyer, lithium, sodium, potassium, and rubidium occupy summits on this curve. The properties of the elements are found to be characteristically different according as they occupy portions on the descending, ascending, or lowest portions of these curves.

We cannot examine more closely here into the interesting relations between properties and combining weights. But the most interesting point of all still remains to be touched upon. In a first glance at Mendelejeff's table we cannot but be struck by the fact that gaps occur in it in which no element is placed. These places have yet to be filled. They represent the elements *remaining to be discovered in the future*. How far the gaps may be filled it is impossible to say, but that many of the absent elements will yet be found we cannot doubt. By means of this table Mendelejeff has been able to prophesy the discovery of unknown elements, and even to describe with exactness their chief properties. In three remarkable cases his prophesies have already been fulfilled. Before 1875 the place now filled by gallium in the fifth series was vacant. Mendelejeff suggested that the place belonged to a hypothetical element, *eka-aluminium*, the properties of which he proceeded to define. In the year 1875 Lecoq de Boisbaudran announced the discovery of a new element by means of spectrum analysis, termed by him gallium. On comparison of their properties it became clear that Lecoq de Boisbaudran's gallium and Mendelejeff's eka-aluminium were one and the same element. The following is the comparison of the predicted and actual properties :—

Eka-aluminium.	Gallium.
Readily obtained by reduction.	Readily obtained by electrolysing alkaline solutions.
Melting point low. Sp. gr. = 5·9.	M.P. = 30·15°. Sp. gr. = 5·93.
Not acted on by air.	Non-volatile and but superficially acted on by air at bright red heat.
Will decompose water at red heat; slowly attacked by acids or alkalis.	Decomposes water at high temperatures. Soluble in hot hydrochloric acid, scarcely attacked by cold nitric acid; soluble in caustic potash.
Will form a potassium alum.	Forms a well-defined alum.
Oxide, El^2O^3. Chloride, El^2Cl^6.	Chloride, Ga^2Cl^6. Oxide, Ga^2O^3.
Atomic weight about 69.	Atomic weight 69·7.

So, too, the metal scandium discovered by Nilson in 1879 is identical with the hypothetical eka-boron of Mendelejeff with atomic weight about 44. Lastly, the germanium of Winkler (1885) is identical with the eka-silicon of Mendelejeff with atomic weight 72.

The greatness of a generalisation enabling us to predict what elements will be discovered in the future, and what their chief properties will be, as well as to systematise the varying properties of the elements now known, needs no discussion to make its importance evident. Since Mendelejeff's discovery chemistry has seen no greater generalisation.

DAVY.

CHAPTER XVII.

DAVY AND FARADAY.

THE foundations of the science have now been laid, and we must next glance at what the workers of to-day have built upon those foundations.

Sir Humphry Davy's work comes next in order. His name has become almost a household word, and there are very few who have never heard of Davy's safety lamp. Davy* came of an old but not wealthy family. After the death of his father he was apprenticed to a trade, and was soon regarded as rather an idle fellow. He used to be continually occasioning explosions and other disturbing phenomena in the house of the gentleman

---

* Dr. J. A. Paris: *Life of Sir Humphry Davy* (1831). Dr. J. Davy: *Works of Sir H. Davy* (1839). Born at Penzance in Cornwall, 1778. Died at Geneva, 1829.

who helped him after his father's death, and who had not quite the keenness of sight necessary to see what the boy might become. But his talents were not to be cheated of their destiny, and in good time he became the great original worker, immortal as the discoverer of the alkali metals and of the safety lamp, and the great lecturer of whom Coleridge said, "I attend Davy's lectures to increase my stock of metaphors."

In 1799 Davy discovered the anæsthetic properties of nitrous oxide (N^2O). This gas is usually prepared by decomposing ammonium nitrate by heat.

$$(NH^4)NO^3 = N^2O + 2H^2O.$$

It is a colourless gas which, like oxygen, supports ordinary combustion. A red-hot splinter of wood rekindles when brought into the gas just as it would do in oxygen. In these reactions the nitrogen of the gas is set free; $4N^2O + C^2 = 2CO^2 + 4N^2$.* But the most remarkable property of nitrous oxide is its effect upon animal life. If nitrous oxide be inhaled by the human subject the first effects are singing in the ears. Insensibility then follows and, if the gas be persistently inhaled, death through suffocation. If air be allowed to enter the lungs when the phase of insensibility has set in, the effects pass off and no evil result follows. A certain amount of excitement

* The reason for not halving this and other equations is that so manipulated they would contain expressions for single atoms (as, in this instance, C), which have already been defined as not existing separately.

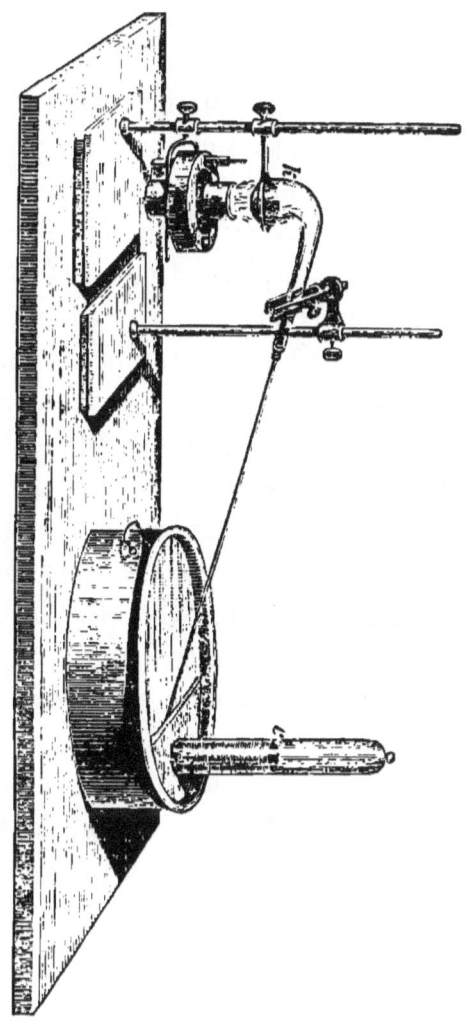

PREPARATION OF NITROUS OXIDE.
Ammonia Nitrate is heated in the retort (k), and the gas evolved collected in the cylinder (c).

is sometimes observed after inhalation, whence has arisen the popular name of laughing gas.

The great discovery of the compound nature of the alkalis was made by Davy in 1808.* His method was to place a small piece of pure potash upon a disc of platinum, connecting this with the negative pole of a galvanic battery, while the upper surface was joined by a platinum wire to the positive pole. Small lustrous metallic globules collected on the lower surface of the potash, some of which burnt off while others became tarnished, and so preserved from further action of the air. The globules were metallic potassium. At the same time that the metal was being liberated a violent effervescence, due to liberation of gases from the caustic potash, occurred at the positive pole. Davy was unable to obtain the metal in large quantities but he succeeded in demonstrating its chief properties. It rapidly absorbs oxygen,† being converted into the oxide (K^2O), and the oxide is extremely hygroscopic, and when combined with water forms, as Davy showed, ordinary caustic potash. Represented by modern equations these reactions become:—

$$2K^2 + O^2 = 2K^2O. \qquad K^2O + H^2O = 2KOH.$$

Davy found that when thrown upon water metallic potassium swam upon its surface, exciting a violent reaction, and dissolved with formation of caustic potash.

---

* "On some new phenomena of chemical changes produced by electricity, particularly the decomposition of the fixed alkalies," &c. —*Philosophical Transactions of the Royal Society* (1808).

† In perfectly dry and pure air potassium, at the ordinary temperature, remains unchanged.

In this reaction he found that hydrogen was evolved and, at the high temperature produced, burst into flame.

$$K^2 + 2H^2O = 2KHO + H^2.$$

The compounds of sodium had been of importance earlier than those of potash. We have already, in the second chapter, seen that sodium carbonate was known to the ancients. The "nitre" mentioned in Proverbs xxv. 20,* is native carbonate of soda, and is given as a translation of the Hebrew *nether*, the same substance being known as νιτρον in Greek, and *nitrum* in Latin.

The discovery of metallic sodium is announced by Davy in the same memoir, and it was obtained by him by exactly the same process. Davy observed the formation of the oxide (Na^2O), and the action of the metal upon water, and further stated erroneously that sodium took fire in chlorine gas.

Some of the knowledge relating to these elements obtained since Davy's discovery may here be briefly sketched. Gay-Lussac † and Thénard heated iron turnings in a gun-barrel, and allowed melted caustic potash to flow slowly on to the hot iron. The iron took the oxygen of the hydrate while hydrogen gas was evolved, and metallic potassium distilled over and was collected in a bent copper tube. The method at present in use was proposed by Curadau and has been

---

* "As he that taketh away a garment in cold weather, and as vinegar upon nitre, so is he that singeth songs to an heavy heart."

† Louis Joseph Gay-Lussac (1778-1850).

improved by Brunner, Wöhler, and especially by Donny and Mareska. It consists in the reduction, at a white heat, of potassium carbonate by carbon :

$$K^2CO^3 + 2C = K^2 + 3CO.$$

The ignition of crude tartar (hydrogen potassium tartrate) provides us with an intimate mixture of charcoal and potassium carbonate. The mixture is heated in iron cylinders coated with clay, and the metal collected in the flat iron condensers suggested by Donny and Mareska. The rapid cooling of the vapour insured by these flat and shallow condensers prevents the formation of the explosive compound, $K^6C^6O^6$, produced by the union of the potassium vapour with carbon monoxide (CO).

The specific gravity of potassium at 13° C. compared with water is 0·875 (*Baumhauer*). The only metal lighter than potassium—unless hydrogen be included—is lithium. At the ordinary temperature the metal is soft and may easily be cut with a knife. The fresh surfaces rapidly oxidise and the metal should be kept under naphtha. Potassium melts at 62·5° (*Bunsen*). It boils at a red heat* and the vapour density suggests a molecule composed of two atoms.

One or two of its compounds may be mentioned. Potassium hydrate or caustic potash, KOH, may be obtained pure by the action of the metal on water.

* E. P. Perman [*Journal of the Chemical Society*, vol. lv., p. 326, (1889)] has quite recently determined the boiling points of potassium and sodium. That of potassium he finds to be about 667° C., that of sodium 742° C.

It is usually prepared by decomposing potassium carbonate with slaked lime, Ca(OH)² (calcium hydrate).

$$Ca(OH)^2 + K^2CO^3 = 2KOH + CaCO^3.$$

If the solution be too concentrated the reverse action sets in and potassium carbonate is produced. This is an interesting example of the fact that chemical reactions depend upon other conditions besides that of the simple affinity of one element for another.

Potassium hydrate is a hard, white, brittle substance. It is used for absorbing carbonic acid in analysis, for surgical purposes, and in the manufacture of soft soap. The last-named article consists of the potassium salts of organic acids.

Potassium chloride is found in the Stassfurt potash beds, and is used in artificial manures, while the bromide and iodide are extensively used in medicine. The tri-iodide KI^3 is a somewhat inexplicable compound on the ordinary ideas of valency.* Oxygen is usually prepared by heating potassium chlorate, $KClO^3$. It decomposes, leaving a residue of chloride.

$$2KClO^3 = 2KCl + 3O^2.$$

The salt is used in the manufacture of lucifer matches, for pyrotechnic purposes, and as a medicine.

---

* It may, however, be regarded as a *molecular* compound of KI with I^2, but the usefulness of any distinction between molecular and atomic compounds is at present a moot point.

Potassium nitrate (saltpetre), KNO^3, occurs as an efflorescence on the soil in various hot countries. It is used in medicine, but most largely in the manufacture of gunpowder. Gunpowder consists of a mixture of charcoal, sulphur, and nitre, the proportion being, approximately, 75 per cent. of saltpetre (nitre), 15 per cent. of charcoal, and 10 per cent. of sulphur. The simplest expression for the reaction occurring when gunpowder is fired is:—*

$$2KNO^3 + S + 3C = K^2S + N^2 + 3CO^2.$$
Nitre + Sulphur + carbon = potassium sulphide + nitrogen + carbon dioxide.

This simple expression cannot, however, be taken as accurately representing what occurs. The first thorough investigation of the decompositions taking place was made by Bunsen and Schischkoff. Abel and Noble have, more recently (1874), published an elaborate series of results on the same subject. Among other results they find that the tension produced on firing powder in a space which it completely fills amounts to 6,400 atmospheres, or 42 tons per square inch. The temperature of the explosion is about 2,200° C.

Potassium carbonate is obtained by extracting with water, or *lixiviating* as it is termed, the ashes of wood. The name potashes arose from this extraction being made in pots. By dissolving it in appropriate

---

* For the sake of simplicity many equations may be written with single atoms. But the reader must not take this as implying the separate existence of single atoms.

acids the other potassium salts may be formed. It is used in the manufacture of soft soap.

Sodium was obtained by Gay-Lussac and Thénard by heating caustic soda with metallic iron. At the present time it is manufactured in considerable quantities by heating to whiteness a mixture of caustic soda, slack, or small coal, and chalk. Sodium is of more commercial importance than potassium, being used in the manufacture of aluminium. When metallic sodium is thrown into water it evolves hydrogen, but the heat is insufficient to ignite the gas. Caustic soda may be formed similarly to the potassium compound.

Sodium chloride, or common salt, is an article of great commercial importance. The total salt produced in England amounted in 1876 to 1,676,000 tons, of which 1,500,000 tons were obtained by evaporating brine and 176,000 were raised as rock-salt.

Sodium carbonate is an article of great commercial importance. It is obtained from common salt by first converting into sulphate by means of sulphuric acid and then acting upon this with coal and chalk. $Na^2SO^4 + 4C = Na^2S + 4CO : Na^2S = + CaCO^3 = Na^2CO^3 + CaS$. This is Leblanc's process (1794). To him we owe cheap soap and cheap glass. He died in a French asylum for paupers. The ammonia soda process consists in passing carbonic acid into an ammoniacal solution of common salt.

The importance of Davy's discovery becomes very

apparent when we thus see the extensive use to which the compounds of these metals are put. From these researches Davy concludes: "Oxygen then may be considered as existing in, and as forming an element in all the true alkalies; and the principle of acidity of the French nomenclature might now likewise be called the principle of alkalescence."* From analogy alone Davy thinks it reasonable to expect that the alkaline earths (lime, baryta, &c.,) are similarly composed of metallic bases united to oxygen. "I have tried some experiments upon barytes and strontites, and they go far towards proving that this must be the case."

His first attempts to electrolyse baryta† (BaO), *i.e.* to analyse it by electricity, were not very successful. Berzelius and Pontin obtained the metal by electrolysis in presence of mercury, whereby an *amalgam* of the metal with mercury was formed. The amalgam was then heated in absence of air when the mercury distilled off. Berzelius and Pontin communicated their results to Davy, who repeated their experiments and electrolysed baryta, barium chloride ($BaCl^2$) and other barium salts.

---

* *Phil. Trans.* (1808).

† The compound of barium first observed was the natural sulphate, heavy spar ($BaSO^4$). It was examined in 1602 by a Bolognese shoemaker, V. Casciorolus. For a long time it baffled analysis. The presence of a new earth was detected by Scheele in an ore of manganese and Gahn recognised it as the basis of heavy-spar. Guyton de Morveau, a disciple of Lavoisier, proposed in 1779 to name this earth barote (βαρύς, heavy) and this name was altered by Lavoisier to baryta.

The metal is best obtained by electrolysis of the fused chloride.

Calcium was obtained by Davy and by Berzelius and Pontin by electrolysis of calcium chloride. Matthiessen first prepared it as a coherent metallic mass in 1856. Calcium plays an important part in nature. The carbonate occurs in enormous quantities in its various forms of calc-spar, arragonite, chalk, marble, limestone, coral, &c., and united with magnesium carbonate as magnesium limestone or dolomite. Quicklime is the oxide, CaO; slaked lime the hydroxide, $Ca(OH)^2$. Bleaching powder is formed by the action of chlorine on dry slaked lime. Calcium sulphate in different states is known as gypsum, alabaster, and plaster of Paris.

Strontium was first obtained by Davy in the same year (1808) by electrolysis of the moistened hydroxide and of the chloride. It is a yellow metal. It occurs in nature as the sulphate ($SrSO^4$, celestine) isomorphous with heavy-spar and the carbonate ($SrCO^3$, strontianite isomorphous) with arragonite.

The discovery of metallic magnesium was announced by Davy in the same paper. It was first obtained as a coherent metal by Bussy. The method proposed by Caron and Deville for its manufacture is now used on the large scale. The method consists essentially in decomposing the anhydrous chloride by metallic sodium. Magnesium is a silver-white metal. The ribbon, in which form it is usually seen, burns when lit by a flame with a light of dazzling brilliancy. It has been observed at sea at a distance of twenty-eight miles. Bunsen and Roscoe have shown that this light is rich in chemically active rays, and have determined its chemical value compared with the light of the sun.

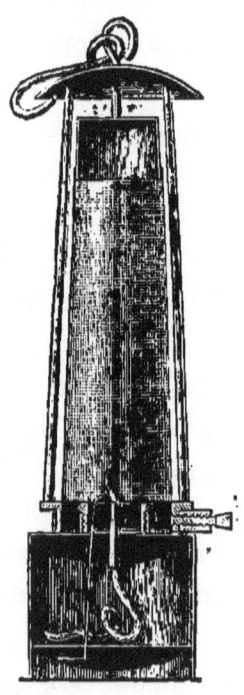

DAVY'S SAFETY LAMP.

Davy attempted unsuccessfully to decompose alumina (Al^2O^3), silica (SiO^2) and zirconia (ZrO^2). In 1809 he published his important paper on chlorine.* This gas was not then recognised to be an element,

* *Phil. Trans.* (1809): "Researches on the oxymuriatic acid," &c.

but was known as oxymuriatic acid, and supposed to contain oxygen. Davy heated the gas with carbon, and obtaining no action was led to doubt the presence of oxygen in it. Tin he found to absorb the gas but the body so formed did not contain oxygen. By a number of negative proofs of this kind Davy established the elementary nature of chlorine.*

In 1815 Davy invented his safety-lamp, and it is to his credit that he took out no patent for it, preferring to make the discovery a free gift. The principle of the lamp depends upon the fact that flame will not pass through fine wire gauze, owing to the rapid conduction of the heat away from the point of contact and the consequent cooling down the gases below their ignition point.

The work of Davy has enriched his science with a number of brilliant discoveries, but the best of them all, as he himself said, was his discovery of Faraday.

Michael Faraday was born in Newington Butts on September 22nd, 1791.† His father was a journeyman blacksmith, and the family afterwards lived in Jacob's Well Mews, near Manchester Square. Faraday himself became errand boy at a bookseller's shop and was afterwards taken on as apprentice. During

---

* The following passage in this paper is worth quoting: "The vivid combustion of bodies in oxymuriatic acid gas at first view appears a reason why oxygene should be admitted in it, but heat and light are merely results of the intense agency of combination."—*Cf.* Hooke.

† *Michael Faraday: a Biography.* By J. H. Gladstone (1872). See also Tyndall's *Faraday as a Discoverer* (1870).

his apprenticeship he was sometimes engaged in book-binding, and books bound by him are now preserved at the Royal Institution. The first chemical lectures he attended were paid for by his brother Robert, who was thus doing more than he could have been conscious of in aid of science. From his shop Faraday was taken to hear Davy lecture at the Royal Institution. Afterwards he was introduced to Davy, and when the latter was injured in the eyes by his investigations of nitrogen chloride he became for a short time his amanuensis. "My desire," says Faraday, "to escape from trade, which I thought vicious and selfish, and to enter into the service of a science which I imagined made its pursuers amiable and liberal, induced me at last to take the bold step of writing to Sir H. Davy expressing my wishes." Davy soon after made him his laboratory assistant, but not till he had earnestly tried to dissuade him from following a scientific career. It would mean poverty, ingratitude, and unrewarded toil. But Faraday was not to be dissuaded.

Faraday married in 1821, though from his position at the Royal Institution he obtained up to 1833 besides a house, coal and candles, only £100 per annum. He had no children. If he had a family he would probably have been deprived of much of his work, for it did not pay. He presents us with the spectacle of a man giving up all for his devotion to pure, as distinguished from applied, science. In his earlier years he undertook commercial analyses

FARADAY.

which paid him far better, and in 1830 he made £1,000 by these means, and in 1831 considerably more. But his researches in pure science multiplied around him, and he at last found that he must choose between making money and adding to knowledge. He did not hesitate in his choice, he did not try to combine both. He deliberately chose to abandon treasure for truth. In the following year, (1832), his total income amounted to £155 9s. Ever after it was even less than that.

Faraday gave up all in order to follow the particular work that he felt he was meant to do. His mind was essentially cast for that of an explorer into the undiscovered countries of knowledge, and he determined to be only what he was. In pursuit of this he refused all other invitations. Thus he was offered the professorship of chemistry at the London University (now University College), but the offer was declined.

The picture drawn of him by Dr. Gladstone, working quietly in his laboratory in the morning with his little niece beside him, never forgetting to please her by conversation or amuse her with some pretty experiment, and all the while engaged upon work of the gravest moment, is charming indeed. If some one called in and his work was interrupted he was never put out or otherwise than pleased to see his visitor. At half-past two he dined, and the afternoon was spent in writing to friends, of whom he had many. Then perhaps he would attend a council meeting, come back for a short time to his laboratory and then spend the evening very happily at home, probably reading aloud to his wife or some intimate friends.

In religion Faraday belonged to the small sect of the Sandemanians, and at their meetings on Sunday he sometimes preached. As he approached his seventieth year the strain of his work became too great for him, and in 1861 he resigned part of his duties at the Royal Institution. His energies slowly waned, and on August 25th, 1867 he passed away.

Faraday's character took the hearts of all who knew him with joy. He was so simple and gentle and self-less, and yet beneath his gentleness lay hidden a cavern of volcanic fire, ready to blaze out at sight of injustice or cruelty. He had a fund of playful, boyish humour which lent added charm to his presence. Thus Gladstone relates how Faraday came down unexpectedly to visit him at Hastings and knocked at the door while he was dressing. "Who's there?" cried Gladstone, but the only reply Faraday would volunteer was "Guess," and the discomfited chemist was forced to go through a long list of names containing all but the right one before Faraday would reveal himself. His kindliness is exemplified by the fact that he would listen with great interest to the chemical lectures of a boy friend of his, aged 13, and applauded the experiments heartily.

As a lecturer Faraday's equal could with difficulty

be found. He contrived by his own earnestness and enthusiasm to bring out new beauties in the most commonplace facts. In his enthusiasm over facts of singular beauty he forgot everything except his own delight in the knowledge. He was raised into a state almost of ecstasy, by force of which he and his audience were alike carried away.

The most prominent results achieved by Faraday were electrical, and of these his demonstrations of the theory of electrical induction are the chief. But we cannot discuss this part of his work here, and must pass on to consider his chemical discoveries, also of great importance. In conjunction with Davy, Faraday experimented upon the very dangerous compound chloride of nitrogen. This body is formed by the action of chlorine upon a solution of sal-ammoniac. It collects as a yellowish oil, the composition of which has only recently been determined.*

Faraday was the first to effect the union between carbon and chlorine. Ethylene, or olefiant gas (C^2H^4), is obtained by treating alcohol with sul-

* This substance was discovered by Dulong in 1811, who continued his work upon it after it had caused him the loss of three fingers and one eye. During Faraday's and Davy's investigation it repeatedly exploded without warning, and sometimes with such violence as to stun the operators. Dr. Gattermann, of Göttingen, has recently (1888) continued the investigation of this substance. He finds that it consists of the trichloride (NCl^3) together with other chlorides. By allowing the chlorine to act for some time, washing the resulting oil free of sal-ammoniac, and again chlorinating, he has obtained perfectly pure NCl^3. He finds that light is a powerful cause of the explosions of this substance. Dr. Gattermann unfortunately states that his eyes and nerves have been so affected as to oblige him to temporarily abandon work on the subject.

phuric acid. This gas treated with great excess of chlorine in presence of light gave rise to a white solid termed by Faraday perchloride of carbon. Expressed according to our present equations this reaction becomes: $C^2H^4 + 5Cl^2 = C^2Cl^6 + 4HCl$. When this body was passed through a red-hot tube Faraday found that it lost chlorine and formed protochloride of carbon. The reaction may be expressed thus:* $C^2Cl^6 = C^2Cl^4 + Cl^2$. The chloride so obtained is a liquid. Faraday also combined iodine with carbon by acting with iodine upon ethylene (carburetted hydrogen) in sunlight. Ethylene diodide, ($C^2H^4I^2$) is thus obtained.

In 1823 Faraday analysed the hydrate of chlorine ($Cl^2 + 10H^2O$) obtained by the action of ice-cold water upon chlorine, and by use of this compound he liquefied chlorine gas.

In 1825, Faraday discovered benzene in the oil obtained from portable gas prepared by Taylor in 1815 by strongly heating fats. His analysis of the new liquid led him to name it bicarburet of hydrogen, its empirical formula being taken as C^2H where $C = 6$. Adopting modern weights ($C = 12$) this becomes CH. The vapour density of the body is, however, six times what this formula would allow and furthermore the hydrogen of the compound can be replaced by chlorine in six stages, so that it must be supposed to contain at least six atoms of hydrogen

---

* These expressions were, of course, not made use of by Faraday. They are the interpretations now given of his facts.

in the molecule. Taking this evidence into account the formula becomes C^6H^6. At the present day this hydrocarbon is obtained by the distillation of coal-tar. The numberless multitude of the *aromatic* compounds (as they are called) are all derivatives of this body. The department of aromatic chemistry now far exceeds in area the other combined provinces of the science. It is difficult to realise that in 1821 at the publication of the second edition of Brande's *Manual of Chemistry*, benzene was yet undiscovered. In the same liquid Faraday obtained a new gaseous hydrocarbon butylene (C^4H^8).

Some of Faraday's chief chemical work was concerned with condensation of the gases. His experiments established the high probability that the ordinary gases were only liquids with a very low boiling point. To appreciate this we may recall that liquids tend to give off vapour at all temperatures. If a little water be introduced into a barometer tube with the mercury standing at 760 mm. and at the ordinary temperature the column is instantly depressed a certain distance. At a certain temperature this depression will amount to half the barometric height. The *vapour tension* of the water now amounts to half an atmosphere, or 380 mm. of mercury. If the temperature of the water in the tube be at last raised to its boiling point (100° C.) the mercury will be driven down to the same level as that outside the tube. The vapour tension now amounts to one atmosphere. In other words *a liquid boils when its vapour tension is equal to the superincumbent atmospheric pressure.* If the pressure upon it be increased its boiling point will be raised. This at once suggests a method for liquefying the gases by pressure. Supposing them to be liquids with low boiling points their boiling points will thus be raised and as the pressure increases will ultimately rise above the temperature at which the experiment is being performed. The gas will then condense to a liquid.

The subject was fully investigated by Faraday,[*] who succeeded in liquefying a number of gases.[†] By sealing up chlorine hydrate in a strong bent glass tube, warming the compound, and placing the other limb of the tube in a freezing mixture, Faraday obtained liquid chlorine which condensed in the cold limb. The tubes used for these purposes must be prepared with care and, properly made, withstand an internal pressure of many tons per square inch. The application by these means of pressure and cold succeeded with a number of gases. Thus, in the case of sulphuretted hydrogen (hydrogen sulphide, H^2S), Faraday brought the material, iron sulphide (FeS) and sulphuric acid,[‡] into the closed limb of the tube, the former being separated from the latter by plati-

FARADAY'S TUBE.

[*] *Phil. Trans.* 1823, p. 160. *Ibid*, 1823, p. 189.
[†] The first gas liquefied was chlorine by Northmore in 1806.
[‡] $H^2SO^4 + FeS = H^2S + FeSO^4$.

num foil. The open end of the tube was then sealed and the sulphide shaken down into the acid. The gas then condensed as the pressure increased. The gases liquefied by Faraday include: sulphur dioxide (SO^2), carbon dioxide (CO^2), nitrous oxide (N^2O), cyanogen (CN), ammonia (NH^3), hydrochloric acid (HCl), hydrobromic acid (HBr), and hydriodic acid (HI), besides those already mentioned.

Other gases, the so-called permanent gases, resisted his attempts. He endeavoured in vain to liquefy hydrogen, oxygen, nitrogen, nitric oxide, marsh-gas, and carbon monoxide. Natterer and Andrews though employing very high pressures both failed in the same attempts, but in 1877 Cailletet and Pictet * succeeded in liquefying oxygen, carbon monoxide, and hydrogen. Oxygen liquefies under a pressure of 475 atmospheres at $-140°$ C., hydrogen at 650 atmospheres. Cailletet liquefied ethylene (C^2H^4), acetylene (C^2H^2), nitric oxide (NO), and marsh gas (CH^4).

Before concluding, mention must be made of Faraday's important discovery of the *electro-chemical equivalents* of the elements. The same strength of current, he found, would in equal times liberate equivalent quantities of the elements. Thus if a current passing for a given time through a solution of copper sulphate liberated 63 grains of copper, it would, under similar conditions, liberate 65 grains of zinc, 63 and 65 being the respective atomic

* See page 299.

weights of these metals. It would similarly liberate 216 grains of silver, or twice its atomic weight; the equivalent weight of silver, compared with zinc and copper, being twice its atomic weight, owing to the fact that silver is monovalent, while zinc and copper are divalent.

NINTH PERIOD.

CHAPTER XVIII.

NINTH PERIOD :—THE MODERN SCIENCE.
MODERN INORGANIC CHEMISTRY.

IN treating of Davy, Faraday, and Dalton, the later developments of their greater discoveries have been shortly discussed. It has seemed clearer and more intelligible to observe strictly chronological order only in the case of the main and fundamental discoveries of the science and those associated with great and illustrious names. In most cases, therefore, the later development has been treated together with the main idea. The chief part of what remains in this chapter will therefore consist in briefly summarizing any omitted results of modern research.

The following table contains the names of elements discovered since the close of last century. The name of the observer by whom the element was first isolated is printed in *ITALICISED CAPITALS*. In many cases, however, compounds were recognised as containing a new element before the element was obtained in a free and uncombined state. Names of workers observing and recognising such compounds are printed in *italics*. The name of the principal worker upon an element, other than its discoverer, is printed in CAPITALS, and any other workers in ordinary type.

Titanium	*Gregor*	1789
	Klaproth	1795
	BERZELIUS	1825
Uranium	*Klaproth*	1789
	PELIGOT	1842
Chromium	*VAUQUELIN*	1797
Tellurium	*KLAPROTH*	1798
Tantalum	*Hatchett*	1801
	Ekeberg	1802
Vanadium	*Del Rio*	1801
	Selfström	1830
	BERZELIUS	1831
	ROSCOE	1867
Cerium	*Klaproth*	1803
	MOSANDER	1839
Palladium	*WOLLASTON*	1803
Potassium	*Stahl*	1736
	DAVY	1808
Sodium	*Stahl*	1736
	DAVY	1808
Barium	*BERZELIUS & PONTIN*	1808
	DAVY	1808
Boron	*DAVY*	1808
	GAY-LUS. & THENARD	1808
Calcium	*DAVY*	1808
	BERZELIUS & PONTIN	1808
	Matthiessen	1856
Magnesium	*DAVY*	1808
Strontium	*DAVY*	1808
Chlorine	*SCHEELE*	1774
	DAVY	1810
Iodine	*COURTOIS*	1811
Lithium	*Arfvedson*	1817
	BUNSEN & MATTHIESSEN	1855

Selenium	BERZELIUS.	1817
Cadmium	{ Hermann	1817
	{ STROMEYER	1818
Silicon	BERZELIUS.	1823
Bromine	BALARD	1826
Aluminium	{ Marggraf	1754
	{ WŒHLER	1827
Beryllium	{ Vauquelin	1798
	{ WŒHLER	1828
Thorium	BERZELIUS.	1828
Yttrium	{ Gadolin	1794
	{ Eckeberg	1797
	{ MOSANDER.	1839
Didymium	{ Mosander	1841
	{ MARIGNAC.	1853
Lanthanum	MOSANDER.	1841
Erbium	{ Mosander	1843
	{ CLEVE & HOEGLUND	1872
Niobium	{ Rose	1844
	{ Blomstrand	1866
	{ ROSCOE	1879
Ruthenium	CLAUS.	1844
Caesium	Kirchhoff & Bunsen.	1860
Rubidium	BUNSEN	1861
Thallium	{ CROOKES	1861
	{ LAMY	1862
Indium	Reich & Richter	1863
Gallium	LECOQ de BOISBAUDRAN	1875
Fluorine	{ Scheele	1771
	{ AMPERE	1810
	{ Gore	1870
	{ MOISSAN	1887
Terbium	{ Mosander	1843
	{ DELAFONTAINE & MARIGNAC	1878
Ytterbium	Marignac	1878
Decipium	Delafontaine	1878
Philippium	Delafontaine	1878
Scandium	Nilson	1879
Samarium	Lecoq de Boisbaudran	1879
Thulium	Cleve	1879
Germanium	Winkler	1885

The existence of others is as yet somewhat doubtful, such as the Yttrium α and Yttrium β of Marignac (1879). Ytterbium to Thulium inclusive were all discovered by spectrum analysis.

Of one or two of these bodies some further mention

must be made. Metallic iodides are found in the ash of sea-weed, and by treatment with sulphuric acid and manganese dioxide (MnO^2) free iodine is obtained from this source. Bromine may be obtained from the same source. It was first discovered by Balard in the salts obtained by the evaporation of sea-water. Cadmium occurs as an impurity in most ores of zinc. Silicon

QUARTZ CRYSTALS.

is, next to oxygen, the chief constituent of the earth's solid crust. It occurs always as the dioxide, SiO^2. This combined with the metallic oxides gives rise to the large class of silicates, compounds which play a very prominent part in geological formations. Clays consist largely of aluminium silicate. Emerald is a silicate of aluminium and beryllium. Felspar is a potassium aluminium silicate. Talc is a magnesium silicate. Serpentine, mica, topaz, &c., are complicated silicates. Pure silica (SiO^2) occurs in crystals as quartz and tridymite. The amorphous * varieties include opal, flint, sand, &c. Davy's discoveries led to the suggestion that silica, like baryta and lime, was the oxide of an unisolated element. Berzelius,† whose immense services to chemistry are but feebly indicated by his prominence in the foregoing table, first isolated the element in 1810, and obtained it in a pure state in 1823.‡ It forms a dark brown powder.

The interesting metal aluminium is next to oxygen and silicon in importance as a constituent of the earth's crust. Its presence in clay and felspar has been referred to. Felspar forms the chief constituent of granite, gneiss, porphyry, &c. The oxide, Al^2O^3, occurs as the mineral corundum. Of this mineral the ruby and sapphire are varieties. Wöhler obtained the metal by acting on the chloride with sodium. The mineral bauxite, a hydroxide of aluminium and iron, is the usual source of the element. From this mineral pure aluminium hydrate is prepared. The dried powder is mixed with common salt and charcoal and made up into balls. These are heated and a stream of dry chlorine led over them. A double chloride of aluminium and sodium distils off

---

* That is, having no regular form.
† 1779—1848.
‡ The process used by Berzelius was to treat potassium silicofluoride, a compound of potassium, silicon, and fluorine, K^2SiF^6 with metallic potassium. Potassium fluoride (KF) is formed and silicon liberated.

$$K^2SiF^6 + 4K = 6KF + Si.$$

and is condensed in a receiver. The double chloride is then treated with sodium. The metal is thus separated, fused, and cast into moulds.

Aluminium is now prepared in this way on a large scale. Its lightness, malleability, ductility, and fusibility render it highly serviceable. Its white colour, its susceptibility to high polish, and its unsusceptibility to aerial action enhance its value and render it an almost ideal metal. Its tensile strength is high, much higher than that of cast iron, and it is exceedingly sonorous. In spite of these manifold advantages and its universal occurrence it has proved impossible to prepare aluminium at a rate enabling it to compete with other metals. Improvements have, however, lately been effected which promise to bring it more into the market.*

Caesium and Rubidium were discovered by Bunsen by means of spectrum analysis, a subject to which we shall briefly refer in the sequel. The spectrum of the salts of Dürkheim water contained two splendid blue lines not before observed. They proved to belong to a new element, the first discovered by spectrum analysis. The delicacy of the spectroscopic test is indicated by the fact that it was necessary to evaporate forty *tons* of the water to obtain enough caesium for investigation. Rubidium was similarly discovered in the mineral lepidolite.

Scheele observed that fluor-spar (CaF^2) was the salt

* See a recent discourse of Sir Henry Roscoe's " On Aluminium; " *Nature*. 1889.

SIR HENRY ROSCOE.

of a new acid. Ampère in 1810 determined the constitution of this acid, HF. But the element itself resisted all attempts at isolation. Davy tried the action of chlorine on silver fluoride (AgF). He expected the chlorine to replace the fluorine thus : $AgF + Cl = AgCl + F$. This reaction actually occurred, but the fluorine as soon as liberated attacked the vessels in which the experiments were carried on, and formed fresh compounds. It appeared incapable of remaining free in the presence of any other element. In 1887 the French chemist, Moissan[*] succeeded by the electrolysis of hydrofluoric acid containing potassium fluoride in obtaining a colourless gas, attacking metals and other substances with formation of fluorides and proved to be elementary fluorine. Owing to its extremely energetic properties it was at first impossible to collect the gas, but more recently it has been collected and its specific gravity ascertained.

Some points of importance still remain to be noticed. By modern observation Cavendish's determination of the composition of atmospheric air has been confirmed. Approximately one-fifth is oxygen and four-fifths nitrogen. This may be illustrated by a simple experiment. A tube closed at one end and graduated is inverted over water, and a certain volume of air enclosed within it. A piece of ordinary phosphorus is now pushed up into the tube on the end of a wire. If left for some time this will gradually absorb the oxygen of the air, and nitrogen will be left

[*] *An. de Chim. et Phys.*

behind. If the air measured originally 20 divisions from the top it will now measure 16. One-fifth, or the amount occupying the space between 4 divisions of the tube, has been absorbed by the phosphorus. The actual method of analysis used by modern chemists is the eudiometric one discussed below.

Besides nitrogen and oxygen air contains traces of other gases, notably carbonic acid and ammonia. The normal amount of the former gas is 4 volumes in 10,000 volumes of air.

The analysis of the air by *weight* was conducted in 1841 by Dumas and Boussingault. They found 22·92 per cent. oxygen to 77·08 per cent. nitrogen.

The analysis of water has been frequently repeated since Cavendish's time.* According to the volumetric method a graduated tube is filled with mercury and inverted over a mercury trough. The tube used for such a purpose is termed an *eudiometer*.† Some pure oxygen gas is next passed up into the tube and its volume carefully measured. The height of the mercurial column in the tube above the mercurial surface in the trough must also be noted, as this by its downward tendency diminishes the pressure upon the gas. The height of the thermometer and barometer must also be carefully observed. A large excess of hydrogen is next admitted, but the total quantity of both gases must not

* Nicholson and Carlisle, in 1800, first decomposed water by electricity.
† From εὐδία, clear weather, and μετρόν, a measure, *i.e.* a measure of the purity of air, or of the quantity of oxygen which it contains.

be more than sufficient to fill about one-sixth of the tube. The tube is now pressed securely down upon a plate of caoutchouc (india-rubber) placed under the mercury, and by means of two platinum wires passing through the glass in the upper part of the tube a spark is sent through the mixed gases. A flame is seen to pass through the gases and combination occurs, the water forming, as Cavendish observed, a dew upon the side of the tube. On releasing the eudiometer from the caoutchouc pad the mercury rises and the volume is found to be considerably diminished. The residual gas is carefully measured, and the observation of the mercury column, thermometer and barometer repeated. The volumes of the gas before and after the explosion must next be reduced by calculation to what they would be at identical pressure and temperature.* The customary pressure and temperature are 760 millimetres of mercury and 0°C. The following numbers are those of an actual experiment,† the volumes being reduced to 0° and a barometric height of one metre.

Volume of oxygen	95·45
Volume of oxygen + hydrogen	557·26
Volume after explosion	271·06

Thus with the explosion 286·2 volumes‡ disappeared.

---

* See *ante* p. 126.

† As given in Roscoe and Schorlemmer's *Treatise*.

‡ The volumes here spoken of may be taken as cubic centimetres, cubic inches, or multiples of any other unit. The actual graduations of the tube are usually in millimetres (measures of *length*) and their

As a large excess of hydrogen was present we know that the whole of the oxygen will have been used in the production of water. Thus of the 286·2 volumes 95·45 are oxygen; the rest, 286·2—95·45 = 190·75, consists therefore of hydrogen. Now the cause of the disappearance of these 286·2 volumes is their condensation to form a very small bulk of water.* Thus we must conclude that 95·45 volumes of oxygen combine with 190·75 volumes of hydrogen to form water, or that 1 volume of oxygen combines with 1·9963, *i.e.* very nearly 2 volumes of hydrogen to form water. The relations of the volumes are thus, 1 : 2, as expressed in the formula OH^2. By exploding his gases in a eudiometer, heated by the vapour of amyl alcohol, Gay-Lussac showed that the volume of steam formed was identical with the volume of hydrogen used. In accordance with Avogadro's law 2 volumes of hydrogen combine with 1 volume of oxygen to form 2 volumes of water vapour.

$$H^2 + O = H^2O.$$
2 vols. + 1 vol. = 2 vols.

Careful gravimetric analyses, or analyses by weight, of water were carried out first by Berzelius and Dulong, and afterwards in 1843 by Dumas and Stas. The method adopted was to pass hydrogen over

capacity will thus depend on the width of the tube. This in no way affects the proportions between them. The numbers refer to divisions of the tube.

* In very accurate experiments allowance must be made for the volume occupied by the condensed water, but compared with the volume of the gases it is a negligeable amount.

heated copper oxide and collect the water formed by its reduction. The experiments of the two latter chemists were conducted with very many precautions. The hydrogen was passed through a series of 8 U tubes containing substances which freed it from every trace of impurity and moisture. It then passed over a weighed quantity of copper oxide and the water formed was condensed in a small weighed bulb, the last traces being absorbed by hygroscopic substances in weighed tubes. The loss of weight of the copper oxide gives the weight of oxygen used, the gain in weight of the second bulb and tube gives the weight of water formed. The difference between the two weights gives the weight of hydrogen in that quantity of water. From these experiments it was found that two parts by weight of hydrogen combine with 15·9608 parts of oxygen. The composition by weight deduced by calculation from the composition by volume coincides with these results.*

The properties of water it is unnecessary to enumerate. It may, however, be well to remind the reader that the density of water increases with a cold till the point of 4° is reached on the Centigrade scale. Water below 4° is lighter than that at 4° and therefore floats upon the warmer water, as does the ice formed from it. In this way the rapid circulation of the water as it cools is stopped, and our lakes and

* The exact composition of water and hence the exact atomic weight of oxygen is still the subject of experiment. Thomsen, Scott, Cooke and Richards, Keiser and Rayleigh are the recent workers in this field.

R. W. BUNSEN.

rivers prevented from becoming a mass of ice. Other substances, such as grey cast-iron, expand similarly on solidification. The beautiful forms assumed by water during crystallisation are sufficiently well known in the phenonema of snow-crystals.

Lastly, we must refer to the great invention of the spectroscope, an instrument of increasing importance to the chemist. Roscoe says, "The spectroscope, next to the balance, is the most useful and important instrument which the chemist possesses." Crookes has remarked, "If I name the spectroscope as the most important scientific invention of the latter half of this century I shall not fear to be accused of exaggeration." The very importance of the subject prevents us from entering into any long discussion of it here. It has come to form a distinct branch of chemical science. In the hands of men like Bunsen and Crookes it has explored the recesses of the rocks for minute traces of hidden treasures, while with it workers like Miller, Huggins, and Lockyer have fathomed the abysses of space and determined the constitution of the stars.

It was first observed by Newton that white light when passed through a prism is split up into coloured rays. Some of the rays are bent more sharply out of their course by the prism than others, and thus if these be received upon a screen they form a band or *spectrum* in which the colours follow the order: violet, indigo, blue, green, yellow, orange, red. Using the light of the sun we obtain in this way the solar spectrum. Dark lines in the solar spectrum were first observed by Wollaston in 1802 and mapped by Fraunhofer, an optician of Münich. Herschel and Talbot observed that *bright* lines in the spectrum might be obtained by heating certain substances in the flame, but it is to Kirchhoff and Bunsen that the

SOLAR SPECTRUM.

interpretation and utilisation of the phenomena of the spectrum are due. Different substances when volatilised in a colourless flame colour it in various ways. Thus, if a little common salt be held in the flame of a spirit lamp it colours it an intense yellow. The sodium compound is capable when thus heated of emitting light rays of a particular refrangibility. The spectrum obtained from this flame is very different from the continuous spectrum described above. It consists of two bright yellow lines. Moreover, if pure white light (lime-light, for instance) be made to pass *through* such a sodium flame before being analysed it will be found that its continuous spectrum is interrupted by a double black line occupying a definite position in the yellow.

Kirchhoff and Bunsen invented their spectroscope

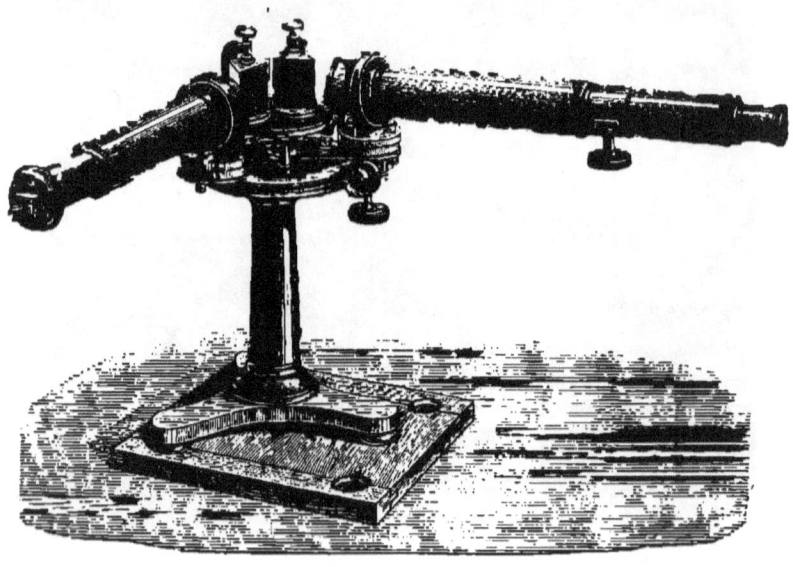

SPECTROSCOPE.

for observing these phenomena. The light is received through a very fine slit and by an arrangement of lenses the rays are rendered parallel before reaching the prism where the light is split up. It then enters the observing telescope where, by means of another lens, an image of the spectrum is obtained, and this is observed through a magnifying glass. An incandescent solid or liquid gives only a continuous spectrum, but where the substance is capable of being ever so slightly volatilised it is found that each element gives a spectrum of characteristic bright lines. So delicate is the test that $\frac{1}{3000000}$ of a milligram of sodium salt can be detected with certainty.

The dark lines in the solar spectrum are due to the absorption of certain portions of the solar light by upper incandescent vapours. Each vapour absorbs in this way the same light that it emits. Thus the sodium line is in the sun represented by a black line in the yellow. But the interesting facts of spectroscopy and stellar chemistry cannot be gone into here. These few words have only been inserted to remind readers that these discoveries are among the most important of the modern science.

CHAPTER XIX.

NINTH PERIOD: THE MODERN SCIENCE.
ORGANIC CHEMISTRY TO-DAY.

SOME short reference must now be made to the immense strides made by organic chemistry since the time of Scheele. Lavoisier was the first to attempt the ultimate analysis of organic bodies. In his later form of apparatus for the determination of carbon and hydrogen in these bodies, Lavoisier burnt his oil or other organic substance in a stream of oxygen and collected the water and carbonic acid formed, employing eight or nine absorption bulbs for the latter purpose. The substantial features of this method have already been described. From his analyses he drew the correct conclusion that vegetable bodies are composed mainly of carbon, hydrogen, and oxygen, while animal bodies contain in addition nitrogen and sometimes phosphorus.

Guyton de Morveau, one of Lavoisier's disciples,

suggested the term of *la base* or *le radical* for that portion of a substance which combines with oxygen. This radical might be either elementary as carbon, or compound as the radical of tartaric acid. The radicals of the vegetable and animal kingdom Lavoisier regarded as usually complex. His researches on fermentation have been referred to. He did not make any wide distinction between inorganic and organic chemistry, but he was an illustrious pioneer in the latter branch of the science.

Berzelius, in 1814, began important investigations into the composition of organic bodies. His method of analysis for carbon and hydrogen depended upon treating the substance with potassium chlorate and collecting the water and carbonic acid formed. Berzelius followed Lavoisier in a belief in the existence of compound radicals. In 1815 Gay-Lussac discovered cyanogen gas (CN).

The belief prevailed at this time that organic bodies could not be artificially prepared. This was the view adopted by the German chemist, Gmelin, in his great *Handbuch*. But the belief in mysterious vital forces alone capable of giving rise to organic products was rudely shaken by the synthesis of urea effected by Wöhler in 1828. Urea is a highly important animal product and is excreted regularly in the urine.* Ammonium cyanate is an artificial

* The quantity excreted by an adult man amounts to from 30 to 40 grams daily (a little over 1 oz.). The formation of the various constituents of the urine forms one of the most interesting chapters in physiological chemistry.

product of the laboratory and may be obtained by acting with an ammonium salt upon potassium cyanate. Now, this salt when heated to 100° C. becomes rapidly converted into urea. Here, then, is the first case of an organic product synthesised from inorganic sources.

In 1823 the great German chemist, Liebig,* began to perfect the methods of organic analysis. His labours on this point culminated in the development of the process actually in use at the present day for determining the carbon and hydrogen in organic bodies. His method consists essentially in heating a mixture of the carbon compound with copper oxide in a long glass tube. The carbon and hydrogen of the substance are oxidised; the water formed is absorbed

LIEBIG'S COMBUSTION APPARATUS. *a*, calcium chloride tube. *b*, potash bulbs.

---

* Justus Liebig (1803—1873) was born at Darmstadt. He was made professor at Giessen, and founded its laboratory. He remained at Giessen for twenty-six years, during which time he published 200

in a tube filled either with calcium chloride or with pumice moistened with sulphuric acid, while the carbon dioxide is absorbed by potash solution contained in the bulbs devised by Liebig. The method customarily in use at the present day differs from that of Liebig in only a few particulars. The combustion is now usually carried on in a current of oxygen gas, the substance analysed being placed in a porcelain boat behind a long column of copper oxide.* Gas has replaced charcoal as a means of heating the combustion tube. The perfection of this method of analysis took Liebig many years to accomplish, but the results of its use amply rewarded the labour bestowed upon it.

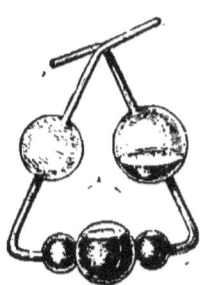

POTASH BULBS.

In 1832 Liebig and Wöhler published their celebrated research upon the radical of benzoic acid. These chemists found that bitter almond oil, benzoic acid and their derivatives all contained a particular group of atoms, or compound radical, involving oxygen as well as carbon and hydrogen, and termed

papers, 20 of them joint works—chiefly with Wöhler. He also published works on organic analysis, organic chemistry, physiological and agricultural chemistry, his chemical letters, &c., and edited several journals. His discoveries include those of aldehyde, chloral, and, simultaneously with Souberain, chloroform.

* To estimate *nitrogen* in nitrogenous bodies with this apparatus all that is necessary is to mix the substance with copper oxide and substitute a current of carbon dioxide for one of oxygen. The nitrogen of the substance escapes as such and is collected over potash solution.

BARON LIEBIG.

by them benzoyl* (C^7H^5O). Liebig gave great support to the radical theory by the development of his true idea that both ether and common alcohol contain the same radical *ethyl*, the former being the oxide (C^4H^5O), while the latter is its hydrate † (C^4H^5O, HO). The work of Liebig, Berzelius, and Dumas further developed this theory, the central idea of which is that the elements of inorganic chemistry are represented in organic chemistry by combinations of elements, or compound radicals, which play the part of elementary bodies. We term cyanogen a radical, says Liebig, 1, because it is an unchanging constituent in a series of compounds; 2, because it may be replaced in these compounds by simple bodies; and, 3, because in its compounds with elementary bodies these latter can be set free and replaced by their equivalents of other simple bodies. At least two of these conditions must be fulfilled if the radical is to be considered a true one.

The work of Dumas and Laurent led to the publication, in 1839, of Dumas's *theory of chemical types*. Dumas observed that the elements of a compound could often be replaced by their equivalents of other elements or compound radicals. Laurent added the observation that when such substitution was made the compound still retained

---

* "Yl" from the Greek ὕλη, matter.

† In our present formulæ the relation between the compounds is expressed by ether (C^2H^5)^2O, alcohol C^2H^5OH.

its essential chemical properties or its chemical type. As an example we may take the case of acetic acid, $C^2H^4O^2$. By the action of chlorine one of the atoms of hydrogen may be replaced, and we obtain monochloracetic acid, $C^2H^3ClO^2$, in which the chlorine plays the part of the hydrogen replaced. The views of Dumas and Laurent were strongly combated, but they held their ground. The observation of reverse substitution in the conversion of a chlorinated body back again into its hydrogen derivative much strengthened their position (*Melsens*, 1842). The facts of replacement had an interesting bearing upon the development of the atomic theory. The fact that in these substitutions never less than two atoms of chlorine react was one of those which led Laurent to the conclusion that the molecule of chlorine must consist of two atoms.*

The older radical theory was modified by Gerhardt (1839) and assimilated to the theory of chemical types. The older theory regarded the radicals as closed groups of atoms, while Gerhardt, though not abandoning the belief in a "residue," which was the equivalent of the radical, regarded the whole compound as forming the chemical unit. Thus, according to Laurent and Gerhardt † alcohol is represented

---

* As examples take the action of chlorine upon acetic acid above mentioned:

$$Cl^2 + C^2H^4O^2 = HCl + C^2H^3ClO^2$$

or upon marsh gas:

$$CH^4 + Cl^2 = CH^3Cl + HCl.$$

† See *ante* p. 296.

by the formula C^2H^5OH, containing the residue OH. The action of hydrochloric acid upon alcohol will be represented as $C^2H^5OH + HCl = C^2H^5Cl + HOH$, or C^2H^5 |OH H| Cl, forming ethyl chloride, C^2H^5Cl, a body first prepared by Basil Valentine and known as sweet spirit of salt.

The classical researches of Bunsen upon the cacodyl compounds were of weighty service to the true radical theory. The source of these interesting compounds is Cadet's fuming liquid obtained by distilling arsenious acid (As^2O^3) with potassium acetate. In a series of researches which are models of penetration and skill, Bunsen investigated the composition of this liquid and its derivatives. "If we examine this group of bodies," says he, "we recognise in them an unchangeable member (Glied), the composition of which is represented by the formula $C^4H^{12}As^2$"* [C^2H^6As]. To this *radical* Bunsen gives the name cacodyl (κακώδης, stinking), from the frightful smell possessed by most of its compounds. Bunsen finally succeeded in preparing the free radical by the action of zinc on cacodyl chloride [$(CH^3)^2$ As]Cl. Taking the group $(CH^3)^2As$, as analogous to the *atom* of an element, the *molecule* of free cacodyl contains *two* such atoms $(CH^3)^2As$—As $(CH^3)^2$, and it has therefore been termed dicacodyl. Soon after this Kolbe and Frankland succeeded in similarly isolating the radicals of the alcohol series.

* *Annalen* xxxvii. 1. (1841).

In 1849 Wurtz discovered the compound ammonias, the existence of which was predicted by Liebig. They consist of ammonia, NH^3, in which one or more of the hydrogen atoms is replaced by an organic radical. Thus if the radical ethyl, C^2H^5, be substituted for one hydrogen atom, the compound $NH^2C^2H^5$ termed ethylamine is obtained. The replacement of two atoms produces diethylamine $NH(C^2H^5)^2$, and so on. The new theory of types initiated by Laurent and which regarded organic compounds as formed upon the *type* of the simple inorganic ones, was much aided by these discoveries. The compound ammonias may be conceived as built upon the ammonia type. Again, Williamson's classical research on etherification in 1850 proved that the alcohols and ethers must be considered as built up on the water type. We thus have

$$\text{Water} \left.\begin{matrix} H \\ H \end{matrix}\right\} O \quad \text{ethyl alcohol} \left.\begin{matrix} C^2H^5 \\ H \end{matrix}\right\} O \quad \text{ethyl ether} \left.\begin{matrix} C^2H^5 \\ C^2H^5 \end{matrix}\right\} O$$

Substituting the hydrogen atoms of water by other radicals we obtain other alcohols and ethers, as for instance,

$$\text{Propyl alcohol} \left.\begin{matrix} C^3H^7 \\ H \end{matrix}\right\} O \quad \text{propyl ether} \left.\begin{matrix} C^3H^7 \\ C^3H^7 \end{matrix}\right\} O \quad \text{and } \textit{mixed} \text{ ethers as ethyl propyl ether} \left.\begin{matrix} C^2H^5 \\ C^3H^7 \end{matrix}\right\} O$$

and so on.

The subsequent discoveries of Williamson and others did much to develop the new theory. The theory must not be pressed too far, the same substance can be arranged on a variety of types, and the formulæ are less advanced than true structural formulæ, inasmuch as they only suggest a certain number of reactions of the compound.

Since 1850 the researches of innumerable workers have completely transformed the science, and the best course to adopt in closing this chapter seems to be to sketch, in what must of necessity be very bare outline, the system of organic chemistry to-day.

First, let us define the range of organic chemistry.* The simplest and truest way of stating the province of organic chemistry is to say that it is *the chemistry of the hydrocarbons and their derivatives.* Let us also start with the assumption that carbon is tetravalent (a fact first pointed out by the great German chemist Kekulé). The primary hydrocarbon thus becomes marsh gas or methane CH^4. Its structural formula is

$$\begin{array}{c} H \\ | \\ H-C-H \\ | \\ H \end{array}$$

all the hydrogen atoms playing a chemically similar part. By the action of chlorine upon this substance we can replace the hydrogen atom by atom, obtaining successively CH^4, methane; CH^3Cl,† methyl chloride; CH^2Cl^2, dichloromethane; $CHCl^3$, chloroform ‡ or

---

* For a discussion of the distinction between the organic and inorganic departments of the science *vide* Chapter VI., p. 116.

† CH^3 is an *organic radical* termed methyl; see p. 365.

‡ This invaluable compound was first introduced into medicine by Sir James Simpson of Edinburgh in 1848.

trichloromethane; CCl^4, tetrachloromethane or carbon tetrachloride. In a similar way we can replace the hydrogen atoms of the hydrocarbon by bromine and iodine, obtaining corresponding compounds as, for instance, CH^3I, methyl iodide. The action of caustic potash upon methyl chloride gives rise to methyl *alcohol*, the term alcohol being applied to hydrocarbons having one or more of their hydrogen atoms replaced by hydroxyl (OH):—

$$CH^3Cl + KOH = CH^3OH + KCl.$$

Methyl alcohol is a convenient source of a number of methyl compounds. The first action of sulphuric acid gives us hydrogen methyl sulphate CH^3HSO^4. The remaining hydrogen atom of sulphuric acid may be replaced by a metal. By various other means, such as the action of an acid on the alcohol or of a metallic salt on an haloid ether (CH^3I, Br or Cl), many other methyl salts may be obtained, as the nitrate, nitrite sulphide, sulphite, silicate, &c. Where an acid is dibasic, as sulphuric acid, we may obtain two salts, for instance CH^3HSO^4 and $(CH^3)^2SO^4$ according as one or both hydrogens are replaced. On oxidising methyl alcohol the first product is termed formic aldehyde.

$$\begin{array}{c} \text{H} \\ | \\ \text{H}-\text{C}-\text{OH} \\ | \\ \text{H} \end{array} + \text{O} = \text{H}^2\text{O} + \begin{array}{c} \text{H} \\ | \\ \text{H}-\text{C}=\text{O} \end{array} *$$

* CHO being the characteristic aldehyde group.

Further oxidation converts it into formic acid,

$$H-\overset{H}{\underset{}{C}}=O + O = H-\overset{OH}{\underset{}{C}}=O.$$

The group $-C\overset{OH}{\underset{O}{\diagdown}}$ or, as it is shortly written CO^2H, is termed carboxyl, and is characteristic of the organic acids.

It has already been observed that the first product of the action of sulphuric acid upon methyl alcohol is methyl hydrogen sulphate, CH^3HSO^4; another product formed under suitable conditions is methyl oxide, or dimethyl ether, $\overset{CH^3}{\underset{CH^3}{\diagdown\diagup}}O.$

When methyl iodide (CH^3I), is treated with silver nitrite ($AgNO^2$), nitromethane (CH^3NO^2) is obtained, being methane (CH^4) in which one hydrogen atom is replaced by the group NO^2.

$$H-\overset{H}{\underset{H}{C}}-I + AgN\overset{O}{\underset{O}{\diagup\diagdown}} = AgI + H-\overset{H}{\underset{H}{C}}-N\overset{O}{\underset{O}{\diagup\diagdown}}$$

By appropriate means we can replace further hydrogen atoms in methane by the nitroxyl group (NO^2), obtaining, for instance, trinitromethane or nitroform $CH(NO^2)^3$. Furthermore we can, as might be expected, replace different hydrogen atoms at one and the same time by different groups, obtaining, for instance, bromo-trinitromethane, $C(NO^2)^3Br$, and so on. It is obvious therefore, that from the single hydrocarbon methane a large number of direct derivatives may be obtained, for there is no theoretical reason why we should not introduce into the molecule of methane these various substituting groups in every kind of combination.

Some important classes of bodies still remain to be mentioned. If we reduce nitromethane by nascent hydrogen the nitroxyl group becomes converted into amidogen—NH^2

$$CH^3NO^2 + 3H^2 = CH^3NH^2 + 2H^2O.$$

The substance so formed may indeed be regarded as ammonia, NH^3, in which one hydrogen atom has been replaced by methyl, CH^3. It is termed methylamine. The two remaining hydrogen atoms of ammonia may be similarly replaced with production of di- and tri- methylamine ($(CH^3)^2$ NH & $(CH^3)^3$ N). Here again we may effect a double substitution, obtaining, for instance, di-iodomethylamine CH^3NI^2, where one hydrogen atom of ammonia, NH^3, is replaced by methyl and the two others by iodine. Bodies of a similar nature may be derived from arseniuretted hydrogen, AsH^3, giving respectively monomethyl, dimethyl, and trimethyl *arsine*, &c. So too from phosphuretted hydrogen, PH^3, analogous *phosphines* are obtainable. Amines, arsines, and phosphines are all of them basic bodies, and, like ammonia, combine with acids to form a variety of salts. By a very superficial glance we are thus able to see how rapidly the number of compounds derivable from even one hydrocarbon swells. But if we take methyl iodide and heat it with zinc the following reaction occurs—

$$CH^3 \mid \underset{Zn}{I \quad I} \mid CH^3$$

that is to say, the zinc takes away the iodine from two molecules forming zinc iodide, ZnI^2, and the two methyl groups are left. They cannot exist separately; each carbon being combined with only three hydrogen atoms has yet power of combining with another atom. The two carbons thus become directly united and H^3C-CH^3, or ethane, is the result. It is methane in which one hydrogen atom is replaced by the methyl group, CH^3. Graphically its formula is

$$\overset{H\quad H}{\underset{H\quad H}{H-C-C-H}},$$

and from it a whole series of compounds analogous to those obtainable from methane may be produced. The only difference is that there being more hydrogen atoms to replace, the number of derivatives is considerably larger in number. Thus we may obtain two hydroxyl derivatives; the first, $CH^3.CH^2OH$, is common alcohol, or ethyl alcohol, as it is distinctly termed, the group, $CH^3.CH^2$ or C^2H^5, constituting the radical ethyl. The second is $CH^2OH.CH^2OH$, having one hydroxyl in each methyl (CH^3) group* and known as ethylene

* At first sight it would seem that we might obtain a body

$$CH^3.\overset{H}{\underset{OH}{C}}-OH$$

containing its two hydroxyls attached to the *same* carbon atom. Such bodies, however, cannot be obtained, losing water at once and becoming monohydroxylic.

glycol.* The acid corresponding to ethyl alcohol is of course acetic acid, $CH^3.CO^2H$, Mono-, di- and tri-chloroacetic acids ($CH^2Cl.CO^2H$: $CHCl^2.CO^2H$: $CCl^3.CO^2H$) and other such derivations are known. Acetic aldehyde is $CH^3.CHO$. Trichloracetaldehyde, $CCl^3.CHO$, is usually known as chloral.

The hydrocarbon next above ethane, C^2H^6, is propane C^3H^8. These hydrocarbons are said to form a *homologous series*, the higher being obtained from the next lower one by the addition of CH^2. Their derivatives are also homologous.

From propane, C^3H^8, analogous derivatives may be obtained, but here some complications occur. Writing out the formula of propane more fully we have $CH^3.CH^2.CH^3$. Now it makes all the difference whether we substitute a hydrogen atom in the methyl (CH^3) groups at the end of the chain or an atom in the CH^2 group at the centre. Suppose, for instance, that we introduce iodine into the methyl group. The formula becomes $CH^3.CH^2.CH^2I$. The carbon atom with which the iodine is combined is attached to one other carbon atom and two hydrogen atoms. It moreover plays a certain part in respect to the rest of the molecule. The introduction of the iodine atom alters its relation to the rest of the molecule. But now suppose the iodine atom in the central group. The formula becomes $CH^3.CHI.CH^3$. The carbon atom with which the

---

* Dibasic acids, &c., can of course be obtained, corresponding to the alcohols.

iodine is now combined is attached to *two* other carbon atoms and *one* hydrogen atom. It plays a part in the molecular whole quite distinct from that of the terminal carbon atoms. The introduction of the iodine atom now alters *its* relation to the rest of the molecule. The change produced in the molecule by the introduction of the iodine atom in the one case is therefore quite distinct from that produced in the other. The two compounds are therefore quite distinct. The first is termed primary, the second, secondary propyl iodide.* It may be well to observe that the two terminal carbon atoms play an exactly similar part in the molecule and that therefore the compound $CH^3.CH^2.CH^2I$ is identical with the compound $CH^2I.CH^2.CH^3$; indeed these formulæ must never be taken as representing the relation of the atoms *in space* but merely as indicating which atoms are directly united to each other. Obviously these modes of substitution in the propane molecule may be repeated with other substituting groups, giving us, for instance, $CH^3.CH^2.CH^2OH$, primary propyl alcohol ($C^3H^5.OH$) and $CH^3.CHOH, CH^3$, secondary propyl alcohol (C^3H^5OH). It is noticeable that the empirical formulæ (C^3H^6O) of the secondary and primary derivatives are identical. The substances are only distinguishable when their rational or structural formulæ are given. Bodies thus

---

* When there is a long chain a large number of isomers may be obtained as $CH^3.CHI.CH^2.CH^2.CH^2.CH^3$; $CH^3.CH^2.CHI.(CH^2)^2.CH^3$ and so on.

containing in their molecules the same number of the same molecules are said to be *isomeric*.* From propane, then, we may not only obtain a series of derivatives strictly analogous to those obtainable from ethane, but the number of derivatives is also much increased by the possibility of forming such isomeric bodies. Proceeding up the series of hydrocarbons we have

$$CH^4, C^2H^6, C^3H^8, C^4H^{10}.$$

The last hydrocarbon, butane, has not yet been mentioned. In this case the hydrocarbon itself may exist in two isomeric modifications and *each* of these gives rise to a long series of derivatives.

The first modification where all the carbon atoms may be written out in a chain is termed normal butane, $CH^3.CH^2.CH^2.CH^3$, the second, isobutane, $CH^3CH{<}^{CH^3}_{CH^3}$ or trimethyl methane. Each of these is capable of forming two mono-substitution products. The alcohol, $CH^3COH{<}^{CH^3}_{CH^3}$, is termed a tertiary alcohol, the substituting group being in primary compounds united to CH^2, in secondary compounds to CH, and in tertiary compounds to C. The primary alcohols when oxidised give rise to acids as we have seen. The secondary alcohols on the other hand form a new class of bodies termed ketones. Thus with secondary propyl alcohol,

$$CH^3.CH^2.CHOH.CH^3 + O = CH^3.CH^2.CO.CH^3 + H^2O,$$

the product being known as ethylmethyl ketone.

* This name was given by Berzelius (ισος, equal ; μερος, a share).

Tertiary alcohols split up on oxidation. We have then

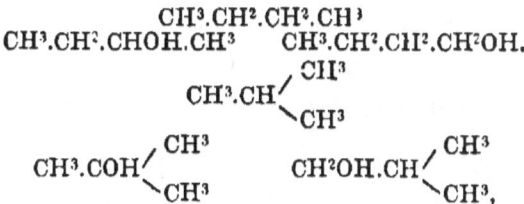

and by introducing various substituting groups we may theoretically obtain chlorine substitution products, alcohols, aldehydes, ethers, acids, ketones, amines, and so forth, in almost any number.

Butane exists in two modifications; of the next higher paraffin, C^5H^{12}, there are three modifications; of the next, C^6H^{14}, five are possible and four known; of the next, C^7H^{16}, nine are possible, and when we reach the hydrocarbon, $C^{13}H^{28}$, it has been calculated by Professor Cayley that no less than 799 modifications should exist. Each of these modifications should give rise to several complete series of derivatives of its own.

But this is by no means the only series of hydrocarbons known to the chemist. Another series begins with the term C^2H^4, ethylene, and like the other proceeds upwards by increments of CH^2. The structural formula of ethylene is—

$$\begin{array}{c} CH^2 \\ \| \\ CH^2, \end{array}$$

where we see that two of the units of saturation of carbon are engaged with each other. The series of the olefines, as they are termed, is characterised by this constitution. Its members tend to combine directly with chlorine and other elements. Thus ethylene produces the dichloride, $CH^2Cl.CH^2Cl$, which is identical with symmetrical dichloroethane. We can also substitute hydrogen in ethylene, obtaining for instance, monochlorethylene, $CH^2:CHCl$. and so on. The hydrocarbons form the series C^2H^4, C^3H^6, C^4H^8, C^5H^{10}, and so on. We may obtain from them a large number of derivatives similar to those obtained from the paraffins, except for the peculiar union of two of the carbon atoms and the unsaturated character or proneness to combination resulting from that union. An example of this group is afforded by the following compounds:

$CH^2: CH.CH^3$, $CH^2: CH.CH^2OH$, $CH^2: CH.CO^2H$,
$CH^2: CH.CH^2I$.

Another important series of hydrocarbons is the acetylene series commencing with the term $CH\equiv CH$, a gas capable of combining with four atoms of chlorine to form $CHCl^2.CHCl^2$. Far fewer compounds of this series are, however, known.

Other series of hydrocarbons are known, but need not be referred to here with the exception of one, which has become of greater importance than all the rest, the benzene series. All the hydrogen atoms of benzene (C^6H^6) are proved to be of equal value in the molecule, and the only way of representing this structurally is by the ring formula proposed by Kekulé:

or, perhaps preferably Ladenburg's modification.

We may obtain from it substitution products much in the same way as from other hydrocarbons. But there are special laws regulating this substitution. Representing the benzene molecule as is commonly done by a simple hexagon we see that we can obtain only one monosubstitution product, all the hydrogens being similar, and three disubstitution products, *e.g.*

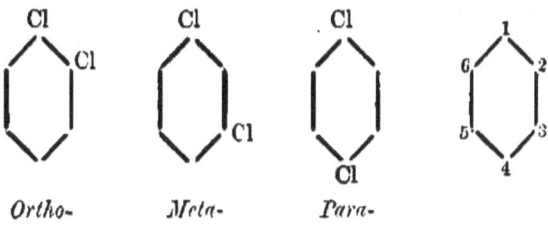

Ortho- *Meta-* *Para-*

known as ortho-, meta-, and para-dichlorobenzene. $C^6H^4Cl^2$ 1 : 6 is identical with $C^6H^4Cl^2$ 1 : 2, the chlorine in both cases being combined with adjacent carbon atoms. Where three hydrogen atoms are replaced by the same element three isomeric modifications may be obtained, but where there is more than one substituting element there is a larger number of isomers.

We may thus replace hydrogen in the benzene ring by a variety of groups just as in the case of the paraffins, and may produce higher hydrocarbons by introducing alkyl radicals, as, for instance, CH^3. We thus obtain $C^6H^5.CH^3$ where CH^3 is termed a *side chain*. On oxidising such derivatives the side chain becomes converted into carboxyl and thus we here obtain $C^6H^5.CO^2H$, benzoic acid. Where there are two side chains as in $C^6H^4{<}{}^{CH^3(1)}_{CH^3(2)}$, orthoxylene, oxidation produces a dibasic acid as $C^6H^4{<}{}^{CO^2H(1)}_{CO^2H(2)}$, orthophthalic acid. By substitutions of this kind we may obtain an enormous number of benzene derivatives, and the reader may at will construct large numbers on paper for himself. It is easy with the constitutional formulæ now in use to predict the existence of numerous compounds as yet undiscovered, and to describe their chief properties, for these undergo a gradual modification of properties as we pass up a homologous series just as properties of the elements become modified with rise of atomic weight.

In many compounds two or three benzene rings may be combined, either indirectly, as in rosaniline, or directly, as in naphthalene

which body is again the source of a large series of compounds. We cannot do more here than thus indicate how in the modern system of organic chemistry the vast numbers of its compounds diverge from a few simple hydrocarbons like the branches of an enormous genealogical tree. The system is so far perfected that the character of the undiscovered compounds is in many cases as plain to the chemists as the character of the elements destined to fill the blanks in Mendelejeff's table. Modifications of properties occur along with rise of molecular weight and change of structure. Thus, as an instance of the former truth, boiling points rise, and often very regularly, as we pass up a homologous series. As an instance of the latter normal compounds have a higher boiling-point than iso-compound. Similarity of structure on the other hand always goes hand in hand with similarity of properties, and thus it happens that all the paraffin hydrocarbons have great chemical similarity, for instance, in allowing their hydrogen to be replaced by chlorine, and that all the primary alcohols form acids on oxidation. It is these strictly defined relations which make it possible to direct research in this department upon such definite lines and make organic chemistry so perfect a science.

CONCLUSION.

IT may seem to some that science becomes less interesting and less beautiful as it advances. This, however, is but a one-sided view to take. The mere facts of science may be dry enough, but the facts have to be interpreted, and so arise deep truths through which we seem to peer into the great heart of nature. There is a poetical side to this, and the poetry of it becomes more obvious as the truths become more deep. Again, the truths which we are able to see and the conjectures we are able to frame only bring us more closely into contact with the vast regions of mystery where knowledge fades into speculation, and speculation into awe. We need fear no loss of the mysterious by the achievements of science, though we exchange a lesser mystery for a greater. The wonder with which in ignorance we look up through the branches of a forest beech and see the giant boughs spread upwards in moveless strength and the floating tresses of sunlit leaves curved back towards us, the wonder with which we watch in its cool nooks the softness of the shadow, or through its recesses the changeful play of palpitating light—this wonder is great. But that is still greater and of more enduring worth with which, by higher knowledge, we watch the same wondrous beauty and see beyond it how, through the myriad cells of leaf and branch and trunk, minute by minute, the life currents of protoplasm ebb and flow, making the green grace of the tree possible by their swift mysterious power: or again, how the gleaming spears of sunlight that shiver into soft glow of colour upon those tiny wind-lifted shields have sped unstayed in their few moments of dazzling life through depths of space, so vast and desolate that before them the mind of man can only wonder in impotence, or recoil in dread, to be stayed at last and fall in fragments at the light touch of one trembling leaf. No need is here to complain that science will leave us with nothing to wonder at. It is only morbid conceit which can forget the great truth uttered by a man who combined the keen observance of science with the lofty insight of the poet—" Poetry is the impassioned expression which is in the face of all science."

In our review of the progress of our science we have

seen it at first advancing slowly through the darkness of ignorance and error. In this darkness it was difficult to go forward, but it was more difficult to go back. After a while the darkness here and there lightened a little, but the first gleams of brightness were too often alluring marsh-lights beckoning to impenetrable morass; the false guides were more treacherous than the night. But as the twilight of doubt broadened into the day of knowledge it revealed ever wider and wider tracts of hill and hollow for us to explore. At last the daylight has flooded mountain rock, and valley mist, and we stand in wonderment before the vision of the newly revealed realm as it stretches before us, from the gold of the sunrise to where hastening night has dropped his purple mantle on the hills. It is a splendid kingdom, but great is the task of mastering it, and great our responsibility if we err. We must have regard to its beauty and not merely to its wealth. We must not forget the beauty of its mountains in our search for the treasure of its mines. We must see the countenance but not forget its expression.

INDEX:

Acid, Acetic, 98, 374
    Hydrochloric, 60, 99, 199
    Nitric, 39, 59, 60, 101, 223
    Organic, 227, 371
    Prussic, 227
    Sulphuric, 60, 62
Affinity, 148, 163
Agricola, 97
Albertus Magnus, 38, 43
Alcohol, 33, 118, 237
Alkalies, 165, 252, 320
Aluminium, 328, 347
Ammonia, 88, 199
Ampère, 282
Antimony, 67, 85
Aquafortis, 60
Aqua regia, 39

Atmosphere, 33, 203, 209, 221, 251, 351
Atomic theory, 257
Avogadro, 279

Bacon, R., 24, 40
Barium, 227, 226
Bayen, 246
Becher, 117, 175
Benzene, 336, 378
Bergman, 225, 245
Bernard of Trevisa, 50
Berthelot, 228
Berthollet, 257
Berzelius, 228, 283, 289, 326, 353, 361
Black, Dr., 94, 161
Boerhaave, 179

INDEX.

Boyle, 121, 151, 179, 248
Bunsen, 348, 358, 367

Calcium, 327
       Carbonate, 89, 167
Carbon dioxide, 89, 141, 219, 241
Cavendish, 33, 83, 183, 211
Chaptal, 65
Chevreul, 228
Chlorine, 225, 328, 336, 338
Chloroform, 369
Combustion, 134, 140, 147, 246, 252
Condensation, 337
Constant proportions, 245, 257, 269
Copper sulphate, 98
Crookes, 134, 345, 356
Cullen, 159

Dalton, 261
Davy, 317
Dulong and Petit, 285
Dumas, 351, 353, 365

Electro-chemical equivalents, 339
Elements, 40, 50, 83, 87, 102, 115, 128, 146, 176, 252, 297, 344

Faraday, 329
Fats, 228
Fermentation, 34, 287
Fusel-oil, 237

Gas, 87
Gay-Lussac, 278, 325, 253, 361
Geber, 15, 38, 298
Geoffrey, 114
Gerhardt, 293
Glass, 27
Glauber, 58, 97
Glycerine, 228
Gunpowder, 49, 105, 134

Hales, 153, 199
Helmont, Van, 86
Hermes Trismegistus, 38
Higgins, 267
Hoffmann, F., 179
Hooke, 137
Hydrogen, 83, 89, 219
       Sulphide, 227

Indestructibility, 157, 235
Iron sulphate, 39, 50, 60
Isomers, 374
Isomorphism, 289

Latent heat, 169
Laurent, 296
Lavoisier, 183, 231, 260

INDEX.

Lead oxides, 180
Lémery, 114
Liebig, 30, 228, 254, 362, 368
Lossen, 306
Lully, Raymond, 34, 50

Macquer, 179
Magnesium, 327
Marsh gas, 267
Mayow, 147, 178
Mendelejeff, 308
Metals and non-metals, 298
Metals known to ancients, 25
Molybdenum 227

Newlands, 308
Newton, 138, 356
Nitrogen, 204
Nomenclature, 253
Northmore, 338

Olefiant gas, 267
Opium, 84
Organic chemistry, 116, 225, 360
Oxygen, 147, 185, 202, 226, 248

Palissy, Bernard, 30
Paracelsus, 79, 94
Phlogiston, 169, 176, 206

Phosphorus, 150, 227
Pliny, 27, 32, 68
Pneumatic trough, 143, 198
Porcelain, 29
Pott, 29, 179
Priestley, 182, 185
Proust, 258
Prout, 284

Radical, 361, 363
Reactions, 163
Réaumur, 30
Rey, John, 178
Richter, 259
Roscoe, 75, 276, 344
Royal Society, 113
Rutherford, 204

Sal-ammoniac, 98
Salt-petre, 49, 101, 134, 145
Salts, 50, 151, 295
Scheele, 182, 225, 326
Silicon, 27, 346
Soap, 30
Sodium sulphate, 98
Spectroscope, 356
Stahl, 117, 176, 200
Starch, 28
Stas, 353
Strontium, 326
Structural formulæ, 304
Suidas, 37
Sulphur dioxide, 200

www.ingramcontent.com/pod-product-compliance
Lightning Source LLC
Chambersburg PA
CBHW030400230426
43664CB00007BB/684